LEE WALBURN

Just My Type

Just My Type

Just My Type

ISBN 978-0-9883261-3-2

book design Dekie Hicks
cover design Shannon Biggers
illustrations Michaele Prince and Lee Field

Wheredepony Press
Rome, GA 30165

FOREWORD

The first words of mine ever published appeared either in the fall/winter of 1955 or the winter/spring of 1956—a time so distant in memory, I have no idea what those words were about. I know only the publication carrying them was called *The West Georgian*, a student newspaper of West Georgia College.

Lee Walburn talked me into it. He was editor of *The West Georgian*.

Neither of us knew then that our lives would be shaped by words, or that words would be our contract for a friendship that has been as binding as the genetics of blood.

It was Lee who persuaded me to apply for a job at the *Atlanta Journal* in 1962, and it was Lee who developed an hour-by-hour schedule for me to follow on the first article I would write for that newspaper's sports department—a call-in report of a game from the boy's Class B and C basketball tournament played in Macon (GA).

I was terrified, but I did everything he told me, because, to be truthful, I was in awe of him. I believed if I obeyed his instruction, I would survive for at least one paycheck.

On March 7, 1962, my first byline appeared in the predate addition of the *Atlanta Journal.*

I was a writer. Officially.

I had a career.

For the next twenty years my ambition in that profession was to write as well as Lee—even for a sentence or a paragraph.

I have learned, of course, that every writer brings the contents of his or her gift to the page in his or her own wrapping—plain or decorative, string-tied or with bows made of curled silk.

Still, I remain in awe of Lee's remarkable skill as a writer, as everyone who reads the collections of this book will be. I proudly, gladly, admit to bias influenced by friendship, but in more than 50 years of practice I've learned a few things about writing taught only by the doing of it, and for me, Lee is, and has been, one of the half-dozen most accomplished writers I have known.

It begins with talent. Lee's is God-given, but fine-tuned in a mill village where taking notice of things was an exercise in survival as well as a primer lesson in human behavior. What he learned from those days would become the one important characteristic of his work: He has always understood his writing was not about himself, but about the people and the events that became his subject matter.

Most writers file away the kind of experiences Lee had in his mill village as notes to be used if needed; Lee absorbed them as part of his life substance. It was in the God-given part of his talent that he intuitively knew his art was in what he took in—what he absorbed—and that the words of his articles and stories were merely expressions of that art.

His exceptional series on the homeless, written as a columnist for the *Atlanta Constitution*, is, for me, proof of that mystic gift. He could never have written so brilliantly of that sub-world of despair and danger without understanding the people of the street before he joined their ranks for a first-hand look. He had seen that longing before, knew the sound and the scent of it, was locked in on the quintessential soul of the series before he began to meet its inhabitants and to build the word pictures that would enthrall readers.

The same can be said of his series on the vanishing cotton mills of the South, a series so perfect for him it was like being flung in his own brier patch, and one written with such force that the late Celestine Sibley insisted it should be submitted for a Pulitzer Prize. (In fact, both the cotton mill series and the homeless series were offered for Pulitzer consideration.)

His piece on Henry Aaron won prizes. His series on the Ku Klux Klan was considered bold and letter-perfect. He calls his profile on the life and influence of the late Larry Williams—the Piano Man—as well done as anything he has ever written. He does not lie about that. I knew Larry, worked with him, have always considered him one of the truly grand human beings of this world's history. Lee got him down right.

But I do not want to suggest that his work is drawn only from the serious and the sensitive, tinted by rainbow shadings of the human dilemma. He would be considered a humorist if you excerpted what he calls his light pieces—glimpses into everyday life—and this collection is triumphant with the sheer joy of those stories. They are, for me, Twainesque—funny, wise, neatly layered in a manner that offers readers a choice of what they take from the readings.

To wit: The natural meanness of Hog Singleton and Nub Carruth; home builders quaking in fear of Lee's wife, Jackie; the peeping Tom episode, and toothpaste on his bullet; the necessity of lying to his mother; Saturday night suppers in the mill village; David Duke at a Klan rally.

All good reading, all tender-felt, all smile-warm.

But here is what you do not find in Lee Walburn's writing: one-line cuteness or boiled-over personal angst crammed into transparent tales of dysfunction. He is not mesmerized by the appearance of his name in print. He does not expect the people of his stories to be a medium for him; he is their medium.

In my view of it, Lee has made only one mistake in his career as a writer: he has never written fiction. He believes he is not suited for it, that his thinking and his fingers are trained for other things. He is wrong, of course. I've pounded on him for years about it. Tried to shame him into it. Nothing works in that regard with the man. I should stop berating him about it, but I think I owe him. He did put me at the machine to make the words I have made for more than 50 years.

And, of course, there's that boy's basketball game in 1962, the one he led me through, step by step.

I only want him to follow me for a while. I know him. He would like the trip.

—Terry Kay

INTRODUCTION

I want to begin by telling you about an old man who one morning revealed the answer to an eternal question, *"What is Life All About?"*

Every Friday I eat breakfast with my buddies at a little cinderblock side-of-the-road restaurant called Dirt Town Deli. The patriarch of the country establishment is named Rowan Hicks. He is the type that has never eavesdropped on a conversation he couldn't interrupt with a tale of his own.

Not long ago he nudged his way into one of our conversations to talk about the latest exploits of his bird dog, "Prime Time." I teased Mr. Hicks about his barging in. He stepped back and I could tell that without meaning to I had embarrassed him. Then he said something that stabbed me right in my heart. He said, *"Well, you know, Lee, all we really have in life is our stories."*

In so few words he had pronounced a universal truth, that stories, woven together, form the fabric of our lives, tell what was important to us and more valuable, who was important to us.

A benign friendliness has usually accompanied my spillage of words in magazines and newspapers. Nevertheless, there was a time, especially during my career at the *Atlanta Journal-Constitution* when I was available to nettle the world or, in my more arrogant moments, to settle world arguments that were baffling presidents, dictators and radio talk show hosts.

I shivered on the freezing streets of Atlanta as I lived with the homeless and wrote passionately about their teetering balance on the rim of reality. I witnessed the inside workings of the Ku Klux Klan, attending secretive regional leadership meetings in an abandoned chicken house in Forsyth County and a cross burning in Bethlehem, Ga. For four months I explored the heartbreak of a vanishing textile industry in the South. Over time, big picture news fascinated me less than the personal lives of those who have had to deal with ramifications of the news.

Granted, there will always be an audience for writers who are perpetually grave, but I trust there are enough of you who won't consider me foolish just because I frequently break out in a rash of good nature in this book, as well as in my latest incarnation as Saturday columnist for the *Rome News-Tribune*. I have decided that if I can't enlighten the world, I will see if I can make it grin.

As old Rowan Hicks imprinted on my heart, when you have a good story, share it with someone. So, with urging from nobody but myself, here are stories that bear my ink-stained fingerprints. They are Just My Type, 50 years preserved in ink.

DEDICATION

This book is dedicated to my mother-in-law, Vivian Miller, who taught me by example how to handle that bully, cancer, and my mother, Myrtle Walburn, who taught me by example how to handle bullies, period. Further, this book is dedicated to everyone who has looked cancer in the eye and refused to blink.

CREDITS

There is an entire section of this book devoted to my life with Jackie Miller Walburn. She was born with the gift of laughter and the patience of a saint, is as self-reliant as a pioneer and as dependable as the sun that will come up tomorrow morning. There is little in life she cannot do and little she won't do if it benefits someone other than herself. She has been willing to take care of all the heavy lifting in life while I worked on this book. She, more than anyone on earth, is Just My Type.

As usual, my daughter, Shannon Biggers, was there when I needed her. Director of Creative Services at Berry College, she designed the cover after convincing me that the book title with which I had fallen in love was not my type.

There is no way I could have met publication deadline had not computer whiz Jane Marie Rainer assumed command of all the old magazine and newspaper articles that were written before computers were invented. How they were translated into new type without involvement of my fingers and brain I will simply chalk up to her magic.

Terry Kay, author of the classic *To Dance With the White Dog* and more than a dozen novels deserving equal acclaim, is my oldest and dearest friend. He is so dear I suspect that he would even commit hyperbole in order to warm my heart with praise that is higher than my writing deserves. Only a person who has reached the summit literarily, can be so free in encouragement for those of us who are still climbing. You may judge for yourself in his Foreward, which he agreed to write if I would limit revelations of our wandering together off the beaten path.

Special thanks goes to Lee Field, whose artwork is the highlight of my column on Saturdays and to Michaele Prince for the pen and ink drawings in this book.

Dekie Hicks of Wheredepony Press has guided me through the process of book publishing. In 50 years of spilling words for a living, I had not the faintest idea of what it takes to birth a book.

Finally, my thanks to Cancer Navigators, the wonderful non-profit organization that inspired and sponsored this book. Without the inducement and privilege of donating every penny of sales to the care of cancer patient navigation, publication of *Just My Type* would never have happened.

CONTENTS

small town life

life off the beaten path

life under spotlights and harsh lights

life with wonder woman

life in different colors

life in the family

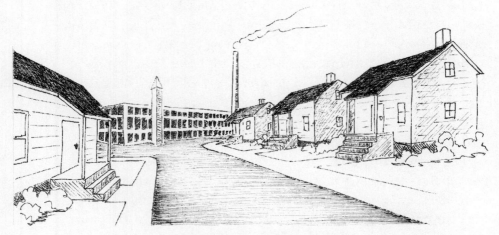

small town life

The Mill Is My Shepherd

I had no idea I was poor. I probably should have suspected, but who really knew the difference growing up in a LaGrange, Georgia cotton mill village where virtually everything but a decent wage was provided by Callaway Mills. *The mill is my shepherd, I shall not want.*

As cotton mills began to hum after the Civil War's devastation, grateful whites emerged from the mountains and Piedmont shacks and thankfully arranged their meager belongings in company houses. They burned company coal in their stoves and grates. They raised hogs and cows in company pastures. They learned to read and write in company-supported schools, baptized the repentant in company-subsidized churches. They heard promises of regular paydays unless they had black skin. The only thing whiter than a cotton mill was the Ku Klux Klan.

I was born into a third generation of cotton mill workers in La-Grange at a time when only a small fraction of its 25,000 residents wore white collars to work, most of them in stores clustered around a fountain and statue of Gen. Marquis de Lafayette downtown. Until I was 4, we lived in a mill house with my Uncle Frank, who rented one for 25 cents per room a month. We shared four rooms with his children, James and Voncille, and our grandmother who blathered endlessly about kinship to Stonewall Jackson.

Later my parents moved our family into Render Apartments. The building had been condemned years before, was ordered demolished, but had not been. A young boy named Jimmy fell through a rotted floor into a bathtub while spying on the woman bathing in the apartment below and broke three ribs.

My family shifted from pillar to post until I was 9. That year Daddy and Mama got jobs in Callaway mills and we moved to a three-room house on East Williams Street. It had three rooms straight through with no hallway. Mama used to say you couldn't heat that house with a pipeline straight from Hell. It had indoor plumbing, but we heated water on an oil stove and poured it into a galvanized tub when we bathed. The house sat barely above ground in the rear but the front rested on tall brick supports; water from the tub ran under the comically tilted house and past the imaginary secret tunnels I dug in the red clay.

I was in the seventh grade before being told I was poor. If I had not read it in the *LaGrange Daily News,* I might have gone away to college before even considering the possibility.

That year I saw a photo in the local newspaper of children boarding a bus. I was one of the kids. The caption read, "Underprivileged Children Visit Shrine Circus in Atlanta.."I asked my teacher what that meant and she said, "Oh, darling, that was just something they had to say to get free tickets." For years I didn't question her explanation.

Her name was Miss Brown and she was one of many who perpetuated an illusion that I was blessed. In the Callaway Mill village of my day, I could play basketball, football, softball or tennis and never have to pay a fee or buy a piece of equipment. I could swim in an Olympic size pool and never bring a towel from home. I could read as much as I wanted at the Callaway Library and never have to purchase a book.

I could sing and dance and act in plays. Bandmaster Vannie Sanders would valiantly attempt to teach me to play a musical instrument, providing the trumpets and tubas and clarinets each time I was game enough to try.

The cotton mill village was indeed paternalistic, and while it perpetuated a historical sense of dependency among adults, it fostered an environment of safety and strong values among its children.

If I were to recreate a chronology of those who orchestrated this loving charade, I would start with two brothers, Howard and Dexter Shuford. During school week they lugged their green bags of equipment to our mill village schools for games at recess. They organized half-mile-long cake races, where I would have always finished last were it not for Jimmy Strickland, who was fat, and Dan Medlock, who had flat feet.

Howard and Dexter put together kazoo bands with washtub bass and hummers made from paper-covered pocket combs. Then, in summers at Callaway YMCA and the Callaway Pool, the brothers kept us in line with flinty stares and tight lips that would intimidate the biggest bully. On Sundays they taught us at the Southwest LaGrange Baptist Church. At age 12 I decided in Dexter's class to be baptized although

I understood more about what he stood for than I did about the New Testament.

At age 13 I became increasingly aware of Mary Florence Moore. She was born with the gift of laughter and a sense that all teenagers needed her tender mercies. Never married, she lived at the Teachers' Home across from the YMCA. She chaperoned the Callaway Teen Club and tolerated no hanky panky at the weekly Saturday night dances. She produced and directed the club's plays and musicals and always had a shoulder available for the lovelorn.

She once did a great thing for me. I was serving as representative to a state convention of Teen Club officers and one afternoon after I led a session she took me aside. She hugged me and then she said, "You are a smart kid, but you talk like a hick. You need to pay attention to your grammar and you need to get your teeth fixed. Otherwise, nobody is ever going to take you seriously."

With how many hundreds of others must Mary Florence Moore have mixed laughter and straight talk and set in motion waves of self-understanding? It just wasn't unusual in that cotton mill village where children spent such little time wondering who was rich and who was poor.

To my way of thinking, it proves you can't always believe what you read in a newspaper.

February, 2012

Frank Childers' Place

For as long as I can remember traveling Georgia 411, they were there, a wiry black man and a little white pony. Sometimes the pony was hitched to a plow, sometimes to the shell of a car sawed in half to make a cart for hauling everything from collards to firewood.

"He must be a hundred years old," I said one night to my son-in-law, Reed Biggers, as I was telling him about the old man and wondering who he was.

"He's almost a hundred. He's 92," replied Reed.

"You know him?"

"He's my friend. Name's Frank Childers. I killed my first buck on his farm when I was 13. My brother met him when he was looking for a place to hunt and he introduced me. Then it kind of became the thing to do for Berry College students. Barbecue a deer, drink beer and sit around listening to Frank play his old guitar."

So it was through Reed that I came to know Frank Childers. He and Reed dropped by Hodge Podge Lodge one day when Reed had taken his friend to redeem food stamps and to pick up some Canadian Mist for Dorothy, who sometimes stays with Frank when the weather gets cold and a little extra body heat is a comfort in the old house that was built before the Civil War.

The next time I saw Frank was the night after Christmas. Reed had bagged a rabbit that he thought would make a fine present. He telephoned Frank to see if it was okay to visit. Sunset was the color of a peeled apricot when we pulled into Frank's yard. Old Bill, the pony, had his nose pressed against a wire fence, staring. A dog barked from under the porch The door opened before we could even knock.

"Let's cook us a rabbit, Frank," Reed said as we entered the room.

"Evuhthang ready. Skillet onda stove. They's some lard onda table."

"You just sit over there in your chair and relax and I'll do the cooking," Reed said. "How you feeling, anyhow?" Doctors had recently removed a large tumor from Frank's abdomen.

5

"Feelin' better. Still can't tote nothin'."

Soon the rabbit was in the skillet and I noticed a signal from Reed to come into the kitchen.

"Ever seen lard foam like this?"

"Nah. Looks kind of like soap," I said.

Within half an hour the chef was serving the rabbit along with some vegetables left over from Christmas dinner. I hungrily bit into a leg. I stopped in mid bite.

"Reed, that was soap!"

We laughed and Frank said, "They's a turkey inda oven."

"Where'd you get the turkey?" asked Reed.

"Mr. Summers at da bank come by, him and his boy. Gimme a turkey and ist new shirt."

"You got some new bedroom slippers, too?" Reed had noticed them.

"Yeah. 'member that ol' white preacher who use hang 'round here an' drank white likker? Well, his wife she still send me stuff at Christmas, even though she left him and move to Texas."

Reed turned to me and said. "The rest of us wouldn't touch the stuff, but one night we all filled up our glasses about halfway to the top with water, and then we gave him his glass full of moonshine. We turned ours up and drank it, and he tilted back his head and downed his. About five minutes later he just fell over backwards out of that chair you're in."

I looked at my watch. "We have to leave before long, Frank. Would you play some blues for me?"

It had been a while since Frank had played for anyone. The old guitar was covered with dust and the nut had fallen off the neck, making it impossible to tune. Finally we found a wood matchstick for a make-shift nut. Frank's long fingers began to feel around over the frets where paint had been worn away from playing for decades in one key.

"Oh, mama, she's gone. Oh, mama, she's gone. Oh, mama, she's gone." He stopped playing.

"Still ain't right. Strings s'posed to sing."

"I'll get it fixed," said Reed as we prepared to leave.

"You gone take me fishin' Reed?" Frank asked as we stood at the door.

"This spring, Frank. Soon as it warms up."

"I be feelin' good by then, I bet. Be feelin' real good. You won' fo'get?"

Reed patted him on the shoulder. "I won't forget, Frank."

As the tires of our truck crunched the rocks of the drive, we took one more look at the silhouette at the door, an old man waiting for spring and a promise.

Feburary, 1985

GOD MOVES IN MYSTERIOUS WAYS

The new preacher was awakened by a thunderous knocking on his front door. He fumbled in the darkness for a light switch and through sleep-fogged eyes saw that the clock beside his bed recorded the imminent arrival of four a.m. Considering the hour he assumed someone had arrived in a state of agitated emergency.

A grimy creature with dirt caked on him like tree bark materialized in the incandescent glow of the porch light. The visitor identified himself simply as Bubba. He said he was there to remind the preacher that the next day was food stamp day. Upon the preacher questioning the significance of such information Bubba told him that the previous occupants of his pulpit had always taken him to pick up his stamps.

The preacher was a man of temper despite having heard the meek are supposed to inherit the earth. He explained with Old Testament ferocity that he did not consider running a shuttle service to the welfare office part of his ministry. Bubba trembled appropriately, having comprehended the emotion, but showed up again after daylight, not having accurately identified the meaning of the tirade.

On the way to pick up the food stamps the young minister advised Bubba he needed to get a car of his own. Bubba just nodded his head and smiled.

A couple of days later the preacher received a call from Bubba's wife, Dula. She told him that each of the previous pastors at the church had always taken her and Bubba into town on Fridays to get groceries. Resigned by then to his fate, the preacher drove the couple to the supermarket. He rolled the cart up and down the aisles, nodding pleasantly to random members of his flock while Bubba and Dula filled the cart with fatback, white flour, lard and sugar.

In time the minister began to learn more about his new dependents. Their only source of income was provided by Dula's blind mother who sewed quilts that sold for $3 each. He learned that Bubba had been abandoned at birth by his mother, who ran off with a man widely considered to be the boy's father. The child was left with his grandfather and grandmother, who kept him chained under a porch when they went to work. They often fed him out in the yard with the dogs.

When Bubba grew up he roamed the streets and people made fun of him. One of the tormentors thought it would be great sport to write a letter on Bubba's behalf to a columnist for the lovelorn in an Atlanta newspaper. Dula, who lived on a farm south of Atlanta, saw the letter in the paper and responded to it.

Since Bubba couldn't read, when Dula's letter came he took it to the fellow who had written the first message. A second letter was promptly dispatched proposing marriage and the proposition was accepted by Dula. The girls father sent a Greyhound bus ticket to Bubba. When he saw his daughter's prospective groom he almost had a heart attack. But he had promised Dula a husband and he stood by his word.

The preacher gradually became adjusted to the couple, but he received a call that alarmed him. Bubba, who knew nothing about dialing a telephone, had somehow reached him and pleaded with him to come over because something bad was wrong with Dula. She died of cardiac arrest before help could arrive.

A few days after the funeral, the local sheriff found Bubba in the cemetery at midnight. He was pumping bullets from a .45 caliber pistol into his wife's grave, apparently the only way he knew to express his grief and frustration.

Eventually the preacher moved away and didn't hear of Bubba for many years. But recently he had the opportunity to visit his former congregation and he asked what had happened to his hapless little neighbor.

One of the members of the church said that for a long time after Dula died Bubba just roamed the streets as he had in his youth. Then one day, as he ambled through the town he was stopped by the Widow Wilson, who owned a profitable country store. She told him to get into her car, and he did. She told Bubba she was lonely, that she was going to clean him up and marry him.

Now Bubba drives around in a big pickup truck with all the latest gadgets on it. He has seven cowboy hats to wear with a different set of clothes for each day. The Widow Wilson has hired somebody else to run the store and—so folks say—Bubba has never been happier.

"God moves in mysterious ways," says the preacher who told me this story, and I guess he ought to know.

October, 1982

KILLING TIME

I have often raised my voice in praise of small towns. But I'd have to say, after a recent odyssey through the textile towns of the South on journalistic assignment, they are a great place to live but not much fun just to visit.

When you are a stranger in a small town, time is like a dripping faucet--a day takes a long time to fill up. I was marooned in Eden, N.C., on a holiday weekend, so lots of folks were out of town, but I got the idea things moved about the same pace regardless. I had planned to fill this particular Saturday with some interviews for a series I was doing on vanishing textile towns. But several people, who the day before had said they would talk to me, started backing out.

The first man said, "Naw, I forgot that I got to mow the grass."

"How about when you get through?" I asked.

"Well, sometimes it takes all weekend."

I called my second interview.

"I got company," he replied.

"How about Monday?"

"I got to cut the grass."

I was faced with a Saturday as empty as my hopes for ever getting my interviews. I was reduced to cruising around in my rental car. When I spotted a flea market, I headed for it. Tell the truth, I would rather have real fleas than spend time in one of these alfresco Kmarts, but I thought perhaps I could do some character studies, pick up on the local idiom.

At the obligatory used-book cranny, two men were discussing literature. "I've read books for 25 years, and I can't remember a damn thing in any of them," said the short stocky man with part of a thumb missing. "So I just stopped reading. I just sell them now. Can you remember anything you've ever read?" he asked his friend.

"Only when I start reading them again," admitted the fat man with the big cigar. "Then it dawns on me that I already read it. Most of the things I remember is from comic books. Wonder why that is?"

He took a draw on the cigar and slowly exhaled a cloud of blue-gray smoke. He hitched up his pants, which gave him the appearance of a large round apple with two toothpicks stuck in the bottom.

"I don't know why people got to knock comic books so much."

"Oh, there's folks got to knock everything," the vendor commiserated. "Even some of them evangelists knock comic books. They knock smoking, too, and a couple of million people are going to be out of work because of it."

"Why don't they knock cocaine?" the apple man mused. "I never heard Falwell or any of that bunch say much about that. Wouldn't it be something if it come out they was on that stuff?"

"Wouldn't bother me none," said the vendor. "I say let them do it if they want to and leave me alone to do what I want to."

Nearby, two families gathered for a chat. "I thought you said if you had another baby you gone give it to us," said one man. He put his hand on the head of a wide-eyed little girl of maybe 4 years and patted affectionately. She stuck out her tongue and tried to bite his hand.

"Unh-unh, I don't want her," he said, but he laughed like he didn't mean it.

I drove out to Eden Park, high on a knoll. I thought I could see the river from there, but I couldn't and was disappointed. Two policemen were sitting in the shade.

"Things a little slow?" I asked.

"It'll pick up tonight," one replied.

"Not for me," I said. "I don't even have a wife here to fight with." One of them laughed.

I visited the local fitness center and offered the girl on the desk a substantial bribe to let me work out.

"Naw," she said, "Everybody would know you ain't from around here." I didn't even bother to ask how they would know.

The Western Steer was cool in the 97-degree vapidness, and the waitress was young and friendly. I asked her where folks went for entertainment on Saturday night.

"Well, they's Daddy Jax on Highway 14," she said. "I go there sometimes, but I done quit drankin'. I was staying loaded all the time. I drunk for breakfast. I drunk for lunch."

Why is she telling me all this, I wondered. She put her tray down and leaned across the table on one arm. "For three years I didn't hardly eat. I got down to 80 pounds. I drunk instead of eat. Then, I got skee-red. I was having trouble driving home at night. I just quit cold turkey a year and a month ago."

"Why did you drink so heavily?" I asked.

"I don't know. Just to have something to do," she said.

I told her I thought I understood.

October, 1986

NOBODY THOUGHT THERE WOULDN'T ALWAYS BE A MILL

MANCHESTER, GA.—Cotton towns have always been defined by mill whistles. Even after the two steamboat-like wakeup blasts at 4:30 a.m. were discontinued, single signals blared at 6 a.m., 2 p.m. and 10 p.m. calling workers to their eight-hour shifts at the factories that lifted the post-Civil War South from its economic knees.

Whistles were audible rainbows, promises that the South's world was not to be violated again. But the whistles don't blow here anymore. The people look down from a hill dotted with square box homes built by the company and stare at the old brick mill. Fuller Callaway started the first cotton factory here in 1910. Then, Milliken and Co. came in the '70s and bought out Callaway, but still there was a mill. The people thought there always would be.

Now, there is only silence. There is no pulse inside the empty three-story structure. Milliken closed the doors in February and the workers, even many of the 80 percent who have been relocated on new jobs, are still stunned. Loss of a way of life, after all, is just as hard to understand as loss of life itself. The grief is still palpable among those who, until the silencing of the whistles, had not known nor cared to learn any other way of making a living.

At times, with low pay and lower expectations, it wasn't much of a life. Nevertheless, it was their life, a curious contradiction of defiance and acquiescence.

On the one hand, cotton millers (they never called themselves textile workers, even after the introduction of synthetic fibers) have been fiercely determined, underpaid workers with obsessive visions of a better life for the kids. There remains among them a general pride of accomplishment and a pugnacious attitude directed toward outsiders.

On the other hand, there is a perplexing society of fear and insecurity. For all of a cotton miller's hopes for the children, few, once caught up in the warp and woof of a weave room, dare to break away themselves. The mill has been the paterfamilias, the touchstone in their lives. Especially in the old days under Callaway.

In those days, if a worker needed coal for the fireplaces, he was never turned away from the factory supply. He paid for it 50 cents a week. If he needed money to prevent a bleak Christmas for his children, he got it. If he landed in jail after too much Saturday, the second hand or the superintendent bailed him out and got him back on the job on Monday.

Under modern management employees had the chance to make more money through production incentives, but the human relationships within the mill vanished. If one fell victim to demon rum, he was gone, not protected. Modern management meant tougher discipline at the same time it added air conditioning and a cleaner environment.

Floyd Ellerbee, a giant of a man with basket-like hands, has performed under both systems. He spent 40 years and three months in the weave room. He says, "There is a difference in a comfortable place to work and being comfortable in your work. I still liked the old ways better."

Off and on, Floyd's wife, Jeanette, has worked 28 years in the mill. The two of them raised their daughter, Melanie, in a house they bought from Callaway for $4.46 a week and paid for in less than seven years. Melanie had 10 years on her record when the doors shut.

So, two generations were leveled by the closing. Floyd will not try to relocate even though his unemployment check has already stopped. He will open up a lawn mower repair business at his home, he says. Melanie has found work at the Goody's plant for less money. Her mother is recovering from an operation and hopes to work there in the future.

"I really loved my job at the mill," Jeanette says. "That's the reason I never tried to learn anything else. Nobody believed there wouldn't always be a textile industry. There always had been."

There is a moribund silence inside the Manchester mill. Only the smell of cottonseed remains, as difficult to get out of the brick and hardwood as it is to get out of the blood. But don't listen for the cotton mill whistle here. It won't ever blow again.

December, 1985

GOODWILL HUNTING

This fall I plan to avoid Dirt Town Deli, my favorite temple of biscuits, bacon, sausage, fried bologna and cheesy eggs up on Highway 27 in Gore. I've been a fairly regular breakfast customer there for three or four years, which is long enough for the locals to recognize my newcomer face, but not my name. Most mornings they are garbed in heavy-duty work clothes and billed caps and I like to think that on those days I am conformably clad. But in the fall when they show up in apparel that renders them indistinguishable from trees, leaves and briars I am noticeably dissimilar. Nevertheless, as a gesture of cautious acknowledgement, one will usually inquire, "Have you gotcha deer yet?"

Not that there is some buck out there in the forest wearing my name tag. It's just that in the country, how you answer goes a long way toward determining whether they bother to place a name to your face. I don't hunt and I've about run out of answers to the query, so these days, if referenced at all, I will be identified as that fellow they ain't seen around here lately.

The bottom line is, I am not washed in the blood, except in terms of that beautiful old song in the church hymnal about the symbolic connection between sacrificial blood and forgiveness, which some would say is not antithetical to the spiritual experience many hunters ascribe to dawn, dusk and gunshot in the woods and fields.

There was a time, before we moved to Armuchee, when my ostracism would have been confined to visits within the boundaries of my wife's rural upbringing, where a boy's first step and first hunt occur on about the same time table. But now, even were I still eating lunch high atop Buckhead, my failure to own a Purdy of London shotgun might identify me as a low-roller ill-equipped to discuss manly achievements over sips of Macallan 25 Scotch. In the corporate world, evidence that you can dispatch wild game with the blast of say, a $100,000 Purdy or a coveted Italian Fabbri is beginning to fill the role among a growing number of power brokers that Rolex, Porsche and a mega mansion used to serve for those in a mine-is-bigger-than yours state of mind.

One morning up at Dirt Town I mentioned to an old timer named Pullis Legg that a female executive in Atlanta told me that a number of women climbing corporate ladders were adapting to these luxurious hunts as an obligatory aspect of power elbow rubbing. Pullis said he didn't think it was all that good an idea. He told me about the wife of a friend of his who was pestering him to let her go deer hunting. Before they went out in the woods he said that some old boys around there were bad about stealing game after it's killed. He cautioned her that if she drops a deer and anybody comes up and tries to take it, to raise her gun to protect it.

Sure enough, she up and shot what she thought was a deer. Shortly thereafter came a man around the bend just a running. She pointed her gun at him and said, "Just a minute, mister, you ain't gonna get my deer."

He said, "Lady, could I at least get my bridle and saddle?"

Sometimes I suspect the fellows at Dirt Town aren't above shooting me a line before going out to shoot their guns.

October, 2006

FOLKS OUGHT TO UNDERSTAND

It is a county of good people and hard work and although some folks there have become well-off by local standards, almost all of them came by their nest egg honestly and with considerable sweat.

If you had grown up there you would have known Hog Singleton. That's not his real name, of course. I will not provide that information since I am sure he would have no trouble locating me even in a city this big.

At one time Hog was a football player of collegiate promise, had not such a career entailed at least a passing familiarity with textbooks. Over the years he became known as the meanest man in the county, moving ahead of an elderly farmer, Nub Carruth, who is still number two, but past his prime.

Meanness in a small town doesn't carry the same definition as it does in a big city. In a metropolis it refers to bank robbings, murders and assorted pillaging. But in small towns it is a term that covers general orneriness and may include anything from kicking dogs to cussin' real heavy.

Hog's meanness has been confined mainly to clearing out local beer joints and to physical disputes with the deputies who try to put him in jail for his own good. There is an occasional adventure with an irate husband, but nobody gets too steamed up about that, it being so personal between the parties.

Nub's meanness, on the other hand, stems mostly from impatience. He once owned a $3,000 bull that he hadn't been able to hem up in the pasture for over a year. So, one day Nub got into his brand-new pickup truck, for which he had just paid $10,000, and headed out across his considerable pastureland in search of the recalcitrant bovine.

When Nub found the bull he tried in vain to pin it against a fence with the truck. Finally, he just gunned his pickup into the side of the bull and knocked it sprawling. The animal jumped up and hightailed it across the grassy field, while his owner was left with a severely injured vehicle spewing steam into the air from its radiator.

Nub's pastureland is divided by a busy highway, which he still crosses as if it were the tranquil, dusty road of his youth. Shortly after his aggravation with the bull he gunned his recently repaired truck across the thoroughfare—as usual not looking left or right—and was struck broadside by a Volkswagen. The little foreign car was virtually unscathed, but the truck was so disassembled the local Chevrolet dealer had to replace it altogether.

The embarrassment of being felled by a Volkswagen had Nub in a particularly foul mood the night Hog Singleton showed up in his yard. Hog had gotten drunk with friends who apparently grew tired of his company and dumped him, unconscious, into a ditch near Nub's farm. When the inebriated giant regained mobility he wandered up to Nub's new truck and, discovering keys in the ignition, figured it was the most logical transportation home.

Nub and his wife, Lovella, were in bed when they heard the motor fire up. The grizzled old farmer grabbed his .357 magnum from the table next to the bed and scrambled toward the window. He tripped and put a bullet hole in the mattress about six inches from the supine body of his spouse. He also deposited three out of five shots into the body of his truck as it pulled out of the driveway.

About three miles down the road the pickup bandit passed out again and ran the truck into a dirt bank. The young deputy who came to arrest him received a broken jaw and a dislocated finger.

To make matters worse for Nub, who was going to need still another truck, Lovella was convinced her husband and Hog had simply concocted an assassination plot that would be made to appear accidental by the alleged theft.

Everybody figured that Mrs. Carruth had finally believed her husband was telling the truth, but not long afterwards old Nub was flattened like a tortilla when his tractor mysteriously ran amok while he had his back turned.

Just the other day the local probate judge saw the recently liberated Hog walking slowly down a sunbaked road and stopped to give him a lift to town. The judge thought the timing was right to lecture his passenger about lifestyle, since it was the middle of the week and Hog was sober as, well, as a judge.

"Hog," said the magistrate, "You're not a bad fellow. How come you do the things you do?"

"Well, judge," replied Hog, "I've tried living straight and living bad and just about everything in between. When I'm all concerned with trying to live a certain way, I ain't happy. But when I just live the way I am, I'm real happy. Looks like folks ought to understand that."

November, 1982

THE HERETIC AT ANTIOCH BAPTIST CHURCH

His hands were sandpaper rough. Big, calloused, working hands as dry and weathered as the tobacco leaves they once tended. After he had devastated a portion of barbecued chicken at the Antioch Baptist Church's spring Chicken Pickin', 72-year-old David Irby folded those hands across his midsection, leaned back in a metal chair and spoke his mind.

"I'm gonna tell it to you honest as I can," he said. "I realize that you can find places in the Bible says women shouldn't be preachers…and a lot of us thought that." He looked toward the front of the narrow fellowship hall where the Rev. Judith Powell had donned an old hillbilly hat and was blushing as she performed her part in a frivolous skit. "But after meeting her, I just think maybe it's all been misinterpreted.

"You see, in a period of five years, I lost a brother, a son, two grandsons and an uncle, all to accidents. I've shed enough tears to float this old church. And what I've found out is that when your heart is breaking and somebody loves and cares about you, you don't care whether it is a man or a woman."

Both this rough-hewn man of the land and the slender, brown-eyed woman of the cloth are heretics. In becoming pastor of this tiny 144-year-old church in the flatlands of North Carolina, the Rev. Powell, in the eyes of the Southern Baptist Convention and the Baptist Home Mission Board, has defied the biblical instructions of God.

In accepting Rev. Powell, Irby and the 71 other members of the Antioch congregation have rebuffed a 1984 SBC resolution that said, in effect, that because of woman's role in the Garden of Eden, and specific scriptural admonitions, no female can serve in a position of authority over men.

Indicative of just how seriously the dogma is taken is the fact that among the 14.6 million members of the Southern Baptist denomination, there are less than one dozen female pastors of their own church. In October 1986, the Baptist Home Mission Board voted to cut off funds to any congregation that accepts a female pastor in the future. In its history, the board has funded only one such ministry, that of the Rev. Debra Griffis Woodbury of Maryland. By contrast, the United Methodists have more than 3,000 ordained ministers. In all denominations, there are an estimated 8,000 ordained female ministers. Only Catholics and certain Jewish sects are as opposed to the ordination of women as are Southern Baptists.

In a letter to *The Atlanta Journal* and *The Atlanta Constitution*, the Rev. Charles Stanley, pastor of the First Baptist Church of Atlanta and former president of the SBC, explained the position. "To insist on ordination is to change God's design for carrying his ministry through his church. His plan calls for distinctive roles for men and women. To alter His plan is to imply we know better than God. The church must always guard against patterning its beliefs, policy or practices after those of the world."

The Southeastern Baptist Theological Seminary at Wake Forest, N.C. , an institution that hasn't always delighted conservative Baptists, disagrees. Last month, they awarded the Rev. Powell, a 42-year- old grandmother, the Warren-Poe Award for Rural Church Ministry. The three-year $800-per-annum stipend will place Rev. Powell, who has a master's degree, with an income slightly above the official poverty level of $7,133. According to her son, Mike, she has been offered three to four times as much to serve other churches in a capacity other than as pastor.

Judith Powell says simply, "God is higher than the Southern Baptist Convention. I did not set out to become a pastor; I was called. Although I ran from it and didn't understand for a long time, I believe that when God created me, he called me to be a pastor. I believe that if he didn't want any woman to be a preacher, he would have made me a man. I am not a feminist. I am a female who has been called to serve God."

Although the Rev. Powell, who grew up in Greensboro, N.C., had made a commitment to the Southern Baptist form of Christianity when she was 17, she was 30 and the mother of two children when she answered a second life-changing call. Two years before, her husband, who was serving in the Air Force, was electrocuted while working a part-time job trimming trees. After a period of extreme confusion, she quit her job as a Southern Bell sales representative and entered Baptist College at Mars Hill, N.C., in 1975. The family managed to subsist on Veterans Administration benefits. She started work on a master's degree from Southeastern in Wake Forest in 1979. She considered the degree strictly in terms of preparation for a career in Christian education.

While in seminary, the Rev. Powell began to serve as a supply preacher. This is permissible in Southern Baptist dogma, for the position is subservient to a male authority. During this time, Charles Dorman, director of student/field ministries at Southeastern became impressed with her work both as a person and student. In 1982, when a selection committee from Antioch approached him about finding a pastor for their little church, he asked, "Would you consider hiring a woman?"

"There was silence for a minute," Dorman recalls, "and then a younger man in the group said, 'Yes.'

"Then I said there is a very special person I want you to meet. When they came out of the meeting with Judy Powell, there wasn't one who didn't have tears in their eyes. This woman has a power."

The membership of Antioch Baptist Church, a white clapboard building so old it has hand-hewn crossbeams in its ceiling, voted to hire the Rev. Powell as its minister at a starting salary of less than $5,000 per year.

When she arrived at the church, the membership numbered only about 50 people—25 new members have been added since her first sermon—and some members had suggested closing its doors. A few of those who attended were not happy about the hiring of a female preacher, recalls Jessie Belle Lewis, who was chairman of the selection committee.

Ed Tippette, a burly retired used car salesman from nearby Roanoke Rapids, liked it least of all. An Episcopalian, he had attended Antioch's services with his wife for years. He even sang in the Baptist choir. But he quit. He refused to listen to the Rev. Powell preach.

At the Chicken Pickin' social ("We have to create our own excitement here," said Deacon Herb Smith, who cooked the birds), Tippette talked about his relationship with the new preacher.

"My wife, Thelma, kept coming home and saying, 'Ed, you ought to come hear her. She's good. She's good.'

"Finally, I came back. What I found was where there had been division in the church, she had brought healing. I found love in this place I had never seen or felt before.

"Not long after that, she baptized me. She dropped me, 'cause I'm so big and she's so tiny, but she did what a lot of preachers before her couldn't do. I love her. And in plain English I'll tell anybody, a woman's got the right to preach if she has the gift."

The Rev. Powell tries to shut the controversy out of her life. She simply accepts that Antioch Baptist is not the last stop for her, that "God may need me somewhere else."

She added, "Like first love, Antioch will always be the special one, whatever happens. But I believe that small churches are where women will serve, and, as for me, that is what I want. This is my ministry, one on one. I can't get in the pulpit and proclaim God's love without knowing each of their burdens . . . where they are hurting."

Last year, she baptized twins in the first baptism ever inside the church. She baptized Herb Smith's brother in a converted grain bin built as a gift of love by Herb. She has baptized others in the Gaston River. From over 160 prospects on her list, she expects more to follow before her work is finished at Antioch. She tries not to think of herself as a pioneer, nor does she dwell unduly on the opposition of conservatives within her denomination.

"Sometimes, it does seem as though we women are just something to get minds off the real issues," she says. "But all it is doing is hurting the individual churches. You go out and try to tell people God loves them and they look at you and say, 'Why, you don't even love each other.'"

April, 1987

MEMOIR OF AN URBAN COWBOY

Poets muse wistfully of cattle meandering peacefully o'er the lea and perhaps I had fallen under sway of Longfellow or Shelley when I traded my city loafers for steel-toe work boots and Carhart overalls. After all, there are no laws against owning cows before you are ready.

I was preparing to retire from my job as editor of *Atlanta* magazine and had purchased a home, pond, cattle barn and 19 acres from banker Steve Kemp and wife, Ellen. For some reason that escapes me now (perhaps delusions of skyrocketing farm land values), we already possessed some 20 adjoining acres of pasture, old barns and pond. Additionally, I had invested in a range of plaid shirts, two wide brim straw hats, Wells Lamont leather gloves, an all terrain vehicle, a slightly-used Kubota tractor and several rolls of barbed wire. It amounted to little more than an empty charade without cows.

Transitioning from city life to pastoral was trendily referred to at the time as achieving balanced life force. Well, there is nothing as expensive or humbling as a big, well-developed, full-bodied misconception.

I was surprised to discover cattle are designated by breed rather than color. By then I had completed a deal for two reds, two blacks, two whites and a brown. I bought a bull. People would look at him and remark, "Wow, that is really one fat bas—rd." So, I called him F.B. All F.B. was good for once a year was to bring smiles to the faces of the girls. The rest of the time he ate, added prodigiously to the atmosphere's level of methane gas and tested the tensile strength of pasture fences. Even in the understanding community of Armuchee neighbors can grow weary of you roaming around Highway 156 in the middle of the night with a bucket of sweet feed and a flashlight while imploring, "F.B., get yourself back in that pasture."

One evening, about dark thirty, my wife and I were repairing an exit F.B. had created. In a torrential rain storm, lightning flashing, we worked frantically to repair the fence bordering the highway because we had to return to Atlanta that night. Berry College's cattle major domo, Ray Larson, was driving past at the time. He later asked our daughter, Shannon Biggers, "Are your parents mental?"

I prefer "budgetarily impaired," which covers time as well as money. When the month neared to market calves (don't name them or you can't do it), I discovered I would need a corral and head gate in order to load them up for transport. I dropped $1,200 quick ones, not counting therapy for radial tunnel therapy on my right arm because I thought a rancher should do his own work. I located the setup next to the old barn that had cost $2,700 to repair even with the help of Decathur Miller, he with a gimpy left arm, I with an impaired right. To ensure bovine hydration after the creek started drying up I had to hire Tommy Dean to repair the pump in the old well house. Another $500 got me a Bush Hog mower to keep pastures groomed so the cows wouldn't be embarrassed. Nobody told me that seven cows and F.B. could consume 60 bales of hay at $20 a bale during a droughty year. With less budgetary impact I could have raised 20,000 pounds of consumable or marketable potatoes on a single acre it would take to raise 165 pounds of beef.

When my black cow, Lisa Left-Eye, began to run a fever and create abstract pasture sculptures, I beseeched veterinarian Dr. Ernest Myers to drive out after work because of what I considered an emergency. Gynecologic examination of Lisa revealed part of the problem was motherhood. Then, when Dr. Myers opened Lisa Left-Eye's mouth for examination he shouted, "Oh, my God!" I feared she and I had introduced Mad Cow disease to Armuchee. Instead, he marveled, "This cow has no teeth. This cow, is Lord, olddddddd!" I thanked him and wrote him a check.

I couldn't have recouped my investment if every one of my cows had produced marketable triplets. Eventually, I found a customer for them. As they were loaded up one by one I offered no comfort to Decathur Miller and my wife as they looked at me with matching scowls.

When both began outright sobbing I swore the cattle were being purchased as pets, not hamburger. "Time to turn the other cheek and mooo-ve on," I said, though with little hope they would appreciate the pun.

July, 2011

BELOW THE SUNDAY LINE: RIFLES OR
LAW BOOKS?

S pring Creek Baptist Church is located below the Sunday Line. Unyielding farmers who live within this imaginary boundary just outside of Donalsonville, Ga., have historically attended services on the Sabbath, then rushed back to the fields to make up for the time they lost while laboring on full-time jobs elsewhere during the week.

The Ned Alday family—quiet, hardworking and respected—lived below the Sunday Line. Now, six of them lie beneath gray slabs of Italian marble in the shade of a water oak and some scrub pines next to their church.

A year ago last November, the congregation at Spring Creek Baptist burned a note, symbolizing the paying off of a sanctuary that sprang from funds that were contributed in the aftermath of the Alday family massacre, one of the most maniacal mass slayings in state history.

Only a few days after the church ceremony, another note the people of Seminole County thought was paid off was found to be still due when the U. S. Circuit Court of Appeals ruled the convicted murderers of the Aldays would be granted a new trial based on prejudicial publicity.

The judges ruled that publicity mounted during the media's exercising of its First Amendment guarantee of freedom of the press had violated the Sixth Amendment that guarantees a speedy and public trial by an impartial jury. The new trial has been shifted from Seminole County.

The Court of Appeals is saying that a group of admitted remorseless killers could not get a fair trial in the community where the crime took place because of unusual influence caused by what the citizens read and heard. The natural question is, given modern technology, is it possible to conduct a trial anywhere free of such information bombardment? The more subtle inferences are that Southern towns are not capable of anything but vigilante justice.

Through the years, there have been rumors that mob violence was narrowly averted in Donalsonville while the accused (Carl Junior Isaacs, Billy Isaacs, Wayne Carl Coleman and George Elder Dungee) were incarcerated there.

Periodically, stories about the Alday slayings contain a single paragraph alluding to a supposed vigilante operation that was halted by the actions of Bud Alday, a surviving brother of Ned and Benny Alday. Benny has been quoted in newspapers and books as having discouraged an acquaintance who came to him and said a group of men had agreed to kill the accused murderers if the family would sanction it. The family, fairly typical of the conservative community, felt that justice would prevail through the system.

In the aftermath of the decision by the 11th Circuit Court of Appeals, I was put in contact with two people who claim to have been a part of the plan to execute the accused. They described in detail how the matter was to have been resolved. One of them said that at about 7 in the morning after the alleged plot was hatched, he received a telephone call, and a voice said, "We've talked with Bud, and Bud doesn't want it to happen. He believes justice will be served."

But even with community anguish over the mass killings continuing, questions asked along the wide, flat streets of Donalsonville about the supposed plot are generally met with silence or outright skepticism. Bo McLeod, the venerable publisher of the *Donalsonville News*, wrote of such rumors, "There are a few screwballs among us who get a thrill out of talking dumb and sounding off about what all they'd like to do to the four men. But they're in the extreme minority, and they are pretty well-known for their lack of sense."

Sheriff Jerry Godby also discounts the validity of such tales. "Sheriff Dan White, [in charge at the time] told me there was a set of keys to the jail just hanging on the wall. If anybody had really wanted to do anything, they could have."

Whether the vigilante plot was real probably is important only as it relates to the Court's attitude. There are those who would cite the lingering rumors of this non-event as verification of the Court's opinion that justice for the Alday killers was not possible in Seminole County.

On the other hand, it must not be forgotten that in the fieriest furnace of emotion in our state since the murder of Mary Phagan in Atlanta, the community placed its faith in justice. Nothing actually happened.

And we must also consider that events such as the ordering of yet another trial when there is admitted guilt serves to remind us there are at least two ways of abusing the judicial system—one as portrayed by men with rifles, and the other as exemplified by men reading between the lines of a law book.

December, 1986

THE NEKKID TRUTH

There is a beautiful little lake called Lahusage near Mentone, Ala. It's a tiny impoundment, supplied by the wild and scenic Little River. The water is so clear it is often Caribbean blue. Several years ago my wife and I were looking at a piece of property there as a potential retirement home.

On one trip we parked our truck and began to walk toward the dam because we had heard there was some structural damage. It was a little past noonday and sweltering, not a day to tarry far away from shade trees. As we neared the dam my wife said, "I hear voices."

Indeed, she did.

High stepping jauntily across the dam from the other side came a pot-bellied good-ole boy carrying in one hand a picnic basket emblazoned with "Roll Tide" and in the other hand a six pack of Budweiser. His date was sort of skipping along and giggling at his side.

She greeted us like she was a member of the Lahusage Welcome Wagon. "Hey there!" she offered. Her voice was husky from too many cigarettes, but lyrical in the way she turned each word into multiple syllables.

"Ya'll new around here?" she inquired.

I told her no, we were just looking. I guess her definition of "looking" wasn't the same as mine. Not much later I was fairly certain of the disconnect. She asked, "Ya'll got any kids?"

Her interest struck me as somewhat intrusive given that we had just met.

"Well, yes, we have children," I replied, "but they are older than you. Why do you want to know?"

"'Cause I'm fixin' to git nekkid," she said.

And she did.

She was well turned out, in a Rubenesque sort of way, and the big tatoo on her right thigh was as *au courant* as anything I've seen on MTV. She didn't so much dive as she joyously belly flopped into the

30

water.

Her date popped the top on a Bud and said, "I hope she didn't go an' offend y'all. That gal shore does like gitten nekkid."

She hoisted herself back up on the dam. As we turned to go, she said, "Y'all have a good day."

It seemed sincere and after all, we were in Alabama where public nudity is no excuse for impolite conversation.

July, 2013

A CASE OF PARADISE NOT FOUND

The man is not a loner because he enjoys solitude. He has tried to blend into the world and people continue to disappoint him. He had lived in Rome for 3,050 days and apparently not enjoyed a single one of them when I first met him at Dogwood Books and Antiques on Broad Street. That meeting was like sticking my finger in a light socket. I wasn't electrocuted, but I was shocked.

"You are much older than your photograph in the newspaper," he said when Dogwood owner Kenneth Stoddard introduced us.

"Well, the picture was taken six weeks ago, so that figures," I said.

"Why do you count the days you have lived in Rome?" I asked as I tried to fashion something resembling a conversation.

"That's how long I've lived here without getting to really know anyone. I've been told it takes 32 years to be accepted in Rome unless you move here when you are young and have money. I've only been here 3,050 days. I'm not young and certainly not rich."

"How hard have you tried to find friends?"

"Well, you can't put a sandwich board on your back and advertise for a friend. Georgians are funny people. I thought everybody thought alike, but they don't. This is a foreign country."

"Have you attended any church functions here, gotten to know people that way?"

"I'm Catholic," the man said. "There are so many Baptists in this town. Religious people worry so much about their salvation they don't have time to be nice."

He told me that his mother, who was past 50 when he was born, was deeply religious. Baptist, he said, but didn't elaborate on their spiritual differences. He described his grandmother as the "grand dragon" of Richmond, Virginia. "She hated Eleanor Roosevelt because she messed up people paying low wages to their maids."

"Why did you move to Rome?" I asked.

"My brother lives here. After I retired from teaching in Richmond, he said, 'Come to Paradise.' It's cheaper here. It's beautiful. The people are wonderful. "

The man moved into a townhouse. "When I was moving in a neighbor said, 'Oh, you have furniture made of wood.' I said, well, I left my concrete furniture at my other home. I was told the association would clean my gutters and take care of grass and such. Well, I had had to buy a ladder and clean the gutters myself. I did see two men cutting my grass. I went out with glasses of ice water on a silver tray, but they didn't even speak English."

"Do you have any special interests?"

"Great books. My recordings of great music."

"Do you ever go to performances by the Rome Symphony?"

"You can't have a symphony with women in it," he said. "When you are used to the Berlin Philharmonic, the Vienna Philharmonic, you can't go see the Rome Symphony. Why lie about it?"

As for books, he approves of a short list of classics. He would not be disappointed to see a big bonfire with what he calls "trash passed off as literature." His choices for fuel would be, "Luther, Calvin...people like that. George Bush, Glen Beck, Rush Limbaugh...although it would be hard to burn a radio...Freud, Darwin."

The man's father, a telephone company employee in Richmond, did burn books. "Every October. He never explained why he did it. He would be out in the yard piling them on and we just helped. He was our father, you know. As a child you didn't know what you liked or didn't like. Your father and your mother told you what you like. You didn't say, I have my rights. You had no rights. He didn't tell us to do it. I don't even know why he did it."

"Do you burn books?"

"Oh, no. It is very hard to burn a book."

Ironically, this little book store appears to offer his most comfortable harbor. Others have met him there, found his opinions different, but honest and provocative, fascinated that he doesn't pull his opinionated punches.

I could tell you his name, but you would somehow have to vault over the wall guarding him to make it meaningful to either of you. I told the man I hoped someone would read about him and turn out to be the friend he hasn't found. It may be difficult to find an exact match and a person can grow weary with the thought of finding someone to fill a space of understanding.

July, 2011

FOR BETTER OR FOR VERSE

Southern Baptist is the predominant religious affiliation in 98 percent of the counties in Georgia, Alabama, Arkansas and Mississippi. That still leaves room for other kinds of Baptists. Mead's Handbook of Denominations lists a staggering array (not limited to): American, National, United, Conservative, Fundamental, General Association of Reformation, Free Will, Landmark, Duck River and Kindred Associations, Six Principle, Primitive, Seventh Day, Two-Seed-in-the-Spirit, Predestinarian and The National Baptist Evangelical Life and Soul-Saving Assembly of the USA, Inc. The only attribute that fits all: "Whatever we are, we aren't them."

I belong to the Southern variety. I say belong, not in the sense I fit perfectly, but in the sense I have been perfectly welcomed by Pleasant Valley North, notwithstanding my quirks, backslides and a brief detour to Methodism in order to qualify for the Wesley Chapel basketball team. With the exception of a few gallons of baptismal water, there's really not that much difference between the two denominations. Both sin. Baptists don't enjoy it.

One thing Baptists and Methodists definitely have in common, we like to sing. Even though Corey Biggers, a member of my bloodline, used to cover his ears and wail, "Don't sing, Papa," I seldom fail to blend in my less than an octave when music director Jason Coffman dials up a hand clapping, foot tapper like "When The Roll Is Called Up Yonder."

I say dials up because nowadays song lyrics are projected onto giant screens. The late Vivian Miller called it "singing off the wall" and she didn't particularly like it. She did approve the guitars, piano and drums, referring to them as "the band." But, all things considered, she had rather respond to a jubilant, "Let us stand now and turn to number 35, "How Great Thou Art." Our hymnals are still in good supply, they just don't have many fingerprints on them.

One day at lunch I asked a lovely friend if there is any singing off the wall at her church. She raised her eyebrows and said, "Oh, my goodness, no! We are Episcopalian."

To my good fortune, whenever the calendar features a fifth Sunday in any month, I still have the option of enjoying the tactile pleasure of a worn hymnal cover and the rustle of pages. Fifth Sunday singing remains a cultural happening at three small, historic churches located in the slender finger of north Floyd County that is commonly referred to as The Pocket. West Union Baptist, Everett Springs Baptist and Mt. Tabor Methodist alternate as hosts, preaching is minimal and the majority of those who leave the pews and come down the aisle at the moment are more inclined toward singing than confessing.

My wife's people, as we say in the South, are from the area. At dual invitation from Uncle Lamar and Aunt Carolyn Miller and Fred and Dean Abston, Jackie and I attended the January 30 Fifth Sunday at Mt. Tabor. It's a lovely little church, its stained glass windows, a wood cross and an illuminated picture of Jesus the dignified symbols.

Our first song was Number 615, "He Keeps Me Singing." Wayne Hopper's booming baritone made my half-a-note-off less conspicuous, although my wife nudged me and indicated I was singing the wrong verse. After nearly an hour of singing with the congregations and humming along with the choirs, I had worked up a powerful appetite and while belting out "I'll Fly Away" my concentration momentarily wandered toward the fellowship hall where awaited homemade deviled eggs, chicken casserole, potato salad, cookies, brownies and six or seven kinds of cake and pie.

Mt. Tabor and Everett Springs choirs presented medleys before Robert King introduced their counterparts from West Union. (As best as my wife explained it, Robert's grandmother was her great grandmother, although it isn't easy to trace all the forks in Jackie's family tree).

"First of all," he said. "I prayed God would grant me a golden voice that I might sing in the choir. He told me, 'I can't do that, but I'll give you a congregation that won't know the difference.'"

It seemed to me Robert was looking in my direction when he said it, but I believe even bad singing is welcome in heaven if it is sincere. We united on "I Just Came to Praise the Lord," and I started planning how to secure a place in line before all the deviled eggs vanished.

February, 2011

WHEN HE BECAME SHE

By the nature of my job I sometimes encounter stories for which I have no frame of reference. The story of J.C., or Phoebe as she was introduced to me, is one of those times. Since there is no way I can offer a proper perspective, I am letting the story tell itself.

Nearly everyone in the family said J. C. would outgrow it all. He was a likable little guy and time would probably take care of his preference for dolls over cowboy guns.

By the time he started first grade, however, relatives were teasing him by calling him "Sissy." So, it didn't bother him too much at first when schoolmates did the same. His outgoing personality made him a favorite of teachers and he easily found a place in class plays.

When J.C. reached fourth grade he began to feel uncomfortable with the teasing. He became a loner. When he was 14, be welcomed the family move from Irwin County, Georgia, to Atlanta, but when he enrolled at a local high school he heard for the first time the word "queer." He was repulsed by the idea of people "doing that." Nevertheless, he could not deny that at times he was attracted to boys.

In his sophomore year conflicting emotions and taunts from his peers almost destroyed his last shred of happiness. One day the ROTC instructor imitated J. C.'s mincing walk in front of his howling troops. Another time, the stress caused J.C. to faint while standing at attention. He swallowed a handful of his mother's pain pills.

He survived and never played with death again. But there were many times when he wished he had died at Grady Hospital. Fifteen years after swallowing the pills he learned of a doctor in Mexico who would perform a sex-change operation.

At two o'clock on the morning of January 5, 1969, J. C. walked across the border into Tijuana, Mexico. When he checked into the Caesar Hotel a pimp approached him and asked if he wanted a woman.

J. C. had not known that a full year of hormone injections was necessary as a prelude to the operation. The doctor told him he could not perform surgery without the treatments, but when he saw the depth of his patient's despair, the Mexican physician agreed to perform a preliminary stage of the operation.

When J. C.. returned home he bought dresses, wigs and other feminine attire. For the first time he signed the name "Phoebe Smith."

A little over one year later, the second operation was completed and word spread back home about the sex change. While the patient was convalescing, neighborhood teenagers began to ride by the house, shouting, "Oh, Phoebe, baby."

Once she had recovered, Phoebe got a job within state government. After a cautious beginning she began to make friends and grow more comfortable in her new role. In May 1971, she attended a four-day convention and had two dates, one with a popular speaker. In the fall of 1973, someone at work distributed an article about her that had appeared in *The Atlanta Constitution*. Her world began to close in again.

One night she was dancing with a man on a crowded floor. Suddenly the couple became aware that everyone had stopped dancing and was staring at them. Later, at a convention party, a young stranger walked up to Phoebe as she stood chatting in a crowd. He asked, "Are you a man?"

"No," she replied, "and neither are you."

When I was introduced to Phoebe Smith she was 45 years old and more comfortable with her past and her present. She wore bright red lipstick and a red pantsuit.

In her leisure time she publishes a newsletter for transsexuals. She said she would like to make a movie of her life or, that failing, open a boutique. She has written a self-published book called "Phoebe."

"If I hadn't told my story," she said, "it would always be easy for me to blame society for whatever goes wrong in my life.

"I have come to the conclusion it is foolish for me not to do what I want to do and to be able to do it without fear of the consequences. If I don't live the rest of my life as I want to, then what I have already done is for no reason."

July, 1983

MUST LOVE DOGS

Briggs Traylor and my son, Steve, were camping on Johns Mountain when the puppy came walking out of the brush and made himself at home. Sat down in front of their campfire like he was waiting for someone to pass him a cup of coffee. Briggs reached over, lifted the visitor into the illumination of the fire, checked out the equipment and proclaimed, "This one's a Leroy."

The next day Steve tracked down the owners of the wandering puppy, fully intending only to restore order to the litter of a glossy-haired bitch in Hayward Valley. Then the inevitable happened.

Steve returned to his home in Marietta rehearsing a speech of explanation to his wife, Carolyn. His best shot was, "Well, Briggs said he would be willing to take the puppy after a week or so." It was a speech he never had to make. Colby and Alix's eyes said from first glance that if these sisters had any control of the situation, which daughters always do, the puppy would be going nowhere.

A dog well chosen is a joy forever. But one that chooses you...well that takes on a more spiritual context. Steve named the puppy the Rev. Leroy Cash, because there was no getting around it—this time the man had been chosen by the dog, as surely as if a circuit rider had showed up at the campfire and proclaimed, "I claim you in the name of the Lord."

Last Thanksgiving holiday Steve lifted the Rev. Leroy, now 17 years old, into the bed of his truck in Augusta and brought him back to our home at the foot of Johns Mountain, one last visit to where it all started. The Rev. Leroy stumbles when he walks, his breathing is labored, he sleeps most of the time. The next time these faithful companions return it will be to scatter the Rev. Leroy's ashes here.

At the very mountain spot where the Rev. Leroy first wandered up to a campfire, Norman and Peg Arey built their home a few years later; built it in a way that made it easy to spoil their pure bred poodle, Cajun.

The Areys had always been poodle people; that is, until the day

Norman arrived at the Hatfield sanitation repository to deposit household rubbish. He noticed a yellow dog scavenging around the edges of the dump, nosing out scraps for a meal. On another visit he saw the dog sitting, half-hidden in the woods, watching children romping on a playground. Norman surmised that some fear, some despicable horror from the past, overwhelmed the outcast's obvious longing for human contact.

Norman was emotionally shaken by the display of timidity and sadness. Week after week he and Peg spread picnic lunches across the road from the trash collection bins and offered food to the yellow dog who would edge toward them and then retreat. Weeks of picnics went by before sanitation supervisor, Vester Stanley, discovered the homeless scavenger rummaging inside an inclosure. He shut the gate and called Norman. The yellow dog, frightened and whimpering, was taken home by Norman and Peg. He named her, Molly.

A year passed with offerings of food and love and still Molly would not come close enough to allow touching. Even a cautious hand gesturte caused her to bolt away and cower. She paced relentlessly. The second year she calmed enough to be fed by hand. She allowed cautious touches. By the third year, Norman could whisper, "Come sit in the circle of safety" and Molly would tippy-toe over and sit between his legs. That year she began to follow every move Norman made, her brown eyes shiny with obvious worship. Now, she wakes him in the mornings by edging onto the bed and tenderly nudging his face. She rides in his pickup truck, her head resting in a way she can keep her eyes fixed on her hero.

When I visit Norman says, "Have you ever seen such a beautiful animal?" I have, but I say the girl is incomparably gorgeous.

When I think of Molly and the Rev. Leroy it's easy to understand the lyrics from country music's Josh Turner, "…a dog is the only thing on earth that loves you more than it loves itself." Why that's practically New Testament. It's a thought that makes it easier to consider the possibility that there was divine intervention in the lives of two stray dogs.

December, 2012

LET'S TALK TRASH

Recently I called Chief Magistrate Gene Richardson, Environment Court's reincarnation of Roy Bean, legendary "hanging judge" of the old Wild West. I wanted to know if he had ever imposed capital punishment on anyone caught littering. I was hoping he had. However, despite his legendary intolerance of dimwit blubberhead untrainable trash-spreading morons he said that once or twice he stopped just short.

"You do not want to come into my court on a littering charge," Judge Richardson said. Even though it was a telephone conversation it sounded to me as if he were struggling to avoid saying a bad word. I'm not sure most of us could employ similar restraint lacking training in courtroom etiquette.

Judge Richardson is perplexed by cavalier attitudes toward litter. "I had one fellow who was just bent out of shape when I fined him $450 for emptying a tray of cigarette butts out his car window. I asked how he would like a little jail time to go along with it."

I determined from our conversation that should I decide to sit by the roadside and shoot the tires out from under the next redneck who tosses McDonalds, Wendys and Bojangles garbage along our road frontage it does not legally qualify as pest control. I have clocked time and mileage from all three establishments clustered on Martha Berry Highway. It is easy to conclude it takes approximately eight miles to eat a Big Mac, a Wendy's Value Meal or two chicken biscuits. As for the accumulation of Mountain Dew bottles, aluminum beer cans and smokeless tobacco cylinders, there is no way to pinpoint their place of origin. The demographics, however, are apparent.

I swear this is true. Last year my wife and I were driving home, impatiently trailing an old pickup. A husky German Shepherd rode majestically in the truck bed. As the truck neared our driveway the dog dipped its head and came up with a plastic bag of garbage that he tossed out at our address. We could only surmise doggie see, doggie do.

42

To label that driver a good ole boy would elevate his status, so I will stick with redneck. I'm not sure I could make the same distinction as did President Jimmy Carter's brother Billy who once said, "A good ole boy is somebody that rides around in a pickup truck…drinks beer and puts them in a litter bag. A redneck rides around in a pickup truck, drinks beer and throws them out the window."

Mary Hardin Thornton is director of Keep Rome-Floyd County Beautiful. At times she must consider her title an oxymoron given the degree of difficulty attached to her mission. Almost every newspaper story about cleaning up Floyd County's rivers and roadsides will have Ms. Thornton's name and a quotation embedded somewhere in the text. She always is articulate and composed. But, this time, the way she said, "It's just a bunch of sorry redneck people", her point could not have been made more powerful by outright cussing.

According to Keep America Beautiful statistics, 81 percent of littering is intentional, 55 percent by motorists flicking, flinging or dropping. Top suppliers of the habit are fast food establishments. If anyone at headquarters is caught mentioning the term biodegradable packaging he or she is shipped out for electric shock treatment. Apparently, litter begets litter. Ms. Thornton surmises that a visual of orange-clad prisoners spearing and sacking roadside trash creates a mindset that tossing garbage out the car window is actually a good thing because it provides something for jailbirds to do. Last year 51 billion pieces of litter were picked up along roadsides. That's 6,729 items per mile per year. My wife and I picked up that much Thursday.

The late L.R. James was security officer at Berry College. Whenever he found a bag of trash near the campus he would open the bag and rummage through the contents, searching for a name, an address, a phone number, anything that would give a clue about the owner. Then he would call on the phone and announce, "Mr. So And So, I have the bag of garbage you left near Berry College. I will wait for you to come pick it up." To those who responded that he could go soak his head in the campus reservoir L.R. would remind them he was an officer of the law. He would outline the consequences if he had to deliver the package to their home. Sometimes vigilante justice is all that works.

March, 2011

HYSTERIA AS A BREAKER OF ROUTINE

He was not the late Wayne Minshew. He was simply late. Nevertheless, the morning Wayne failed to show up at Thurston's for his breakfast glass of orange juice, Mitzy Hutchinson felt in her heart he must be dead. He had not missed that day-starter in five years. Neither had he failed to show up for lunch at her restaurant, so regular in his eating habits he just sits down at his booth and tells the waitress, "I'll have lunch."

They know that on Monday's Wayne's lunch consists of dessert. On Tuesdays he has a half Dante Dry panini ("unwet, but succulent"). On Wednesday and Thursday, lunch is one of Mitzy's giant toffee cookies. Friday is Buffalo wings ("dry, spicy with a halitosis reach of 24 inches").

Rhonda Washington and Stacy Abernathy were at Thurston's the morning Wayne Minshew didn't show up for orange juice. They tried to calm Mitzi who was almost incoherent. Her beloved customer must be dead, she wailed.

Mitzi knew she wouldn't be able to bear the scene at Wayne's apartment so she dispatched Rhonda and Stacy on a frantic trip of morbid discovery. They called back with the sad news that Wayne's car was still parked in the lot. Something was obviously wrong. But, what to do?

Mitzi didn't think two ladies could handle discovering Wayne's body, so she told them to come back to the restaurant. She asked a customer named Larry, who didn't even live in Calhoun, if he would hurry to the apartment and confirm the sad results. Larry could find no way of getting into the apartment, however and called to say there didn't seem to be a car in the lot.

A little after that Wayne strolled into Thurston's. After he had been properly berated for scaring the beejeezes out Mitzi he explained he had spoken at a United Way meeting. But could he please have his glass of orange juice?

Near the end of July I received an email from Wayne. "Lee and Jackie: You guys might want to come to Thurston's one day over the next two weeks. Don't ask why. It's too sad."

I printed out the email and hurried to show Jackie. "Mitzi obviously has some terrible disease. So terrible Wayne can't bear to discuss it in an email."

Jackie read the note and said, "Maybe Mitzi's not sick, she's just sick of getting up at four o'clock in the morning and working all day. Don't you think we should find out before we go to pieces?"

I emailed Wayne, "We will meet you at Thurston's tomorrow."

Wayne was waiting at his sidewalk seat. I thought it strange he was smiling under the circumstances. Inside, Thurston's was overrun by customers. Mitzi was taking orders and bouncing back and forth to the kitchen, amazingly cheerful for someone who had precipitated such heartache in our life-long friend that he couldn't even bear to tell me in the email.

Well, actually, he had. I, unfortunately, had not gotten around to reading that one. It said, "Crisis averted! At the end of last week a teary Mitzi had the place sold. But today Mitzi reported she can't let go. I still have a hangout."

Since it was Thursday when we met, Wayne had a giant cookie for lunch. Jackie had a Caesar salad and soup, I had a panini and soup. It was almost three o'clock before Mitizi had a break. She alighted momentarily at our booth, but seconds later, clued in to the subject we were in the process of clarifying, she scurried to the kitchen and retrieved the petition that helped change her mind.

It is a lengthy document lobbying against any non-holiday closings of Thurston's. Among other things it said on behalf of regulars in booth five, " Whereas the affixed signatures accompany this selfish, it's all-about-us petition, etc., etc...."

The petition was signed by Bobby Cox, Hank Aaron, Vince Dooley, President Jimmy Carter and others whose signatures were not quite as legible (although I think I spotted the scribbled autograph of Jorge Mario Bergolio, who is now better known as Pope Francis). Doesn't matter. Wayne forged them all on the petition that may be remembered in the history of downtown Calhoun as the impassioned document that saved Thurston's.

August, 2013

Six Flags Over Armuchee

Mark Twain understood one of the great laws of human nature, that Work consists of whatever someone is obliged to do and Play consists of whatever someone isn't obliged to do, but can't wait to do it. Twain also knew that the way to make someone covet something is to make it difficult to obtain.

It's called reverse psychology. Twain explored that special kind of mind manipulation in "The Adventures of Tom Sawyer." Aunt Polly has sentenced Tom to whitewashing 30 yards of board fencing on a glorious day better made for swimming. Which is what Ben Rogers intends when he comes across Tom haphazardly swishing his brush across the boards. When Ben makes fun of Tom working on such a day, Tom says it isn't work. Ben scoffs, "Oh, come, now, you don't mean to let on that you like it?"

Tom resumes whitewashing and says, "Like it? Well, I don't see why I oughtn't to like it. Does a boy get a chance to whitewash a fence every day?"

Tom convinces his buddy that whitewashing a fence is so much fun Ben gives him his apple for a chance to paint. By the time Tom has similarly conned other friends he has traded fence painting to Billy Fisher for a kite, Johnny Miller for a dead rat and a string to swing it with and has acquired from other friends twelve marbles, part of a jews harp, a piece of chalk, a kitten with one eye, a brass door knob, a dog collar with no dog, four pieces of orange peel and an old window sash.

I've often wondered if reverse psychology works as well in real life as it did in Twain's classic novel. For example, could Coosa River Basin Initiative's crusading Joe Cook convince Wright Ledbetter and other officials in Ledbetter Properties it would be more fun to wade in Burwell Creek than to pave over it? All I can say is what worked for Tom Sawyer worked for me.

Back a few years ago I purchased enough property to raise my first and only herd of cows. Once it dawned on me I wasn't cut out to be a cowboy I probably should have thought about who or what would replace the cows as lawnmowers.

Because of hip surgery I have been restricted over the summer by immobility as well as an edict from my wife, "Don't do anything stupid." As a result our pasture began to resemble Madonna's underarms.

Just about the time I was ready to defy my wife (what husband hasn't momentarily gone insane?) newlyweds Michaele and Bob Prince, as innocent as Ben Rogers, dropped by on the way to check on Michaele's bee hives near our house.

Michaele noticed my authentic Lavender Mountain Hardware checkered shirt, which would immediately tell anyone I either was about to do farm work or go get a pizza at Mellow Mushroom. She said something like, "Hey, whatcha got going on, gentleman farmer?"

"It's a beautiful day and I plan to have me some fun bush hogging," I lied.

"Bush hogging is fun?" Michaele was skeptical.

"More like relaxtion. A lot like meditation, just riding around on my Kubota, maybe listening to a little music as I mow."

Michaele pondered that thought. " Could I bush hog your pasture? I always wanted to drive a tractor?"

Michaele teaches art at Armuchee High School, my pastures needed an artist's touch, so I handed her my tractor keys. I've never seen anyone more convinced she was having fun. Now she cuts my pastures more regularly than I get haircuts.

Bob, retired math professor at Berry, shyly confided he had always wanted to pilot a zero-turn lawnmower. He said he would like to have something to do while Michaele bush hogs. I reluctantly told him okay, but he would have to wear a seat belt because my Hustler is NASCAR certified. I don't believe I've ever seen a happier pair of newlyweds.

In another month or two my pasture and lawn will begin to put on brown coats for winter.

I suspect that for Michaele and Bob it is going to be a lot like Six Flags Over Armuchee is closing for the season.

September, 2013

life off the beaten path

THE BAD BOY OF SUMMER

The baseball game was boring and Skip Caray has a low tolerance for boredom. Boredom means he has to manufacture his entertainment, to dance a little bit with the devil. So, bored stiff during broadcast of a Braves game, he made an abrupt U-turn away from his color commentary. "Joe," he said to his broadcast partner, "What do you do with an elephant with three balls?"

Startled into momentary silence, Joe Simpson braced for the bomb to drop. And then Skip slid in his punch line: "You go ahead and walk him and pitch to the giraffe, silly."

Although he wasn't on-screen at the time, I could see in my mind the trademark Caray smirk and a snort, snort for emphasis. We've known each other for three decades and at the height of his most disruptive moments, I can visualize him even when I can't see him.

Skip is a yanker of chains. A foul ball goes into the stands and he announces it was retrieved by a fan from Alpharetta, knowing that at least a few will get a laugh out of the absurdity and some will even believe it.

As talented as any announcer to pass through Atlanta and funnier than most, Skip amuses not everyone, however. WSB gets a ton of complaints about rudeness on his pregame show.

Although he can use sarcasm the way Zorro used his sword, in response to such criticism he is now billing himself as a "kinder, gentler" Skip Caray. Yet, I suspect it doesn't mean he won't berate a caller over the 1,400th request that he explain the infield fly rule. It doesn't mean Skip won't say to listeners and viewers when a game is beyond recapture, "If you will promise to patronize our sponsors, you have permission to go walk the dog."

As curmudgeons go, he was precocious. I've known him since he broadcast and I reported Atlanta Cracker baseball games in the '60s. Over the years, I've watched program directors and other thin skins try to turn him into Father Teresa. And he does try to accommodate them. Sometimes. Briefly.

Personally, having once had the pleasure of serving as his liaison with the "suits" when I was marketing the Atlanta Hawks and he was broadcasting the games, I think I can say with confidence that any attempt to sandpaper the edges off Skip Caray is the triumph of hope over reality.

Management often got nettlesome when Skip didn't fall into line as the team shill or when he labeled some promo he was required to read, as "stupid." When the powers insisted I do something about his irreverence, I would just say, "Yeah, right."

Skip is to program directors what a roller coaster is to a weak stomach. Here is a now ancient example. The television station where he was briefly employed derived a substantial amount of its advertising dollars from wrestling promoters. Skip was told to read the wrestling results on the nightly sports segment despite his taking every opportunity to proclaim pro wrestling phony and not a real sport. He reluctantly read the results, but for his own amusement he sometimes made up new names for the winners and losers. Advertisers started complaining and wrestling fans, who are wound tight anyhow, were threatening him.

The station manager begged him to "go easy, these guys are advertisers."

Skip said, "I may promise, but once I get started, you know I can't stop. Why don't we let someone-else do it?"

They decided on Linda Faye, the "weather girl." Although she would later marry former Georgia Tech football coach, Bud Carson, Linda knew virtually nothing about sports and, thus, seemed a safe bet. She did know about "happy talk" because television formats required, as they do today, interchange between the various personalities. So, to fulfill her happy talk obligation, Linda says, "Well, Skip, tonight I know something about sports that you don't. I have the wrestling results."

To which Skip replied, "Sorry, Linda, but you don't know something I don't. I was at rehearsal."

I was privileged to watch one of the Caray firings. Well, not the dismissal, but what led up to it. Those who remember the good old days will remember the Brave-Falcon Lounge, a popular dispenser of beverage. On this ill-fated day, Skip had invited Frank Hyland, the veteran AJC sportswriter to join him at the Brave-Falcon and thence to the television station where Frank would be that night's special guest. The broadcast began at 10:30 p.m. They started drinking at the Brave-

Falcon at 5.

I was watching the news that night. Skip would command, "Frrrrrankk. Give us some scores!"

Frank would reply, "Seven!"

"Anymore, buddy?"

"Three!"

And so it would go. Each time they roared with laughter and slapped the anchor desk. When Skip received the inevitable post-show call from the station manager, he said, "Don't bother to talk about it. I know I'm fired."

Not so long ago, but longer between visits than we should allow, we met for lunch at Fishbone. What we had for lunch I don't remember. We drank water without freshening it up and I don't guess I'll forget that.

So, maybe he is kinder and gentler after all. And it maybe his signature old shtick, the allusions to post game cocktails, won't ring with the same authenticity anymore. Even livers eventually lose their sense of humor and beg for mercy.

Oh, well, maybe not.

"Listen up in the second inning," he said.

A smirk began twitching at the corners of his lips. And I knew without question the bad boy of summer would be dancing with the devil again tonight.

May, 2002

STRANGER MALONE

Stranger Malone, ninety-five-years-old and not counting, checked his schedule on a three-year pocket calendar and said he could meet me for lunch on Friday. He suggested we agree on the appointment right then because he is next to impossible to reach on the telephone. Usually busy or gone was the way he put it.

I had met Stranger earlier that evening at The Harvest Moon Cafe on Broad Street in Rome. He and Russell McClanahan play and sing there on Thursday nights, their compensation a good square meal and the tips that accumulate in a Kroger coffee can. That is, they play there if Stranger doesn't have a gig somewhere around the Southeast, or a television show, or a school program. Altogether Stranger will perform more than 100 dates, down from a couple of years ago when two hundred engagements, including playing string bass with the Rome Symphony, was a normal schedule. In 2002 he played six dates in three states in a single week. In 2001 he performed a concert of "hillbilly" music in Sweden.

He was outfitted for our Friday lunch as he had been for the three-hour performance of vocals and smooth licks on clarinet, flute, guitar and string bass: tweed coat, subdued tie of blues and greens, silver hair swept precisely back from his forehead, moustache neatly trimmed, his remarkably luminous eyes the crowning touch.

My exuberant reference to the previous night's show notwithstanding, Stranger didn't think he was all that sharp. He loses a little something when he doesn't perform every day, he said. He massaged his fingers as we talked, saying they felt stiff on the guitar, which he has been playing only 22 years or so, although he had unleashed a nice riff when he led off the show with a bouncy "There'll Be Some Changes Made."

Sometimes I take friends to the Thursday night shows at The Harvest Moon and they stare at Stranger Malone as they might gawk at a face on Mt. Rushmore or some other wonder and sometimes winsome ladies ask to have a photo made with him. His string bass is taller than he is, but he still has the charisma and mischievous grin of a George Burns without the Las Vegas glitz. A woman drops a five dollar bill in the coffee can and whispers to her date, "Is he really 95 years old?"

Simone de Bouvoir, in his 1970 work, "The Coming of Age," observed "There is only one solution if old age is not to be an absurd parody of our former life, and that is to go on pursuing ends that give our existence a meaning..."

So Stranger continues as he started, and here is some of what has happened between then and now. He was not born Stranger, but neither was he christened Kasper, which is the name that appears on official documents. His parents named him Kaloy, but he decided he would rather be called Kasper, the name of one of the Biblical Wise Men, "because in those days, there were no birth certificates and your name was whatever you called yourself."

He grew up on a tobacco farm in Paducah, Kentucky, and he could read music by the time he could read books at age three. His first job was playing sax in the orchestra pit of a silent movie house in 1924. In 1926 he recorded with Riley Puckett and the Skillet Lickers, a legendary band out of Atlanta that sold millions of the records many historians designate as the genesis of country music. He recorded his latest song on an album last year. Doubtless, that is the longest span of musical recordings in the world.

He toured with Pee Wee Hunt, accompanied Rudy Valee and Louis Armstrong, toured with Jack Teagarden's big band as well as Kaye Kyser's, all famous in their day. He has played string bass with the Denver Symphony and the Arizona Symphony. He taught music for 13 years at the University of Arizona. When radio stations had their own bands and musical programs, he played in scores of them from the Mexican border to the Canadian. He can recall the station letters of every one. He once performed on a luxury liner in the Orient, played and sang for tourists in a Turkish hotel. He lived in Germany for 20 years with his second wife before moving to Rome where there are more opportunities for his music.

He had passed through Rome many years prior to his residency in Germany and that is where he got the name, Stranger. He was hitchhiking about 1925 or 1926 when his ride stopped in Armuchee on the outskirts of Rome. A band was playing there for an auction. He joined in and someone yelled, "Hey, who in the world is that little stranger playing hell out of that saxophone!"

While he is a wonder, Stranger Malone is not a novelty. His career has earned him a place in the Georgia Music Hall of Fame. He performs around the Southeast with some marvelous artists out of Atlanta, Mick Kinney and Roger Bellows. Stranger doesn't drive, so he boards a Greyhound bus in Rome and his tour partners pick him up at the bus station in Atlanta.

Music historians widely recognize him, but there is a side to Stranger that most people don't know. His apartment at the old Greystone Hotel near The Harvest Moon is a virtual library of great books. Since leaving school in the ninth grade he has spent a lifetime educating himself and he bristles when writers "make me sound like some pool room dropout. There's a big difference between formal education and what you know."

He has relentlessly studied history, philosophy and classic literature. He concentrated on the New England Poets exclusively for 10 years, Emerson alone for three. At lunch one day I hung with him for awhile on John Steinbeck, but then he moved along to some Europeans not even vaguely familiar to me and I was relieved when he got back to my level with some chat about Gore Vidal.

The last time I saw Stranger at The Harvest Moon Café was the night before a gig at The Moonlight Café in Birmingham. He said he planned to read until 2 a.m., which relieved me of some guilt for insisting on a few encores after his 9 p.m. finale. In answer to my request, he picked up his guitar and started strumming an almost hypnotic melody while he recited a poem he had written.

"Just one more," I pleaded. Stranger reached for the flute he bought in 1929 for $20 and in a room that had grown almost empty of diners he began to play "Amazing Grace," so haunting it misted the eyes of those who remained.

As I was saying goodbye, he handed me a tape labeled "Stories by Stranger Malone." "I've written 26 stories," he said. "They may be a little spicy for the Bible Belt, and they need a little editing I suppose."

And I left him there dining on that night's payoff of vegetables and cornbread, part of him old and wise as yesterday and part of him as young and unexplored as tomorrow.

June, 2005

THE UNSINKABLE ERNA ASHER

If you have not read *The World According To Garp*, or seen the movie, you may not understand when I say Gene Asher's late mother was a lot like Garp's mom, Jenny Fields. That's just a shorthand way of saying Erna Fromme Asher was the same kind of indomitable, awesomely eccentric personality who at times considered herself the only person marching in step.

She was graduated from the University of Wisconsin just after the turn of the century. At a time when women armed with English degrees usually became schoolteachers, she became advertising director for the J. M. High Company on Whitehall Street in Atlanta. She worked there until she married Baron Asher, partner with his brother in a clothing store.

In the 1930s, the Depression swept like a deadly virus through small businesses and the Asher store lost strength and died. Erna Asher managed to get a job in a grocery store, her wage enough food each week to feed her family. In the evenings she told fortunes for a small fee, a practice that paralyzed Baron with fear that his wife would be hauled off to jail.

Gradually, Gene's mother helped lift the family from the pits of economic disaster. She talked the owner of Plaza Drugs on Ponce de Leon Avenue into letting her open a cosmetics department. She also trained to be a practical nurse. And when the family's finances stabilized, she spent her spare time going door-to-door collecting used clothes for the poor children who lived near what is now Atlanta-Fulton County Stadium. She never forgot those times when she had depended on the same charity.

Her energy was legendary among residents of their apartment complex. She was given to arising in the middle of a sleepless night to play college fight songs on the piano. She had a cat named Pumpkins who also played the piano, so well, in fact, the cat was written up in the old *Journal-Constitution Sunday Magazine*. When the apartments changed ownership, the new proprietor did not appreciate nocturnal feline concerts and lodged a series of unrewarded protests.

The Asher family suspected it was the disgruntled owner who eventually poisoned Pumpkins. So sure was Erna Asher that after the funeral she crouched in some bushes under the owner's window and meowed at the top of her lungs all night long.

Nevertheless, Erna considered herself among the most normal of the apartments' residents. She was so captivated by the foibles of some of her neighbors she wrote a book about them; about the doctor who walked around naked in his room, occasionally pausing in front of a window; about the resident who shot a man on a streetcar; about Mrs. Belski, whose mind was still back in the old country and about the insipid Mrs. Rogavin who had a foul, motorized mouth and a loose daughter.

Always impulsive, Erna astounded the family and neighbors during World War II by announcing she had joined the WACS. She was stationed at Daytona for six months at which time America's enemies, contemplating the possibility that Erna Asher would indeed see combat, began to surrender and she came home.

But she was in the service long enough to understand the terrible fear and loneliness of military men. When Gene was wounded in Korea she called him at the hospital and asked if there was anything he needed.

"Yes," he replied, "I need some Scotch. They won't let me have any."

Two weeks later a package arrived. The Jewish chaplain opened the bundle and said, "What a nice mama. She has sent you hair conditioner, tonic and after-shave lotion." The other patients were horrified later to see their wounded comrade swigging contentedly from a succession of Mennen bottles.

Later in his mother's life, Gene and his father decided it would be good for her to visit her relatives in the North. She had reached an age where she did not want to leave her family, however, and postponed each trip with an imaginative excuse. Three times the family embarked for the train terminal only to have Erna demand a retreat to their home.

On the fourth try, Gene and Baron Asher actually convinced her to board the train. The father and son retired to the cafeteria in Union Station for a victory cup of coffee.

"It will do her good to be away from us for a while," Gene said.

When they got home the two men were astounded to find her in the kitchen, going about her housework.

"Mama, what happened?" Gene asked in disbelief.

"You know who was on that train?" replied his mother. "Mrs. Rogavin. I'm not riding any train with that Mrs. Rogavin."

December, 1985

BREAKFAST WITH MR. EARP

Mary Lang had already served the 66-year-old fourth cousin of legendary Wyatt Earp a Dirt Town Deli breakfast when I sat down across from him. Sometimes she gives Vernon Wyatt Earp some bread or a pie to take home afterwards. "Mary thinks I'm like a little kid," he said. "Children think I'm one of them, too. I play with them after church and make them laugh. I just know how children think."

Some days Mr. Earp drives from Trion and brings his shiny black Fender guitar or his banjo now that the brakes have been repaired on his 2000 Chevy Venture Van. "Would you like to hear me sing like Johnny Cash?" he asked. I said sure and so he licked the fingertips of his left hand and played an unmistakable Johnny Cash riff flawlessly on the bass strings. His rich baritone replicated the singer's famously distinct voice on 'I Walk The Line.'"

He could see that I was astonished. "I can do Elvis if you want me to," he said. I nodded approval. He arose from his chair, bony knees and shins protruding like popsicle sticks beneath khaki shorts, sandy hair cascading over his forehead, hips shimmying as he wailed, "That's all right, Mama…that's all right…"

I complimented Mr. Earp and asked him to tell me more about himself. He cheerfully accommodated my curiosity. He said he had a few jobs over the years, but, "I have mainly been retired. My nerves went down on me early, so they retired me. The Army called me when I was young, but they said I didn't weigh enough. I was sent to the Job Corps up in Illinois. I gained some weight there. I wrote short stories about hillbillies that were published in the Job Corps publication. I was a Peace Maker for them. I could help settle any problems between the races because they liked me. I dated a Chippewa Creek Indian girl who was pretty. I like ladies, but I couldn't marry the one I loved.

"One year Beverly Finster hired me at Finster Gardens as an artist and gardener, but the doctor said he thought that was a little too rough for me because I had a chemical imbalance. They retired me. They gave me every kind of medicine known to man. But, I haven't seen a doctor since 2009. I was ordained as a minister in 2006 and God healed me.

"I used to volunteer at a Mental Health Day Care Program. I used music and art and my sense of humor to help them. I studied art at Floyd Junior College and I got my GED. I don't mean to brag, but my intelligence is above average. Doctors said I was born about a genius. I don't understand the average mind or why people do certain things. That's why I didn't like baseball or football, just nature and music and art."

Mary, Crystal Hicks and Crystal Holbrook have tacked a few of Mr. Earp's drawings on the Deli walls. For the most part, however, he has gained deserved recognition as an expert on plant life in north Georgia. "I started by checking out books at the library," he said. "Then I began buying my own books when I had money. I spent years of hard work in the fields and by the '90s I had documented every native plant from the Tennessee line to Atlanta. I know the scientific and common name of every one."

I asked him to name the rarest plant he has ever found. "A yellow slipper orchid," he said. He added the scientific Latin name.

"Whoa, I have no idea what you said," I admitted. He ripped a napkin from our table ring and wrote Cypripidium Caleousus. He was also pleased to have discovered and documented Northern Hackberry or Celtis Occidentalis. He spelled that one for me, too.

"He's got a lot of other talents you need to ask him about." The voice came from my left and belonged to Rowan Hicks, Dirt Town Deli's patriarch. It would be outside his nature not to join an interesting conversation. "Mr. Earp is an expert knife thrower and a master with a bull whip," Rowan said. "And he can climb a tree like a monkey."

"I guess I'm just a really happy person," Mr. Earp said as I paid my check at the front counter. "I love people and I'm glad they love me."

October, 2011

A SHRINE TO ECCENTRICITY

Does it ever cross your mind that some people have more fun than we do? Does it ever occur to you that Dos Equis beer picked the wrong man for their television commercials when Sam Edwards was available all along? After all, he is the most interesting man in Armuchee.

I don't say that just because the guy who cooks the famous Samburger at Schroeders Deli on Martha Berry Highway (To call the Samburger ordinary would be like calling Chateau Lafite Rothschild Pauillac 1996 a table wine) has taken midnight strolls in the White House clad only in his fruit-embroidered undershorts, read Dostoevsky's *Crime and Punishment* while spending 29 days in a New Orleans jail, swam laps in Rome's famous Travi Fountain, gave up his job as janitor to serve as an escort for President Jimmy Carter, served as campaign advance man for both Carter and Presidential candidate/astronaut John Glenn, produced a documentary, published a book, crashed an ultralight aircraft, had his skull crushed by a mob while working for the U.S. Army Security Agency in Thailand, had a near-death experience, simultaneously courted red-headed twins from Nebraska, babysat a President's grandchildren, ran for the Georgia House of Representatives, dropped out of Calhoun High School once and two colleges twice each before enrolling in law school, served as a reporter in Afghanistan, contributes opinions online to the Huffington Post and lives in a tree house.

The tree house was never designed to appear on the front page of the *Atlanta Journal-Constitution*. It wasn't designed to appear internationally on television, including HGTV. It was designed to give Sam Edwards a chance to start yet another novel, maybe even finish one. In order to write he needed a place to sit. To sit he needed a place to go home to. To provide for a place to go home to, he needed money, one of life's inconveniences he hadn't been all that worked up about since dropping out of high school in 1969. So here he was once again weighing the intrusion of reality into fantasy. His best option was to join a new restaurant venture with old buddy, Haley Stephens, who told him to just go out to the restaurant's back lot in Calhoun and build some place to write after work.

Behind the restaurant is a 200-year-old pin oak. Sam sank half dozen poles into the ground and built, eight feet off the ground, a 10X12 foot "office." Then he added a second room of similar dimensions and another, and another, until he ended up with 1100 square feet of structure wrapped around the tree in a U configuration. The building inspector looked at the house, its three sections of roofline, none matching, and exclaimed, "Who designed this thing?"

"I guess I did, sorta as I went along," Sam said. "You know, I really didn't mean to build this thing. It's kinda an evolution of a mistake."

"I don't believe that could be put any better," the inspector said.

Beams for the structure had come from an old, neglected barn, floor boards from a 160-year-old slave shack, ceiling for the sitting room/ library from plywood crates salvaged from a police raid on a marijuana warehouse, rusty tin from his partner's father's stash of useless stuff, green chalk board from an abandoned school building, marble squares from the floor of the town's first bank, floor joists and windows from an old train depot and a new bedroom made from the 18-foot fuselage of a Piper Navaho airplane that belonged to NASCAR driver Jeff Purvis before it crashed on a beach at St. Simons Island. It appears to be flying straight through the house.

There is no way to make this long story short. You may examine a photograph of the tree house on the wall at Schroeders. You will notice that Sam has added a master bedroom. Originally, it was Haley's 18-foot ski boat. Sam has equipped it with bed, flat screen TV and other amenities such as beautiful stained glass. A bathroom with sink and shower is located in a submarine that was abandoned once its use as a prop in a 1960s Elvis movie was finished.

It would be presumptive to label the Kiowa Hawk helicopter that serves as the television and game room as the "last" addition. Rather, it is the most recent addition. After all, Peter Pan didn't grow up and quit flying.

I asked Sam one time if he turned out the way his parents expected. He laughed. "They expected me to be either a preacher or a criminal. I wound up somewhere in between. My granddaddy was a Baptist preacher, my mother a Sunday School teacher. The family has an unbroken line of preachers stretching back to the American Revolution. The World Book Encyclopedia was the first book in our house that wasn't a Bible. My grandfather was continually asking me, 'Sam, did you get The Call yet?'

"One day I said, 'Grandpa, I finally got The Call. This voice said, 'Sam, Don't Do It!'"

May, 2012

FROM RUSSIA WITH LOVE

I never liked pinstripes, but it was the commercial period of my life and there I was in New York City in my best suit, pretending I was happy the world's largest advertising agency had bought my Atlanta public relations firm. My partners and I had made the deal with high hopes, but lately had concluded we were little more than a keepsake of the Jimmy Carter presidential days when everybody up North had to own a trinket from the South. Now I was heading home with a head full of corporate confusion and a belly full of bull.

From a honking, clanking squadron of taxis terrorizing Lexington Avenue, one driver peeled out of formation in answer to my hand signal He pulled smoothly up to the curb, in noticeable contrast to most New York cabbies who consider it great sport to see if they can throw the motor through the hood when they stop.

I put my travel bag on the rear seat and slouched down beside it. After what must have been several vacant-minded minutes, I was vaguely aware that the little cabdriver was attempting to make conversation. He had a thick accent that was very difficult to understand, the kind to which passengers usually reply, "Uh huh," "I see" or "How interesting."

But it was hard not to pay attention to Alex Bruslowsky. He complimented the sun. He complimented the people out walking in the sun. He praised the big buildings and the pigeons that roosted on them. "I love this country," he said.

"How long have you been here?" I asked, not really interested, but too Southern not to feed him the cue he obviously wanted. Alex, it turned out, was Southern, too, having lived in some little town with an unpronounceable name in a lower extremity of Russia. He has a wife and two sons who came to America with him. His mother and father could not come because his father has "jail" written on his identification papers because he had spent 15 years in prison.

"You know why?" Alex asked. "I tell you why. My father's father was

64

capitalist. Stalin took him and shoot him. One day, when I small, the soldiers come and get my father for jail. He say, 'Why?' And they say, 'Because you father was capitalist.' 'But my father dead,' he say. 'That don't matter,' they say."

When Alex grew up he married and fathered two sons. One day his wife begged him to take his family to America. He told her it would be impossible because he could not leave his parents.

"Then I will go without you," she told him. "I want to be free. My life has no meaning."

"You would destroy our family for this freedom?" I asked.

"She say, 'Yes.' Just like that,"

It took four years, including two years of being fed by a Catholic organization in Brussels before Alex unraveled red tape and sailed by the Statue of Liberty. He was a mechanic — a very good one — and as soon as possible he applied for work at a big garage in New York.

The owner told him he would hire him, but could pay him only $3 an hour because he could not speak or write English. He took the job and six months later he was taking home over $200 a week. Then, having learned some broken English, he told his boss he was leaving to become his own boss. A friend loaned him $1,000, another loaned him $2,000. He scraped together enough money to start his own taxi company. Each week he worked 17 hours six days and on the day he took it easy he worked 10.

"One day I call my mother and father to tell them what happen to Alex. My mother say, 'Alex, I cannot believe you work for you self.' My father get on phone and say, 'My son, I love you so much and I so proud.' Then there is buzzing and phone stop working and I do not get to talk to them anymore."

Alex began to cry softly as he took the exit to La Guardia Airport where he had been hundreds of times before and, I am sure, made the same unashamed speech each time. He pulled up in front of the Eastern Airlines freight entrance and said, "I hope you have nice trip."

"Alex, pardon me, but I think the passenger entrance for Eastern is down that way," I said, pointing farther down the road.

"Oh, no," he said with alarm. "I always deliver here. Nobody ever say to me, 'Alex, you are wrong.' I hope you not mad?"

"My goodness, you're right, Alex. This is the right gate. I haven't been to New York very often and I get so confused by it."

Alex smiled and as he drove away he gave me a big wave until he was out of sight. As soon as I was sure he couldn't see me, I picked up my travel bag and began the long walk down toward the entrance to Eastern Airlines' ticket booths.

October, 1982

REMEMBERING LEWIS GRIZZARD

MORELAND—Nostalgia sometimes shows up like an engraved invitation and you say, why not just go? I can't say exactly why Jackie and I were thinking about Lewis Grizzard that day. Best as I recall, we were watching television and Jackie wondered aloud what Lewis would have had to say about Michael Jackson's pajama parties and that led to imagining what he would have written about Kobe Bryant's version of room service and next thing we were headed down to the Lewis Grizzard Museum in this little town that straddles two sides of Alternate Highway 27 like an aging saddle.

We probably should have called first, but somehow it seemed more appropriate to just drop in, the way Lewis used to drop in, knowing that my wife would cook him cornbread to go with a bowl of her vegetable soup. The last time we were here was 10 years ago, a Tuesday on the twenty second day of March, when we said goodbye to Lewis at the United Methodist Church. The sun was in a decent mood given the occasion, the dogwoods wore their best pink and white and the azaleas added some bright red for accent. But as for Lewis, he was represented primarily by the laughter and tears within the stories that were told about him and amateurish recitations of the outrageous tales he had made legend in his newspaper columns and books. The physical Lewis was being cremated in Columbus, a circumstance somewhat antithetical to his version of a South that still loved open caskets at funerals and the singing of "Amazing Grace" and "Precious Memories."

Dust sprayed from eighteen wheelers has blackened the cream clapboard siding of the museum, the maroon trim is dark as rust. The right side of the old building donated by the John Abner Webb family is empty. Its intended symbiotic relationship to the museum was as a convenience store, but did not flourish. A typed notice on the windowed door at the left, through which is visible much of the museum's collection of Grizzardabilia, says, *"If you wish to visit the museum other than during regular hours of operation, please call in advance to make an appointment. 770-304-1490."* There are no regular hours. I called. Nobody answered. The precious memories have not lingered to the degree that this little building has become the tourist attraction that was hoped for and the Lewis Grizzard Storytelling Barbecue and Southern Celebration shut down after coming up $3000 shy of expenses in 1996.

But just because the little museum in Moreland has not become the Lourdes of humor, doesn't mean the patron saint of sass isn't missed by thousands of readers--admitting in the same breath that such an assertion probably inspires a whirlwind of gasps from those who have built a protective fence around political correctness. I can just imagine executives at the *Atlanta Journal-Constitution* breaking out in night sweats at the thought of waking up to column after column of ruminations about same sex marriages, though Lewis was much more concerned on a personal level with no-sex marriages.

Bottom line: *I* miss him. *I* miss the reason he gave to pick up a newspaper. He offered a voice (one of the few incentives left for ink and paper in this era of instant news on the internet and television). For sure it was a mischievous voice, sometimes with a lampshade on the author's head, but three times a week he invited me to his party. It never really bothered me that I didn't always drink from the same punch bowl; his smart ass white boy southern fried persona that translated from the print page right to the stage and commercial prosperity was mainly a carefully crafted shtick: *I believe in women's lib. I've liberated three of them already. Note to immigrant Yankees who complain it's not like it was back home. Delta is ready when you are."* Blood pressures would steam and whistle on any given morning like he had personally lit a fire under every tea kettle of liberal opinion in Atlanta. He wrote 18 books and sold hundreds of thousands of them. His stage monologue, more than 100 appearances a year, commanded up to $25,000 each. Four hundred and seventy five newspapers reprinted his columns each week. He did something no local columnist has done since his death and that of Celestine Sibley. He sold newspapers.

Even if he had lived another ten years Lewis would have turned just 57 this year. He would still be young by the standard of modern actuarial tables, but so old when measured against current society's moralistic threshold as to make one wonder if he would still be employed by those who wanted him to be funny so long as he didn't offend anyone. It was an expectation that caused his editors in his last days to treat some of his columns like a naughty kid that needed a mouth washing with soap.

While his irreverence made detractors break out in hives, those who still mourn his passing, remember him more for the verities of life nurtured in this little town where shopping in Newman was considered going uptown. He could cause you to reach for the phone and call home when he wrote about his Mama. When he wrote about the death of his black lab, Catfish, it made you hug your dog.

Admittedly, Lewis could be a pain in the ass, both on the printed page and off (at least three of his four wives would agree), a summation that reminds me of the breakfast story. Lewis simply had to be the center of attention and even breakfast called for high drama, whether in New York or Ludowici. The way his step brother Ludlow Porch told me the story, one day they dropped in for a bite at a rural, family-owned restaurant. A teenager waited tables, the mother worked the cash register and Grandpa was back in the kitchen cooking. Seeing that the young waitress was very busy, Ludlow placed his order quickly. Lewis, on the other hand, was just warming up.

"My dear," he said. "I will have two slices of bacon, almost crisp, but not quite. I will have biscuits, darkly browned outside, fluffy as a cloud inside. My eggs must be prepared precisely. Please convey this message to the chef. I will have two eggs over; the yolk must crawl but not run."

Shortly afterwards the waitress returned and set Ludlow's order before him. Lewis waited impatiently for her return with his plate. When she displayed no inclination to service his growing hunger he finally got her attention and called her to the table. "Young lady," he groused, "may I expect my breakfast any time soon?"

"Don't 'spect so," she said, "Grandpa said he didn't want to f— with you."

As I wiped the smudge from a window pane and peeped into the Lewis Grizzard Museum, I laughed and thought to myself that Grandpa sort of reflected the attitude of those who were taking Lewis a tad too seriously when his funny, fragile heart gave out for the last time.

May, 2004

CONFESSIONS OF A SECRET WHACKO

When are you really dead? Is it when they lower you into a grave, or when people stop telling stories about you? In the first sense further mention of Ludlow Porch would be shamefully late as an obituary. In the second sense, here it is four weeks after his fatal stroke and I'm still talking about him.

For more than a decade WLAQ broadcast Ludlow's syndicated Funseekers show from 9 a.m.-noon. It was tame stuff compared to today's venom pits because Ludlow believed a radio personality didn't have to be angry or insulting to be funny. Telephone lines would light up with callers weighing in on such weighty matters as teaching newcomers how to speak Southern (Example: "How's ya mama'n 'em?") Those who called Ludlow's show with tongue firmly in cheek he affectionately called WHACKOS.

Ludlow visited Rome many times. He helped Sandy Davis raise funds for Hospitality House in 1995 and 1996. He broadcast live from the Forum in 2002 and 2003. In 2005 he appeared on stage to benefit restoration of the Desoto Theater. That night he mentioned to the audience that I had sometimes logged airtime when his show was broadcast five nights a week from 10:15 p.m. until two in the morning on Atlanta's WSB. He revealed that I was as secret WHACKO.

Several times he recruited me as co-conspirator in harmless spoofs. Sheltered by fictitious identities, I portrayed variously, a financier who wanted to buy The Omni arena and move it to Coweta County, a senator from South Georgia who was introducing legislation to outlaw jogging and as a soldier of fortune who was forming a volunteer militia to invade South Carolina. I appeared as a gene manipulator who had developed a new breed of cows called Boney Brownies. Their legs were as short as those of a basset hound. Needing just one strand of barbed wire to keep them in a pasture, farmers saved a great deal of money. A caller from Norcross, catching the spirit, said he had begun to feed his cows sawdust and they were passing perfect two-by-fours.

Sometimes humor was used to stick a needle into the vein of a serious subject like racism. An African-American who called regularly under the pseudonym M.T. Head often had a sugarcoated, but instructive point to make. When Ludlow mentioned he had trouble understanding jive talk, M.T. Head said, "You just let a brother walk up to you and say, 'Stick'em up,' and see how fast yo' hands go up."

For most part the audience consisted of harmless, lovable insomniacs. But, there was one show that almost fried the telephone lines at WSB. It convinced me that if a fake news item is ridiculous enough, most people will believe it. Ludlow introduced me as Jonathan Jones, an official of the NCAA, guardian body that judges sins and sinners in collegiate sports. I announced that henceforth no two universities would be allowed to have the same sports nickname. In a lottery, Mississippi State had won the right to be called "Bulldogs." Georgia would have to select a new team name. UGA could no longer serve as mascot.

All Hades broke loose. WSB telephone lines exploded with University of Georgia fans, some weeping, some cursing, some promising to open up a can of whupass on Mr. Jones. Ludlow was relieved he had a seven-second delay button. Hysterical Dawgs called totally mystified Vince Dooley at home, long after the iconic coach's bedtime. The *Atlanta Constitution* became desperate for story details. When we realized extent of the furor we tried to tell listeners the previous two hours were just a spoof. By then they thought we were just trying to cover up the truth and kept calling.

As I left the building, as incognito as possible, Ludlow was still explaining. The switchboard operator scowled at me, "Are you the idiot who is on the air with Ludlow?"

I said, "No, m'am, I'm just going to check under his car for bombs."

March, 2011

SCATTERED, SMOTHERED AND COVERED

Waffle House is Cindy Roberson's stage. Impertinence is her act. She's ham on wry, her snarky putdowns are comic valentines. She's like that special girl in fourth grade. Razzing you is her way of showing she really likes you. Cindy serves comeuppance along with my grits and eggs. "Be honest, don't you regret marrying him?" she asks my wife if I dare request an extra packet of jelly. I fake indignation and add an extra dollar to her tip.

Lest you wonder why her taunts amuse me, let this wolf in sheep's clothing explain. Deciphering The Waffle House Code has been high on my bucket list for a long time. (by comparison The DiVinci Code is no more complicated than Rubic's cube). I needed help from someone on the inside to pull off the caper. Cindy was the perfect mark. She wears medals for good service like a halo around her visor. Her work blouse is embroidered with "All-Star." She had to pass a 300-word test on Waffle House operations to get that.

I knew she knew "The Code." She knew I knew she knew. She came clean. Now I have cracked the mystery of Waffle House grill masters' legendary memories.

There are no touch screens, no inventory control system at Waffle House. Technology consists of waitresses armed with ball point pens, pads of paper and lungs like Tarzan. Orders are just shouted in the general direction of the grill. How do they possibly remember?

As all loyal Waffle House customers know, the menu is a celebration of infinite possibilities. There is no dish that that can't be prepared at least six different ways, so the mathematical equations become staggering. A placard boasts Prepared 844,739 Ways. I believe it.

Waitresses shout orders from every direction, like rat-tat-tats from machine guns scattered about. Each order is trusted to the grillmaster's memory. Or so I thought. Waffle House is no different from any other magic show. There is a trick:

Cindy shouts her order to grillmaster Gwen Paramore who has an array of condiments at her fingertips--packets of mustard, catsup and mayonnaise, little tubs of butter and jelly. How Gwen aligns the condiments on a platter provides coded verification of exactly what has been ordered. For example, Cindy, Kathy Coker, Samantha Hunter or Melissa Edgeworth might turn and yell: "ribeye medium, eggs scrambled with cheese, hashbrowns scattered, smothered, covered, chunked and diced." Gwen immediately takes a dinner plate from a shelf. She turns it sideways and places a butter cup in the middle of the plate (ribeye steak medium). She places a jelly packet on the platter edge closest to her and aligns it vertically with a sliver of cheese on top (scrambled eggs with cheese); a little mound is built consisting of tiny pieces of potato, onion, cheese, ham and tomato (hashbrowns, scattered, smothered, covered, chunked and diced). A reasonable percentage of time you actually get what you ordered.

Grillmaster memory is definitely the most famous idiosyncrasy defining Waffle House. But, the famous juke box that caters to no fleeting musical fad and heroic employees who keeps Waffle Houses open when other restaurants dive for safety contribute significantly to legend. Sober after church or tipsy at 4 a.m. the Waffle House is your lighthouse and the light never goes out.

In fact, FEMA administrator Craig Fugate has declared Waffle House his leading indicator as to what degree of destruction to expect in a natural disaster. "If you get to the Waffle House and it's closed, the situation is bad."

The Waffle House on Martha Berry Highway has closed just once that Cindy can recall. It took government force to shut it down. During the chaos of last year's April 27 tornado, as electrical systems collapsed, "We cranked a generator, set up a giant fan to suck the grease and smoke out the door and kept the grill fired up. The Health Department hired a locksmith to come padlock our doors. That was the only thing that could stop us."

It takes a lot to stop Cindy. She's nearing completion of a degree in cosmetology. "I'll serve a cup of coffee with every haircut," she says. If she tells you your hair looks like a family of raccoons bedded there it is only because she likes you.

December, 2011

THE FUNNIEST MAN IN AMERICA

When the funniest man in America opens his front door, he is still glistening and freshly fragrant from his ready-for-the-road shower. Wispy white tendrils of hair diverge damply over the circumference of his perfectly round head. His pale blue shirt, open two buttons down to expose a gold chain and a tuft of white chest hair, is comfortably untucked over white trousers, ebbing and flowing with each tidal shift of his perfectly round belly.

He is stoked from the packs of Camel Turkish Jade mellow menthols, the Winston 100s and the Camel Wides lying on the island top in the middle of an antiseptically white kitchen in his stately home north of Atlanta. On a normal day, if any day is normal for one of the wealthiest comedians most people have never heard of, James Gregory will drink 30 cups of coffee and smoke three packs of whatever cigarettes are on sale by the carton. "I would smoke more," he says as he lights one, "but I just don't have time." Strap a propeller to his butt right now and he might take off like a helicopter.

He takes a puff and checks his watch. The Funniest Man in America is one of the last of the old-time traveling cavaliers of capitalism and he obeys an old-fashioned salesman's canon of punctuality. In 20 years, he has never missed a performance. He has never shown up late for an interview. Vinnie Coppola, Gregory's protégé and opening act, understands that if he hasn't arrived by precisely 3 p.m., he might have to hitchhike to North Carolina, where gigs are scheduled for Friday and Saturday night at Harrah's Cherokee Casino. Coppola saunters through a side door with 10 minutes to spare, close enough to tease his mentor's nerves, but margin enough to deflect a lecture.

At 3 p.m. James Gregory leads a little procession of Vinnie, a writer and a photographer to a milk-white 1993 Cadillac Brougham that sits next to an ink-black Corvette. The brawny Cadillac and flirty Corvette live in the original garage that is next to a newer garage that shelters the 1970 Buick Riviera, the 1964 Chevrolet Impala and the rare 1963

Chrysler Imperial South Hampton coupe.

The Cadillac's massive trunk waits like a hungry whale for big black travel cases of caps, T-shirts, CDs, DVDs and VCR tapes. Setting up an improvisational shop before and after his cash-churning stage shows in comedy clubs, casinos and tiny town theaters, James Gregory has sold more than 200,000 pieces of trunk-transported merchandise, nothing less than $15 an item, as he smokes, sweats, autographs and ignores the inevitable awakening of a coming appetite.

He opens the Cadillac's trunk and fits together a puzzle, a few tiny overnight bags stuffed with wrinkle-resistant clothes wedged among bulky luggage crowded with merchandise. Satisfied that an intrusion of apparel won't impact the customary alignment, he offers this golden rule to Vinnie: "Don't ever forget that the biggest of the two words in show business is 'business.'"

That rule is the one thing James Gregory never forgets. In the world of non-famous comics, he is a phenomenon, a 57-year-old salesman who at the age of 36 parlayed a few "open mic" appearances for fun at comedy clubs into what has become a cottage industry. He substituted funny stories for encyclopedias and kitchenware, and without a TV show, his own radio show or an advertising budget, sells humor through word of mouth. His.

He works talk radio like a healing evangelist works the halt and lame, and on more than 300 days a year he advertises himself without buying a minute of time. He averages guest roles on 155 live syndicated morning drive-time shows a year and about 75 more shows in the afternoon. A radio tower in the smallest burg is a lighthouse that blinks him toward a new set of customers.

His drive-time humor is the weapon of the underdog, release for the traffic-clogged road rage of anyone headed for a bad day or coming home after one. For five or 10 minutes, he awards commuters with a golden scepter of personal superiority as he rags on dumb-asses, eccentric relatives, health addicts, modern parents, out-of-control environmentalists, medical infomercials and violence in the schools. The scant minutes Gregory has in the morning and afternoon are often like an audio version of a family album:

"...Uncle Robert's dream is to own a two-story mobile home. . . . You know on them job applications where it asks Nearest Relative? He put '12 miles.' Where it says In Case of Emergency, Call? He put 911."

His fans hear and spread the word he is coming to town. They are much like his old customers who would buy a stove, tell a friend how much they enjoyed doing business with him and then return themselves to buy a refrigerator. Similarly, two people see his comedy show, they bring two people next time he performs, those four bring four more to the next show, in effect, a comedy pyramid scheme that has made him, if not rich, wealthy enough to purchase homes and automobiles for a slew of relatives, pay doctor bills for friends and family, purchase $10,000 in lottery tickets each year and own the house on the hill that if it were not for the $15,000 to $20,000 a week he can earn by leaving, he would not.

Truth is, he loves money more than he hates leaving home even though afternoons are spent in Ramada Inns, watching Court TV and smoking and reading tabloids during commercials, trying to care that *The Globe* thinks Brad Pitt has had cosmetic surgery. He takes showers in thimble-sized bathrooms with generic shampoo and soap bars, drying off with towels management encourages him to use more than once. The last puff of a cigarette is his good night kiss.

Two hundred miles away from his Atlanta home, Asheville has only this to offer the salesman: 99.9 KISS Country. He will barge in the next morning as the mountain folk head for work. He may talk about whacko environmentalists: "A spotted owl! A damn spotted owl! When was the last time you went into a pet shop and said 'Oh, damn, you appear to be out of owls.' "

He will be locked and loaded on nicotine and caffeine and waiting for the perfect setup. Depending on the cue, he may even abandon the spotted owl and tell his customers some other story they've probably heard a dozen times, so funny that it matters not at all that it is so familiar they could lip sync. They will perk up when he says he will be in Cherokee that night and the next.

When life is a road show, years fly by while hours crawl and even eating becomes an anticipated event. As darkness and dinnertime descend on Asheville, James eases the Cadillac onto the freeway and, within minutes, concludes the exit numbers are not corresponding with the directions given by the desk clerk. He retreats like a general temporarily in disarray, but refuses to concede the battle and relaxes as the exit numbers begin to descend correctly on the new route encircling downtown. Now he is really hungry and announces the approach to each restaurant like a culinary tour guide on a food strip of Mexican, seafood and steak houses. When a passenger offers Denny's as a facetious alternative, James whips sideways behind the steering column and snaps, "Get one thing straight, don't piss on my parade."

There is a wait for a table in the smoking section of the Lonestar. He sips a dark beer at the bar with his entourage, though ordinarily he does not drink. But neither does he often wait. He is momentarily silent, though not often does he run low on conversation. But neither does he often travel with anyone for whom food is not worthy of a poem, a rhapsody, or at the very least a prosaic observation that doesn't piss on his parade.

The waitress says her name is Monique and this is her first night at the Lonestar. "We will be a pain in the ass, but we tip real good," James says, first thing, and he begins an inquisition. There are those who select surgeons with less inquisitiveness than James Gregory evaluating a menu. He wants to know how the cook will prepare each delicacy, what will be its appearance, how long the calves' liver has been frozen, whether the carrot cake is homemade and whether it will be soft and moist if you touch it with your finger. While he is deciding if he will have room for an 18-ounce strip he decides on two bowls of chili with a missile-sized jalapeno atop each, poppers and chicken wings and hot links that he has sent Monique to the kitchen to measure and which he shares with his guests, including the second refill of the spicy sausages. Afterward, he calls for the 18-ounce steak, and recoils in disappointment at the news there is none in the kitchen. He orders two 9-ounce strips instead. Later, he gives Monique a tip by which all future tips will be measured.

At precisely 7:10 the next morning, he has sipped his pot of coffee, smoked nine cigarettes since 5:30, and slipped into one of eight pairs of Stars and Stripes pants. He has not eaten in order to rasp the edges of his alertness when he settles on to the stool in front of a mic across from a sleepy jock at 99.9 KISS Country. The newcomer jock, Drew Montgomery, tells his audience, "We're visiting this morning with The Funniest Man in America." He apologizes that his on-air partner who, incidentally, is his wife, is back in Memphis where their home was recently introduced to tornado-like winds and insurance adjusters.

Tornado is a cue tossed to James Gregory from the Gods of comedy. He lowers the Diet Coke from his lips, replaces a chip on a platter of salsa dip. The mic becomes an auditorium.

"I come from tornado country and I have come to this conclusion watching the news in recent years and it is that a tornado has never touched an intelligent man's trailer. Think I about it. You have never seen on the evening news a tornado victim from a trailer park in a three-piece suit. You know, monogram shirt. Going, 'Yes, this was rather devastating. A tree fell on the Lexus. And there is quite a bit of rubble in the hot tub.'

"I believe that when a tornado hits, the news director of the TV station says, 'Get out to the trailer park and interview a moron.' Here's who they interview. The husband is always frail. One hundred and twelve pounds. One hundred and eight without the belt buckle. Wears a John Deere cap. Got a tattoo. Usually with something misspelled. Got a tire gauge in his pocket in case his trailer don't seem level. He's standing next to his wife. His wife weighs 400. She's wearing those tight, tight polyester pants . . . Why do they wear that? I know they are fat, but they aren't blind. Do they stand in front of a mirror and go Awww Riiighttt? Come on . . . Don't . . ."

As he leaves 99.9 KISS Country James Gregory spots a Bojangles' and a Krispy Kreme separated only by a concrete divider, just the way he would have designed their proximity were he the land planner. After biscuits and meat and coffee and a cigarette at Bojangles', it is a pleasant walk next door to the Krispy Kreme where he orders a dozen hot, plus a strawberry-filled anachronism for Vinnie, who with every bite must swallow ridicule from his mentor for his deviant taste buds.

The road through Cherokee, North Carolina is a tiny scar in the mountains; the few side roads are spaced like stitch marks. No one would come here on purpose were it not for Harrah's Cherokee Casino, owned by the Eastern band of the Cherokee Indians. The casino is separated from a cream-colored hotel and, inside, hundreds of Southerners dressed in service station chic sit almost motionless on stools facing obelisks of temptation glowing in a dark room. Hundreds more slouch at digital games of blackjack, poker and craps, drained of intensity as dealers push buttons to release virtual cards and dice and the only personal touch is to take their chips or to hand them more. At 8 p.m., the traveling comedy salesman, who is catching a nap in a cheap motel room 300 yards away, will rake in part of any swag that remains and, in exchange for a cardboard ticket, will give them back the smiles and laughter they lost in the dark cavern.

It is easier for a camel to pass through the eye of a needle than to determine what will make people laugh, much less inspire them to pay for the privilege, the way they would pay a plumber to fix their clogged commode or the grill master at Waffle House to prepare them an omelet. Humor is so subjective, no comedian, no theory, can fit all influences.

A few weeks before the show in Cherokee, at The Punchline in Atlanta, the venue was packed for the second time in one night, I watched a man in a red shirt with beer bottles lined up like little brown soldiers on his front row table. This obviously was not the first time the man had seen James Gregory. He started laughing even before delivery of the comedian's coup de grace lines, "He just died. Don't nobody know why he died. He just died. (Pause. Inhale. Pause. Exhale. Eyes widen. Jaw drops into a duh). I think it was the stab wounds." On the other hand, Sigmund Freud might have handed his business card to a young woman at another table who never laughed, never even smiled, turning frequently to nibble at the neck of the man who massaged her shoulders and whispered in her ear.

Neither reaction resembled that of a large woman on Friday night in Cherokee. She struggles from her seat and walks out, her lips tight, during Gregory's signature obesity routine although scores of equally large women bounce with laughter in their seats.

"Awwwwww ...damnnnnn! Obesity is a disease? If obesity is a disease, why can't I park in the blue spaces?"

He flashes the casino audience with his belly, leaning back so that it hangs out onstage like a celestial body suspended in outer space. He rubs his hands around and around his midsection as if it were stamped with an official license for political incorrectness. He pauses, pauses, pauses. His cheeks fill with air and his eyes bulge like Louis Armstrong high-noting his trumpet. He sissifies his voice in a way that makes the audience understand he is adapting the voice of those sensitive, politically correct harpies whom he is gleefully offending. The air escapes slowly, slowly, "Awwwwwww…Gaawdddd!" and he points to his stomach. "Just where in the hell do you think I caught this? You think I stood too close to a fat lady and she sneezed on me?"

The common denominator of stand-up comedy is character. He is, in fact, an actor and he can make an audience see Cecil's 82-year-old daddy on his 12-horsepower riding mower racing the next-door neighbor in his motorized wheelchair. He doesn't just crack off one-liners, he tells funny stories. But he also tells stories funny, often taking minutes to get to the punch line. The buildup is often as hilarious as the payoff as he exploits his Southern accent with a series of cackles and whines. The character of his material somehow fits the character of the performer as well as the character of the audience, whether the customers are The Punchline's ironic mixture of Buckhead and Douglasville bloodlines, or Dalton's heartland working class.

Sue and Wayne Gibson have traveled from Atlanta to Cherokee to hear him for the third time in six months. Usually they take several friends with them if he is performing near Atlanta. A man standing in the souvenir line near them after the Saturday night show says, "Why hell, I seen him 10 times. Oh, hell yeah. If he was here tomorrow night I'd come back again. Everthang he says is the truth. He can even make me laugh at myself. You know what I mean?"

That his routine doesn't change all that often doesn't matter to them, no more than it matters to those who have memorized every episode of The Andy Griffith Show or Seinfeld or never miss a showing of The Rocky Horror Picture Show. "Humor, like music, doesn't have to be new as much as it needs to be great," James says in a reflective moment as he sits smoking a cigarette in the afternoon shade of the Ramada Inn overhang. "I learned that from George Jones. He told me one time, 'James, anytime I have a new hit song, my fans want me to sing it. But if I don't sing all the old ones they love, they won't come back to see me.'"

One hour and 10 minutes after James Gregory begins his casino routine, the near-capacity crowd rises from their seats, applause rolling, echoing. He calls Vinnie back from the shadows for a two-minute close while he walks about as fast as he will ever walk anywhere, a snail sprint ahead of the crowd that must file past his table of merchandise on their way out. For a few minutes customers swirl in a perfect storm as the obese and the wiry, the smoker and non-smoker, the trucker and the accountant, the foul-mouthed biker babe and somebody's sweet daughter jostle to purchase the T-shirts proclaiming "The 2003 We Need More Fat People Tour," the "It Could Be a Law" ball caps, and an assortment of recordings of his live acts.

Vinnie sells three items. Brenda Ferrari, the comedian who followed Vinnie's opening act, is still dressed in the padded slacks and shirt of her Etta May character and sells enough to make the humor bazaar worthwhile. Although the two young comics have seen it before, they gape in wonder as James Gregory sells $1,200 worth of merchandise in 30 minutes on Friday, then puts a little more than $2,000 in his pocket off Saturday night sales. It is pocket change compared to his performance fee.

His bag of merchandise is light now and he rolls it on its tiny wheels with the weary slouch of a blue-collar worker trudging home from a shift, toward the exit in back of the dusky stage, the whites of his eyes streaked with tiny red fatigue lines above the glowing tip of a cigarette. Even with money in the pockets an alley is an alley and the one behind the casino where James Gregory has parked his Cadillac changes more in attitude than appearance, depending on the day of the week. Near midnight, after the Friday night show, gales of laughter do not follow each snippet of conversation and when it does not, the intermittent silence echoes the loneliness of life on the road.

"You want to go with us to eat?" the star of the night asks Brenda Ferrari. She has nothing else to do. Someone she cared about used to travel with her, but that grew so tiresome for both of them she hasn't considered a replacement companion. It's either old movies on TV or tag along with the man who amazes her. So, she says "Sure" and doesn't piss on James Gregory's parade. She repeats "Sure" to the most famous comedian most people never heard of—who was drinking lukewarm coffee from a baby bottle while still in diapers, who at age 10 was smoking cigars in Tom Morgan's barber shop in Lithonia, working 37 hours a week in Reese's Grocery, who made his high school classmates laugh by outrageous faux sneezes during study hall, who made his gym mates laugh with him instead of at the yellow patches on his underwear or the gold pants and purple shirt his mother bought him though she couldn't afford them and who he visits every Monday he is not on the road to tell her how much he loves her.

His pockets bulge with rolls of cash and he has fixed the ticket count for two nights on the accounting side of his brain, to be checked off against the casino's version when its check arrives. He lights a cigarette, eases the Cadillac into the night and quickly it becomes a white minnow gliding through a dark sea.

Vinnie has to pee. James is hungry. A convenience store offers redress for both discomforts. James draws a large cappuccino from a machine, selects a few bananas and a Klondike ice cream bar. He discovers state Highway 369 on the map spread across a dashboard the size of a pool table and repositions the Cadillac toward the west. Sunday he will sleep late. Monday he will visit his mother in Lithonia. His one prayer, that he not die on the road without telling her he loves her, will have been answered again.

In the ink of night he remembers it is Saturday and he has not checked his lottery tickets. A passenger asks him what he would really do if one day in defiance of the billion to one odds, he won. The Funniest Man in America takes a puff on a Winston and repeats the tagline from his show that epitomizes every traveling salesman's dream of striking it rich. "I tell you what." Pause. Deep breath. Lip-fluttering release of the breath. " If I win the lottery…if I win the lottery…you won't ever see my fat ass again."

And The Funniest Man in America isn't kidding.

January, 2004

life under spotlights
and harsh lights

ENGLISH BROKEN HERE

Not much to distinguish me from any other columnist. Write a little essay, make a little point, draw a little paycheck. I pen a few lines about dogs and divorce, hopes and happiness, love, pestilence, death and disease, sprinkle in a curmudgeonly opinion or two, make a few speeches, eat some stringy chickens, hide from civic-club program chairmen looking for a speaker.

At least, my obscurity seemed assured until I committed THE ERROR. The dastardly deed occurred in November, but I have just now summoned strength enough to discuss it. The truth is, I thought that if enough time passed it would go away. Unfortunately, each time I look at the issue of November 3, 1985, there it is, glowering at me like some graceless grammatical goblin, "…who invited my wife and I to join them…"

I quit counting at 53 the number of letters from readers who caught this ungrammatical combination of words. Guardians of the nominative case get the shivering fits when I is used as the object of a verb.

Among the more generous comments from readers were those who reproached me for shattering their image of me as a grammar purist. I suppose this is as good a time as any to admit that column writing is similar to making movies. The actors depend on stuntmen for the tough scenes, and columnists rely on copy editors. The biggest difference is that in the movies, only the stuntmen bleed if things go wrong.

Alas, most columnists are just slothful gobs of ungrammatical flab who suffer from dangling participles and ingrown infinitives and without copy editors would constitute a continuing embarrassment to their former English professors. Columnists depend on copy editors the way Sinatra depends on bodyguards.

Nevertheless, I would not have anticipated the outbreak of literary dyspepsia that led to such remarks as, "I have enjoyed your weekly articles from time to time, [at] others I have wondered why the magazine wasted the ink. That one 'I' ruined an otherwise delightful vignette, and Georgians need as many good examples they can get."

Another said, "This puts you just a notch down along with scores of 'educated' preachers [Christ died for you and I], sports announcers and news/weather persons."

Still another remarked, "I was thinking that your work should be held up to my 16-year-old as an example of good, entertaining writing, when I was struck dumb and numb...."

One reader, obviously taxed to articulate adequate disgust, scrawled across a copy of the column, "What's the matter with you? Been hangin' around somebody from Ohio?"

I was relieved to get at least one letter from a lady willing to give me the benefit of the doubt. "Please tell me it was a computer error," she pleaded.

Several word warriors invoked the name of my late English professor at LaGrange College, Miss Jennie Epps. Said one, "...and you have the gall to promote yourself as a student of Dr. Epps, who is no longer here to defend herself."

I even received a call from another of my English tutors, a beloved man from whom I drew my earliest collegiate inspiration in the field of literature.

"I can't talk for long, my wrists are bleeding," he said.

"You are ashamed of me, aren't you?" I said with a whimper.

"Yes, but also forgiving. Most of my poorer students would have never had the audacity to toy with the written word as a livelihood."

I have thought of every excuse possible for my fall from grammar heaven. Those who signed their letters received communication from me explaining that it was not a mistake at all but an experiment in improvisational language. Obviously that's an excuse ahead of its time because not one was familiar with jazz English.

The scholarly *Dictionary of American Regional English* was my last hope for support. It is a magnificent work that was started In 1906 and is so thorough that the first volume—some 500 pages—goes no farther than "C." I don't expect them to get to "Z" in my lifetime.

The author points out there is a vocabulary of use and a vocabulary of recognition, but even that didn't seem to cover my sin. About the only thing I could find that adequately expresses the depth to which I have fallen is on page 341. It is a mountain expression often used by my wife's Aunt Zula:

"The boy ought to be bored for the simples."

January, 1986

DEAR SONG AND DANCE MAN

Jimmy Lavalle Townsend did it to me again. Sat right there at the Old Hickory House drinking his steaming coffee and smoking those God-awful cigarettes, knowing he was dying of cancer, knowing I knew he was selling snake oil again. And still, I bought another bottle.

I was a corporate executive at the time, a smug, pinstriped, clean-shaven, soft-ass remnant of what was once a pretty good newspaperman. I had been offered the editorship of the *Atlanta Journal-Constitution Sunday Magazine* in a delusional conspiracy between Townsend and Executive Editor Jim Minter. "Bad Man," Townsend said, his basset-hound eyes protruding from his ravaged face, "ain't, by God, no place to hide. I'll always be after you. I chose you as a pup, gave you your first magazine piece to write, anointed you, prepared a place for you. Besides, it don't matter you don't know a damn thing about putting out a magazine. I'll be there to show you everything you need to know."

He lied, of course, which would be of little surprise if you had known him. He went ahead and died. He left me and the hundreds of others he had conned into thinking they were special, left us with our lips pursed from the bitter brew of reality, left us to doubt we could ever really reach the places he said we could fly to.

Thirty years ago this month he invented *Atlanta* magazine. He blew into Atlanta like a strange, warm wind that stirs the dust and makes the skin tingle with an indescribable feeling that something you have never seen before is about to happen. Chamber of Commerce Vice President Opie Shelton was no match. Townsend convinced him that what Atlanta needed was a city magazine that would shovel away all that chamber boosterism crap, would gain the city national credibility, and that he, incidentally, was just the man who could do it.

Jim Townsend's *Atlanta* magazine attacked the central nervous system, stopped the heart for a beat, opened tear ducts and shook the throat with laughter. *Time* magazine called him "the father of city magazines."

He was hot. Clay Blair wanted him as senior editor of *Saturday Evening Post; Good Housekeeping, Town & Country, Southern Living* all bid for him. Townsend was so hot he simultaneously edited Atlanta, New Orleans and Cincinnati magazines, hustling back and forth in a Lear jet he conned out of an admirer.

Cocktail hour began at 10 a.m. Four years after he drank the first cocktail of his life—a bourbon and orange juice that drew laughter from those who insisted his preferred drink of ginger ale didn't fit the image of an editor—he was an alcoholic.

Oh, he was a snake-oil salesman, all right. Writers, illustrators, photographers, graphic designers couldn't resist him. He didn't pay them much. Sometimes he didn't pay them at all. "Dear Heart," he would say, his manner so regal there was the feeling of having been summoned to the Round Table by Arthur, "let me tell you why you are going to do this story I have in mind."

Money always became insignificant when you considered that you were the only living, breathing human being capable of bringing the insight, language and heart required by that particular article.

As Townsend lay dying in April 1981, a few of us sat in his room at Northside Hospital. We timed the ominous intervals between breaths. The phone rang constantly. A great photographer was in Egypt when he heard. A plumber with never a published word to his credit called and said it was Jim who had convinced him he was born to be a writer. When Jim died, Dr. Stanley Winokur forgot that doctors don't cry.

At St. Philip's Cathedral, a then-young Pat Conroy delivered the eulogy. "0' Townsend, 0' Dear Heart. We knew you were a con man. But Jim, I swear to you we did not know, none of us knew until the final sickness that you were such a brave man. But you, old editor, old buck-and-wing man with a hat and cane, came awkwardly strutting from out of the wings, out from the shadow of cancer, and taught all of us how to join the flow of the dance…In your last dance, we could hear your voice again, and it said, 'Write it down. Write it all down.' "

May, 1991

BOBBING FOR CELEBRITIES

Celebrity journalism. Now there's an oxymoron that will make you wish you had decided on a career in nuclear physics or grill master at Waffle House. Celebrity journalism is the hellish abyss in which so many otherwise substantive national magazines are trapped. More than a few employ at least one person whose primary responsibility is to pooch kiss whatever posterior blocks the path to a brief, innocuous interview and photo session with whichever star is the cover dessert of the month.

City and regional magazines seldom have to walk what is perhaps the most humiliating of all journalistic gauntlets. But occasionally we get hoisted on our own petard. We start out thinking what a great idea it would be to do an entire issue on Atlanta's contributions to the world of music, complete with a bonus CD of locally-induced melodies. In the momentary euphoria of such a bold thought, we temporarily forgot that we would have to row our boat through a Sargasso Sea of "publicists."

Veteran country music reporter Miriam Longino agreed to produce one of the features. We decided to splash a few admiring words on our pages about Alan Jackson. He's that tall-gangly boy from Newnan who writes and sings well enough to draw applause even from the legends of country music. Small town boy who's a star now. Wears clean jeans with a designer rip at the knee. Has a publicist who intercepted Miriam's request for an interview quicker than a French veto. "Will it be a cover?" Flaks always ask that. They teach it in flak school. "Out of the question if it isn't a cover." Alan isn't especially interested without a national audience either, Miriam was told—as if Alan ever heard of her request behind this publicity Maginot Line.

Okay, we know when to punt. Travis Tritt. We will interview old Travis. He lives out in Paulding County. My son David used to come home from school talking about this neat kid in his Cobb County middle school who imitated Elvis. When Travis grew up he installed air conditioners for awhile. The background of a good ol' boy without a doubt. One of the few country singers who has kept the common touch, we convinced ourselves.

Uh oh, red alert! The good old boy has a publicist. Just like Garth Brooks, who also has a tall hat and a college degree in marketing. The press agent/ manager/whatever, seemed more concerned with the quality of *Atlanta* magazine's makeup artist than its writing. Would the photographer also make publicity shots for Travis? In the process of offering mass assurances to this and other picky criteria, Miriam innocently revealed, "We want to talk to Travis' friends about how it feels when someone they grew up with becomes a big star." The publicist freaked. Game called on account of imaginative angle. Perhaps we had slightly overestimated the extent to which Travis had stayed in touch with his roots. We moved on, our ears ringing with no's.

Well, just damn. Didn't used to be this difficult. I thought back to Willie Nelson. I interviewed Willie at least three times and never talked to a publicist. One time I was to meet him at his hotel room and he showed up an hour late, but with a big grin on his face. "I was out jogging," he said, "and met this fellow. We sat down on the curb and started talking. I just forgot about our meeting."

Willie didn't have a word guardian to shield him from columnists or fans out on the street. He had nobody demanding to know circulation figures and the angle the story would take. There was just Snake, his road manager, who was sitting over on the bed with his razor blade, scratching the grit out of a leafy substance in a shoe box. Willie looked right at me with those piercing eyes the entire time, as if I was almost as interesting as the stranger at the curb.

That was in the mid 70s and I was writing a freelance country music column for the *Atlanta Journal-Constitution*. They paid me $25 a week. By the time I tallied my expenses, I only went in the hole about $50 per column. The expense didn't matter. I drank beer once with Tom T. Hall. I had dinner at Roy Acuff's house along with Rheba McIntyre. I saw Dolly Parton backstage at the Opry without her wig. I have a hand-written letter from her. She drew a little butterfly in the upper left-hand corner of the envelope.

Let me tell you why she sent that letter. One night I drove up to Lanierland Music Park to see her perform. She had promised me an interview after the show. The weather, though, was yielding to an artic influence. Cows in the pastures had to turn their rumps against the stinging wind. Dolly did two shows that night. Afterwards she stood at the edge of the stage and signed autographs. Her hands took on a bluish tint from the cold, but she didn't turn away a single seeker of autographs.

By the time she finished singing and signing, it was near midnight. Her road manager, seeing how tired she was, tried to shoo me away. Dolly said to him, "Aw, shoot, now," and she started talking. She later wrote to thank me for the column, even though I had expressed alarm over her flirtation with pop music.

At the time, Willie and Dolly were as big as it got in country music. He was leader of the brilliant Texas outlaw movement. Dolly had become a favorite late-night TV guest. Johnny Carson was saying to Dolly one night that he would surrender an arm for a glance at certain attributes that left America slackjawed and shamelessly curious. She just laughed at the crudity and America embraced her wigs, lipstick and self-deprecating humor.

Name dropper, you sneer. Okay, guilty. Truth it is I, not they, who remembers these encounters. But that's the point. It didn't matter that I wasn't someone to remember. I had a newspaper column and their fans wanted to hear from them. They didn't hide, they didn't take my audience measurements like they were trying to see if the suit would fit. Even stars like Willie and Dolly welcomed the line of communication I provided, as limited as it was. They spoke to their fans wherever they could, whenever they could. They were just good old boys and girls showing respect for the good old boys and girls who made them celebrities. And the only spin doctors they needed in those days were the radio jocks hunched over their turntables late night and early morning in cities big and small.

June, 2003

IN DEFENSE OF JERRY LEE

The photographs are faded. The newspaper clips have yellowed. The pages in the album wear the scars of a thousand openings. On one page is a picture of Jerry Lee Lewis' second wife. A child has taken a ball point pen and added a mustache and devil's horns. The child was Jerry Lee's third wife, his 13-year-old-cousin Myra.

Myra is 32 now, divorced over five years from a man who sings and plays the piano like a hurricane: a man who reportedly lives like he plays and sings: a man who affectionately calls himself "The Killer."

A few weeks ago "The Killer" was arrested outside Elvis Presley's mansion. It was alleged he was shouting loudly, waving a pistol, and, in general, raising hell. Shortly afterwards he was hospitalized with "pneumonia." Myra flew to Memphis to be with him.

"I told him I was going to give you an interview," she said. "I told him that maybe people would understand the pressures he has had to live with. Pressures that make him act like he does. How the world has just tried to flush him away. How he's been crucified for things nobody would raise an eyebrow over nowadays."

This is the story that Myra told me:

"After Jerry came up to Memphis and recorded 'Crazy Arms' at Sun Records, he, my daddy and a drummer named Russ Smith formed a musical group. Jerry Lee was 20 or 21. By then he had been married twice. Before that, he told me, he was kicked out of Wauxahachie (Tex.) Bible School because of the way he went wild when he played a piano.

"That summer, the whole family was touring and Jerry Lee used to kid and flirt with me. I didn't take it all that serious. I figured he was just being kind to a kid. But I idolized him.

"That fall I went back to school. One night he came by the house and said, 'Yesterday I had a girl go by the courthouse and pretend she was you. We got a marriage license.' Two days later he drove me over to Hernando, Miss., and we were married by the Rev. M. C. Whitten.

When Daddy and Momma found my marriage certificate on the dresser, they just about died. That night Daddy came into my bedroom. He was crying so hard. He took a leather belt and gave me a whipping.

"From that time on, I took care of Jerry. Lee. I cooked for him. I picked out his clothes. I drove the car. I handled all his money. I even worked with the income tax people. For a while, I loved it. From the time I was 10 I wanted to be a housewife. Momma and Daddy had had my little brother because I begged so hard for a baby to take care of.

"After he recorded 'Whole Lot A Shakin' Jerry Lee went from making $30 a night to thousands of dollars. He used to come in with $20-30 thousand in a suitcase because he didn't like checks. He'd just hand it over to me.

"Then we took a tour to England. The press there went berserk when they found out he had a 13-year-old wife. And there were a lot of questions raised about the legalities of his first two marriages. They ran this headline there in one paper ("Child Victim: Clear Out This Gang"). The whole world got in an uproar. I couldn't figure it out why they couldn't see that I was grown.

"Our life got like the Keystone Kops. After our baby was born I was left at home while Jerry Lee was on the road. Then, when he came home it was chaos. The whole band would come with him. They would stay up until 5 a.m. and sleep until 3. I was taking care of them. All that was needed was an orange trash can and I could have called myself Howard Johnson.

"One day I took a gun and put it to my head. But I could not go through with it. Instead, I just walked away without telling anybody. I got an apartment and later filed for divorce. Most people spend their life trying to get out of a rut. I was determined to get into one.

"What I didn't realize at the time was that Jerry Lee was not demanding I do all this. It was just me giving it to him anyhow. And what man won't take a substitute mother?

"I wish everybody knew the real Jerry Lee Lewis. He was kind and generous. He paid millions out for me. I used to order Cadillacs by color over the phone. And nobody ever writes about all the money he has given to charities and the church. He'll wind up back in the church one day, you know. He feels so guilty because he thinks he has misused his talents on the public stage instead of in the church where his mother wanted him to be.

"Sure he's got weaknesses. He was raised where rules and regulations didn't mean anything. Everybody just did as they damned well pleased. He's never adjusted to big cities. He's a gentle person, but, well, he's the kind who pushes a point too far. Like in front of Elvis'.

"Nobody stops to think of all the tragedy this man has had. Things that get to him sometimes. Our son, Steve Allen Lewis, drowned in a swimming pool on Easter Sunday 1962. His son, Jerry Lee Jr., was killed in an automobile accident three years ago. His mother died of cancer right after I left him.

"Nobody takes all that into consideration when they call him a wild man. All anybody remembers is, Jerry Lee Lewis married his 13-year-old cousin.

"Dammit, we weren't even first cousins. We were second cousins."

January, 1977

THE AUTHOR WHO WORE HER
UNDERWEAR INSIDE OUT

At Olive And Burns' memorial service, my wife and I wore our underwear inside out. Olive Ann thought it patently silly to wear seams next to the skin, chafing and irritating like some cotton and polyester mosquito. So, she didn't. So, we didn't.

In the 10 years I knew her she said lots of other things I listened to; not in the manner of accommodating friendly, entertaining chatter, but more in absorbent awe that one whose head seemed so full of air at times had an attitude about God and Life that is worth pondering.

She lived 65 years and wrote one book, *Cold Sassy Tree.* I won't say it's my bible—I especially favor the one that advises, "Do unto others as you would have them do unto you." But, like a lot of mystified people holed up in mental caves waiting for some guru to answer what is life, I never felt particularly close to the truth until Olive Ann told me through the pages of her novel.

She sat down at her typewriter the day after learning she had a lymphoma that would be painful and increasingly devitalizing. Nine years later she had produced a remarkable book about Southerness that, had it been written by someone named, Twain, would probably be hailed as a classic.

Olive Ann's iconoclastic theology is imparted through the voice of E. Rucker Blakeslee, whose grandson, Will Tweedy, narrowly escapes death when he drops down between the rails to avoid a train that seems hellbent on running over him. He asks Grandpa if he thinks his being alive is God's will, if God wills who lives or dies. Grandpa replies:

"Life bullies us, son, but God don't! He had good reasons for fixin' it where if'n you git too sick or too hurt to live, why, you can die, same as a sick chicken. I've knowed a few really sick chickens to git well, and lots a-folks git well thet nobody ever thought to see out a-bed agin 'cept in a coffin. Still and all, common sense tells you this much:

everwhat makes a wheel run over a track will make it run over a boy if 'n he's in the way. If'n you'd a-got kilt, it'd mean you jest didn't move fast enough, like a rabbit that gits caught by a hound dog. You think God favors the dog over the rabbit, son? …Ever noticed we git well all the time and don't die but once't? Thet has to mean God always wants us to live if'n we can. Hit ain't never His will for us to die— 'cept in the big sense."

Will asks Grandpa about prayer and gets this answer: "All I know is that folks pray for food and still go hungry, and Adam and Eve ain't in thet garden a-theirs no more, and yore granny ain't in hers, and I ain't got no son a-my own to carry on the name and hep me run the store when I'm old."

Near the end of the book, consumed with pain and facing his own death, Grandpa Blakeslee finally even figures out prayer. His second wife, Love Simpson, implores him to have faith and pray. Grandpa tells her: "Well, faith ain't no magic wand or money-back gar'ntee, either one…Hit means you don't worry th'ew the days…means you respect life like it is—like God made it—even when it ain't what you'd order from the wholesale house."

Grandpa added that he believed there is only one legitimate prayer, "Lord, hep me not be scairt.

"When Jesus said ast and you'll git it, He was givin' a gar'ntee of a spiritual healing. Jesus meant us to ast God to hep us stand the pain, not beg Him to take the pain away. We can ast for comfort and hope and patience and courage, and to be gracious when thangs ain't goin' our way, and we'll git what we ast for."

A gospel worth pondering from a woman who wore her underwear inside out.

October, 1990

OUTSIDE THE WHITE HOUSE

The night is breezeless and still, as if the earth is holding its breath. The lights that bathe the White House are soft as moonglow. It is the lights that draw the park people, I think, like summer mosquitoes and moths to a porch light. They seem to flit and buzz more than walk and talk, these eccentrics who are insatiably curious about the place where our presidents live.

The man who claims to be king of the United States squats for hours in LaFayette Park. Unmoving on his cramped haunches, he stares at the white edifice. He arises during the day to attend to bodily functions, grab a free meal at noon from the truck that feeds the homeless, or to make an insane charge against the fence around the White House. But at night he squats.

If the night is reasonably cool, some of the park people play tag or bum cigarettes. As I talk to Bob Edwards, who lives within an imaginary 6-by-6-foot boundary of sidewalk brick, some of them crowd close so they can hear our conversation, fetid breaths sometimes close enough to cause an involuntary shifting of position. A man whose deformed right arm is permanently frozen like the backswing of a bowler interrupts to ask Bob, "Don't you think that man is the greatest president in history?" His left hand gestures toward the place where Ronald Reagan lives.

"He's a great actor," replies Bob. The man nods, smiles appreciatively and moves on.

There is thunder off across the Potomac and Bob slips into an undersized denim shirt. All day he has stood in the sun wearing only dark blue running shorts and there is a smear of brown across his slender midsection where the day's sweat has mixed with street dust. He and a 56-year-old bearded man named Charles Hyder share a 24-hour vigil in protest of nuclear arms and one or both are always there between two plywood signs, one with the legend, "Reagan, History Awaits You," and another that reads, "Peace, Equality, Compassion." Their ponchos, a change of clothes, an emergency cup for urinating into, some books and leaflets, constitute their belongings.

Ryder, a solar physicist, has been there for almost a year, freezing in winter, soaking in the spring and sweltering in the summer. Edwards, a psychology major, joined him about two months ago. After listening to Hyder's spiel, he just set up camp with him, making it somewhat easier for the original homesteader to take a break without leaving the place attended by someone not familiar with the cause of disarmament.

During the day cars often slow down in front of the two men and passengers thrust their heads from the windows and curse. Some yell, "Get a job, you communists."

Sometimes Bob confuses them by shouting back, "Get a truck, you car driver." Its absurdity strikes him as fine humor.

He has been slugged an estimated half dozen times. "I'm a pacifist," he says, "but sometimes the humiliation of it is hard to take." He has been shot in the back and stabbed in the chest, but both times before he joined Ryder. For someone who has dedicated his life to protesting violence, he seems to attract it like tall trees attract lightning.

Bob says he is doing this for his children and for all children. It has given him a purpose in life. It has been a struggle to regain personal equilibrium these last two years after he split from his wife, also a psychologist and anti-nuke activist.

I ask him if he thinks his vigil will contribute anything toward world peace. He hands me a piece of paper with a quote from Edmund Burke which says, "No one makes a greater mistake than he who did nothing because he could do only little."

I am conscious of a trickle of sweat on the back of my neck. I give Bob Edwards a dollar and walk away, wondering if it is the weather or Bob Edwards that has made me so uncomfortable.

September, 1988

PEACH COBBLER POLITICS

Robin McDonald and I were exactly one minute and 37 seconds late. Our state's impatient governor was already tapping his foot on the loading dock behind the state capitol which is where he had gone to elude his security force. As he settled into the front seat of my car, he said, "All right, let's see this place you've been raving about."

Zell Miller does not forget. Doesn't forget old enemies, doesn't forget old friends and, most of all, doesn't forget old conversations about new places to eat. Once, in a fit of hyperbole, I had described a recent culinary discovery as the place "where God eats lunch."

"When I get back from the Democratic Convention and Barcelona," he said, "I want to try it."

Within days of his return, he was on the phone. "Can we go tomorrow?"

One of the endearing qualities about Heath's Grocery on Cascade Avenue is that the governor of Georgia has to take his food out in Styrofoam containers just like everyone else. There is no place to sit down.

But there is a big oak tree that shades the bleachers at John A. White Park softball field, and a gracious breeze arrived unexpectedly with measurable relief for the governor, who, unfortunately, has to wear suits and ties to work. Not to belabor my insistence that there is some sort of cosmic influence on Mrs. Heath's food, but the felicitous breeze didn't really surprise me. The first time we took a bite of Mrs. Heath's peach cobbler in this same park, bright sunshine broke through clouds as dark as a villain's beard and I'm reasonably sure I heard the faint sound of harps.

For those of you who complain that I often fail to provide details in this space, Gov. Miller's lunch included rutabagas, black-eyed peas mixed with limas, squash, boiled okra, corn bread, raw onions, fresh tomatoes, two containers of iced tea and whatever he could spear off the plates of his companions.

Once during the meal Robin tried to sneak in a reporterly question, having surmised that the rutabagas had induced an altered state in which the governor might be susceptible. He washed down a bite of corn bread and said, "Dad blame it, Robin, I came here to eat."

Between courses he did toss her a tidbit, realizing that while some folks must have a cigarette after a pleasurable experience, a reporter has to ask a question.

"Here's something nobody knows," he said. "I was sick as a dog when I made the speech at the Democratic Convention. I was running a temperature of over 100 degrees. Shirley had been bathing me with ice trying to get the fever down. And I had to cut five minutes from the speech. I sure hated to throw away some of those lines."

"Such as?"

"I'm not telling. I'll use them later."

And he will. He has a reverence for good lines, especially country music lyrics. What other state has a governor who is a dues-paying member of ASCAP and has given us the immortal tune, "You Can't Ration Nothing That I Ain't Done Without?"

Robin wanted him to talk about the controversy he stirred up when he called for a new state flag because he felt the current one was created as a direct affront to black citizens.

"I wish it hadn't divided the state so much," he said with a sigh.

It is an issue so volatile that *Atlanta Constitution* Editorial Cartoonist Mike Luckovich received death threats after publishing a panel on the matter.

The governor poised his fork over the peach cobbler. It seemed a signal that he was ready to change the subject. A taste, a grin. Then a bite of the blackberry cobbler. Then the sweet potato pie. An outright smile told me that Robin and I have probably ruined forever our favorite source of noonday nourishment. Despite assurances, there is always a chance that in a desperate need to influence votes, Gov. Miller will take a politician or two to lunch there, and as beneficial as it may be to getting his way on some bill, it can't do much for the ambience of the grocery or the neighborhood. I would have felt better if he had said, "Read my lips. No new customers."

October, 1992

NOBODY ELSE TO BLAME

om was her friend. Funny, sometimes outrageous, but always reliable. On the times her love affairs exploded, his friendship was safe harbor for her heart. "Tell you what," he said, "if you aren't married by the time you are 30, I'll marry you."

On her 30th birthday she called Tom from Washington, D.C. Her voice seemed half a laugh, half a tear. "Well," she said, "I'm still not married."

"On second thought," Tom said, "maybe we better make it 35."

"Are you gay?" She blurted it out as a joke.

"Yes."

"Oh, Tom, I'm kidding."

"I'm not," he said.

He doesn't know exactly when he contracted HIV. He found out for certain last year that the disease has evolved into AIDS. When he told his associates at *Atlanta* magazine, he did it with his usual mixture of rock-ribbed honesty and humor. He called a meeting of our staff and laid it out. He saw the faces pale with shock and anguish and tried his usual shtick. "Like I told my Mom, look at it this way. At least I'm not a druggie."

When friends say, "Tom, you're not going to die, they'll find a cure," he indulges the fantasy just as he does his mother when she assures him, "You're going to be OK."

He cracks about his enrollment for disability benefits as if it is material for his stand-up routine. "What happens if they find a cure for this crap? Do I have to come out of retirement?" The jokes are for us. The tears he saves for himself because he is a realist.

Tom has read everything there is about AIDS. He knows the odds. And knowing has given him two options: to be angry and bitter ...or just angry. He chooses angry because he says that he refuses to be bitter. Bitterness comes from blaming others, and he blames only himself. There is evidence, he says, that homosexuality is genetic. His mother and two of her sisters each have three sons and one daughter. In each family there is one son with reddish hair and in each case, he is gay. Even if genes are a factor, Tom understands that both homosexuals and heterosexuals can exercise behavioral options, and for that reason he doesn't believe one penny of research money should be diverted to AIDS from other catastrophic diseases such as cancer.

"AIDS can be controlled by your own actions. Cancer can't," he told me one day in May. "I'm appreciative of any funds that are raised for AIDS research, but I wouldn't want it at the expense of other diseases that attack people who have no choices."

Very few of us are willing to take responsibility for our problems anymore. Victimization has become the excuse du jour. America has become, literally, a society of victims. We can justify almost any dereliction, any destruction, any delinquency in the name of victimization.

Those who consider themselves victims strike out senselessly and virulently. But there is a higher order of human beings.

Tom belongs to the order of those who have made mistakes and are concerned less with where the blame lies than where responsible human dignity resides.

July, 1992

NO, LAUGHING MATTERS

The trouble with the Georgia Legislature, if I might say so on the occasion of their annual January assembly under the Gold Dome, is that the public can't take a joke and the politicians can't tell one.

Humor deprivation was never more in evidence than during last summer's "Cheetahgate." A notion spread that public agitation over an R&R junket hosted by lobbyist Rusty Kidd for five of our state legislators would dramatically change the course of influence peddling during the coming session. As you may recall, Mr. Kidd pitched a party for five lawmakers at a South Carolina resort last summer and forgot to leave The Cheetah Club exotic dancers at home. There was a sudden shower of public outrage about this oversight, upgraded to hurricane status by the media.

Now, don't get me wrong. I'm not saying, "Boys will be boys." Count me with those who want lobbyists branded with a scarlet letter. But frankly, my chief disappointment, having harbored no illusions about the piety of politics, is that no really good tales emerged from the escapade. In the old days, no matter how solid or synthetic the sin, at least one tall story would have been memorialized in smoke-filled poker games at the Henry Grady or Georgia hotels.

Laughter was considered so important to Old Guard politicians that a "designated laugher" was brought in whenever important city or county officials visited. He was provided with a free room, food and drink. He had a booming, raucous laugh that seemed to trigger the tickle box of everyone in room. His assignment was to do nothing but laugh at the tales recited in notorious Parlor A at The Georgia Hotel.

One of the legends that always drew a guffaw, concerned "a Very High State Official."

The VHSO was known for dispensing gracious rewards of paved roads in exchange for personal favors. Once he "requested" that a state legislator stand guard in front of the VHSO's Georgia Hotel room while he kept company with a female constituent. The legislator was embarrassed but didn't dare say no.

Colleagues, aware of what was going on, paraded past, always asking the embarrassed politician what he expected as his reward.

"An intercourse highway," he would say.

His brilliant double entendre became a part of the ribald history of the Legislature, as did an escapade a few years later that featured Playboy bunnies. Bunnies were considered pretty bawdy for the times, though today their uniforms would look ridiculously prudish around most swimming pools. I don't recall the exact year, but the senators decided that for the last session they would dress in togas, and someone got the bright idea to also bring a hutch of bunnies into the Senate chambers.

When the ever-vigilant press started making inquiries, Enigma's Bobby Rowan was persuaded by his colleagues to help diffuse the questions. Denial—and the biggest sin of all, unimaginative excuse making—was never considered.

Sen. Rowan primed the reporters with, "I learned, settin' on my mammy's knee..." and had them laughing so hard before he was finished that it was tough to work up a full load of editorial indignation.

If humor was a viable weapon in those days, the most heavily armed were the politicians, like Rowan, from south Georgia. Before chain stores drove the general stores out of business, a politician could sit around potbellied stoves in his district and bank funny stories like currency, to be tossed onto the table like poker chips at the next session in Atlanta.

One of my favorites concerned influence peddling in Washington, D.C. In the '60s it was very important for Georgia politicos to have a brief personal audience with Sen. Herman Talmadge—if for nothing else, so they could impress local voters with their personal relationship with the powerful "Hummon Tamage."

Sen. Rowan arranged such a meeting between Talmadge and state senators Bob Smalley, a Griffin attorney with strong support from business, and Bill Searcey, of Savannah, who had a constituency that included many black voters.

After introductions Talmadge launched his usual routine: "I tell you, what's wrong with the county today is the nigras and the labor unions..." Searcey promptly popped to his feet to protest.

Shifting gears smoothly, Talmadge continued, "Wait a minute, Bill, you didn't let me finish. Now, as I was saying, many people blame our problems on the nigras and the labor unions, but what's really driving this country down the drain are the banks and big businesses...."

That caused the circumspect Smalley to protest on behalf of his business sector benefactors. Frustrated, Talmadge shouted at Rowan, "Gah-dammit, Bobby. If you want me to please 'em all, bring 'em in one at a time."

Rusty Kidd should have known that influence is best marketed one customer at a time. After all, he's the son of one of the wiliest of them all, former state Sen. Culver Kidd, known as "The Gray Fox." Perhaps, rocking on the front porch in Milledgeville, young Rusty grew up hearing the old-timers spin their funny tales about debauchery and deals and mistook hyperbole for historical precedent.

Truth is, the trip to the beach was more silly than sordid. And once discovered, Rusty Kidd and the Daufuskie Five probably would have been better served by forgetting about denial and coverup. They should have followed the advice of English writer Samuel Butler, who observed that a little levity will save many a heavy ship from sinking. I can't speak for the rest of the public, but I say, since we obviously can't beat 'em, at least we should get to laugh at 'em.

January 1996

CUBA

Antonia Garcia took the ring of keys from a hook and led us to the den on the lower level of La Terraza. At this restaurant in Cojimar, Ernest Hemingway once sipped vodka and lemon juice with fishermen in cutoff trousers and listened to their melancholic tales that would become *The Old Man and the Sea*.

Senora Garcia opened the den's wooden shutters in invitation to the breeze from the bay where Hemingway imagined the gnarled old man urging his skiff toward the smooth blue ocean and the fateful marlin. She brought us some little fried fishes and an aqua-colored cocktail named in honor of Gregorio Fuentes, skipper of Hemingway's Pilar. Gregorio is over 90 and Senora Garcia says you can often find him resting on his terrace in the village and he will tell you stories. Nearby is a stone monument to Hemingway. It is pocked by salty wind, rain and bird droppings.

Not so much is left of the romantic Havana that Hemingway knew. The people of Cojimar are descendants of fishermen, but they do not, for the most part, fish. A few miles away in the city, there is music, but no gaiety. Architecture that once was joyously pastel is painfully pale and scabbed. Electricity is a sometimes thing, except in beach-front hotels where the comfort of European and Canadian tourists has become as precious as the harvesting of sugar cane. Bicycles have replaced cars. Gasoline is scarce, directed primarily to rusted buses packed with sweating riders chest to chest.

Cuba provides a doctor for every 136 people along with free medical care. There is little illiteracy. Street drugs are virtually nonexistent. You can make love relatively free from the specter of death, for everyone old enough to have sex is tested for HIV. Anyone testing positive is quarantined in a sanatorium. Food is rationed. The economy is in such shambles the Cuban government would even be friends with the United States if we would let them. But we are so obsessed with taking away Cuba from one man, Castro, that we maintain a smothering embargo that is choking the life from his 11 million subjects. Killing them for their own good.

The island has the feel of a giant hospital room with out-of-town relatives waiting patiently for the last breath so the estate can be divided among them. Ninety miles away in Miami, expatriates are tense with the anticipation of regaining family estates appropriated in the revolution. There are organizations such as the Cuban American National Foundation, which for $25,000 will promise you a piece of the action, a business turf in Cuba when Castro falls. To them, in the 34 years since the revolution, Cuba has been nothing more than a freeze-frame. Soon, the motion picture will start again. Their ears strain to hear the slightest insinuation of mambo music and dice rolling across a craps table.

Cry for Cuba, but not for the people. They endure. Their failed communism is without the disillusionment you see in Russia. They rejoice in their inner strength, in themselves. They do not impose their heartbreak on others. Almost every conversation about their economic peril is prefaced by, "Despite the current crisis, we are proud." Proud has become a national mantra. Strange how important the word is here among the ruins when a recent study by the Roper Center revealed that even in good times, the people of America are pessimistic about their country and themselves.

Wayne Smith of The Friendship Force and I were in Cuba to arrange a cultural exchange of baseball teams, the one passion shared jointly by our countries. The essence of The Friendship Force is reciprocity, in which the homes in each country become the homes of the visitors for a short time.

As anxious as they are for any kind of progressive relationship with the USA, Cuban officials would not agree to this type of exchange, insisting that their guests stay in dormitories.

At one point our interpreter, Pedro Pablo Oviedo Lopez, took me aside. His smile, which had seemed as personally relevant as his arms and legs, had vanished.

"The officials are too proud to tell you that we cannot have you in our homes during the current economic crisis. I would gladly give you my bread, my food for one day, but I cannot give you my family's food for a week. I truly wish it were otherwise. We would be proud to be your friends."

That night in a Havana restaurant a woman named Beatrice played the piano beneath an ironic mural of a plantation, romanticized as one might portray a scene prior to our own defeated South of 1866. Beatrice had dark lustrous hair. Her posture was regal. On her, the faded gown was as noble and imperishable as the drapes worn by Scarlett O'Hara. *You must remember this*...I became aware that the lyrics from "As Time Goes By" were singing through my mind as she played the theme from "Casablanca"...*the fundamental things apply*...

Her dark brown eyes seemed to ask me, Don't you remember? Don't you remember how glorious it is to be proud?

September, 1993

DOLLY PARTON COMES TO SEE ME

I have gone and played hob now, for I am pretty well certain I have lusted in my mind. The other day Dolly Parton came up to the office because I am the country music critic for the *Atlanta Journal-Constitution*. She had on this purple blouse that you might call a tee-shirt, and, to tell the truth, I can't remember what else. One wise guy remarked that Major League baseball commissioner Bowie Kuhn had ruled her ineligible for the Braves' wet tee-shirt contest as being, "over qualified."

Take my word for it she is pretty enough to take to the dance. She's got a good wit about her, too. She read the column where I said she ought to quit worrying about those white-neck music fans. Granted she sings just about any kind of music good, but when you've heard her sing country, you don't care to hear that other kind.

Anyhow, she stared me right in the eye and said, "Now you better like my new rock 'n roll album when it comes out." When she saw the look on my face she giggled and whacked me a good one on the back. "Aw, I was just kiddin' you," she said. She talks just like regular people.

I like the way she doesn't mind the fun being on her. She told a magazine writer that one time she tried being a Women's Libber, but when she burned her bra, it took the fire department three days to put out the fire. I thought that was pretty funny.

I have just about given up on her taking my advice to stay pure country. Although she hasn't come right out and said it, she must figure she did all right making her own decisions before she ever met me.

To cite some examples, she made the decision to leave Porter Waggoner's show and everybody said that was a mistake. Then after she proved everybody wrong, she decided to branch out from country music (I say the jury's still out). She fired her old manager and hired the one that handles Cher and some of those glamour people. She even fired her Travelin' Family Band, which was just that, her family.

I told her she must be pretty tough. She let me know quick enough that ladies are not tough. "It's just that I've had to make some hurtin' decisions."

Being a country girl, she is not afraid of hard work. Before she came to see me she had already done live interviews with radio stations WPLO, WGST and WQXI. That was before lunch. She hadn't even gotten to bed until 2 a.m. because she was doing a show at the Great Southeast Music Hall. I asked her why in the world was she working so hard. "Just like most people, more money," she said.

"More people are listening to me and that means more money. I figure if you gonna kill yourself working, you might as well shoot for it all."

You know, her TV show didn't do all that good. She said the only episode that worked was "the one where those Hollywood people didn't write the script. I do better when they they just let me be me."

I think that's the reason her stage show is so good. I went to see her at the Great Southeast and there wasn't much difference from when I saw her at Shorty Hamby's Lanierland except some of the audience had funny looks in their eyes, from something they had been smoking I suppose. Dolly was cracking jokes and singing "Coat of Many Colors," "Tennessee Mountain Home" and all those old good ones.

"Why," I said to her, "you haven't changed all that much."

"Well, I ain't the one who has been writin' all them stories," she said.

I'm not about to get into a war of words with Dolly Parton. I don't think I have enough ammunition.

October, 1977

SWEET MEMORIES FROM SWEET APPLE

When people ask me about my journalism heroes, Celestine Sibley is one I mention. As I recall it was about four years ago when Kenneth Stoddard at Dogwood Books and Antiques found for me a copy of Celestine' autobiography, *Turned Funny*. I had lent my first copy to a friend who moved away without returning it.

Some columnists vomit troubles and it is labeled literature. Celestine absorbed life's ups and downs like nutrients, her writing rich as good earth. She could write about her father, Little Henry Colley, the 6-foot-6 inch no-account from whom she and her mother fled when she was a small child and make you weep for, rather than deplore, his sorriness. She could make you appreciate the patient waiting of Jack Strong, her companion for 30 years, whom she finally married just before his death. She handled with literary restraint the deaths of two grandchildren and the absence of two other grandchildren who were "kidnapped" and hid by their father, one for six years and one for 10. She usually drew a laugh writing about her mother, the beloved "Muv," who was technically a bigamist when she married Bob Sibley after running away from Little Henry. She quoted her mother as analyzing that first marriage, "I didn't know I was driving my ducks to a bad market."

Whether Celestine was writing about the last petal of someone's life or the first bloom of flowers, readers recognized her honesty. When I was a columnist for the same newspaper, Celestine's fan mail was delivered in huge cardboard boxes. People routinely wandered in off the streets to take a seat and say, "Miz Sibley, I need to talk to you about my troubles." A colleague once remarked, "Well, you know, she's the only Bible some people got."

She never lived in a new house. Yet Sweet Apple was as well-known, through her columns, as the Governor's Mansion. It was actually two cabins. She bought the first and an acre of land for $1000. She bought the second cabin for $700 and joined them together. Jackie and I spent an evening or two there, with snow-white petals from her Bradford pear covering the ground like lace, sipping a drink and simply listening to her. She was the most fascinating storyteller I have ever known.

Celestine became a reporter for the *Mobile Press* at age 15. After that she did everything there was to be done on a newspaper. She covered the weather bureau, city hall, the county jail and rode with revenuers during Prohibition. She was a Hollywood columnist. Those who know say she was the best there ever was at covering the Georgia Legislature. In 1995 the General Assembly declared her an official state treasure. In the days before the AJC became sensitive to slave trade she reported on a full-time political beat, wrote five columns per week and found time to write more than 20 books. Though she lived in the country, she loved he throb of the city, writing that she loved Atlanta "like women love men who look like the butt end of a mule and act worse."

When a day care center at Bowen Homes blew up in 1980, she reported with soft precision about the mothers at the Grady Memorial Hospital morgue, "…They went in silently, fearfully, and they came out to stand in the sunlight and lean together, weeping noiselessly. One woman put her head down on the iron banister and wept soundlessly for long moments before relatives led her away. Another stood on the curb staring blindly at the street and the little group of waiting people. Tears coursed down her cheeks. 'Nothing…I can't say nothing,' she whispered."

The next day Celestine wrote a column. "…a group of us waited in front of the morgue and I looked at a pretty blonde young reporter, daughter of a friend of mine, and I wanted to say, 'Run, honey, run fast. This job will break your heart. When you are old, you'll be like old Grady Hospital, the receptacle of everybody's sorrows and pain.'"

Oh, how I loved her. Only someone who had felt life's razor edge could be so prepared, week after week, to deflect the blade away from her readers.

August, 2012

PIANO MAN

Sometimes, even if Larry Williams has really needed his four hours sleep after an into-the-early-morning piano gig at Dover House, the warm, silent intrusion of sun through a window will prove startling enough to wake him. As often as not he will already be sitting quietly, a Merit smoldering in an old brass ashtray, his supple fingers deftly guiding small tools in the shaping and nourishing of delicate bonsai plants. In the morning his pet parrot imitates the hacking cough that rips the solitude into ragged little chunks, but not so bad as in the old days when Larry smoked four packs a day instead of three.

If it is not summer he will put away his plants and tools at 7:45, wriggle into some trousers and a Ban-Ion shirt he tossed across a russet overstuffed chair the night before. He will light another cigarette and drive his 1974 Audi Fox to a place he used to live and pick up his 16-year-old son by his second broken marriage and drive him to school, not because he has to, but because it will be his only chance to see the boy and learn a little more about him as he grows taller and away from his father.

Larry likes the feel of his fingers on the steering wheel. He likes the feeling when his fingers controls the tools that shape his bonsai plants and the way they feel when he returns home and spends part of the day dialing friends on the telephone and when he taps the ashes off those cigarettes. His mornings and early afternoons are filled with things for the fingers to do. An Army psychiatrist at Ft. Robinson during World War II told him never to let his fingers grow idle. Busy fingers have a way of shutting off contact with the place where nightmares live, the place that caused the nervous breakdown when Larry could no longer face the realization he was training young Americans to kill faceless people with bayonets.

Most of all, Larry's fingers love pianos. Pianos keep him sane. All the other things just occupy his fingers until they can touch a keyboard in the darker shades of evening when arrives at the Dover House piano bar.

Night in a piano bar smells like regret, with the breath of an alcoholic and the lungs of an emphysema patient. At precisely 8:30 each night he settles into a side booth and exhales his own soft cloud of cigarette smoke while his soup and sandwich and cup of coffee (half off the menu price) are prepared. He has already played a piano from five o'clock until eight at a Holiday Inn six miles away. The gig provides money, no longer considered extra, but rather a necessity. By the time he pays other members of his trio, he takes away less money than in 1940 when he had his own touring big band. Back then he was a jiving fool on the vibraharp and his biggest hero was himself.

Sometimes the soup, sandwich and coffee argues with his stomach and sometimes there is a throbbing beneath his shaved pate. He simply waits patiently as possible for nine o'clock and a predictable miracle. That's when he wedges his stocky frame amongst sound equipment, a bass player and a drummer. That's when his fingers begin to absorb the healing powers of the ivory keys.

Most nights he will open with a solo, maybe "Misty," which he gives a little more upbeat treatment than might be expected of such a song. Sometimes the crowd will lift their eyes and smile almost as one when he makes a solid jazz run, like an old athlete who walks onto a playground full of basketball hotshots and tosses up a smooth hook that says, "There was a time, man. There was a time." But he is careful not to set a standard too difficult to challenge, because the song is not so much a performance as a key that opens the gates to a kingdom of illusion.

For the rest of the night Larry Williams subjugates his own performer's ego, turning the night over to his customers. One after another, accountants, waitresses, salesmen and assorted people of the night emerge from dimly lit booths and into a brief spotlight as they satisfy a peculiar human longing to be read differently than they are.

Some of the customers-performers have been singing two, maybe three nights a week for 10 years with the man at the piano. For them, he borders on deity, having become a granter of expectations, a recognizer of the unrecognizable. For them the routine is familiar and accepted on faith that it is right. Obediently they will glide alone to the microphone, sing two songs, acknowledge the applause and return to their stool or booth to wait the inevitable compliment.

"I got goose bumps tonight," someone will whisper. There will be a soft touching of hands. Soft touchings are important at the Dover bar. Soft touchings are not challenging, not likely to be rejected, not likely to result in a situation where a person is chosen or rejected on any basis other than singing. And nobody's singing is ever rejected.

Two songs and sit down. Wait for a compliment. The rules are immutable. That way the man at the piano does not have to appear judgmental. If Frank Sinatra walked in he would sing two songs and sit down. He would sing the way the man at the piano wants it to be sung. It is his world. He created it, fashioned it from a notion that illusion is good; that if a person has illusion he or she will eventually find reality.

Larry came up with the idea in 1973. He called it the Mutual Admiration Singing Society. Since then MASS has been incorporated, sings to itself five nights a week at whatever bar Larry is playing, finds time to raise money for good causes like the Salvation Army and waits for something wonderful to happen. Its members know that despite long shot odds, it has happened before. Some of the regulars have made it professionally.

Dennis Pennington is singing at clubs in Orlando. Nancy Wilson sings with a band in Atlanta. Marne Andrews has played bit parts in plays and movies. Wendy Walker had roles on TV soaps. There is always hope of a step beyond MASS. For some the hope is as modest as escape from the stagnation of nine-to-five reality. For others it is as basic as the need to be loved, to be chosen.

Being chosen is what MASS is mostly about. In their real world the members are not always chosen. And in reality there is not much applause. Applause is important. The man at the piano makes sure there is never a night without applause for those who take up their identity masks and follow him. And when he roams nightclub to nightclub, as a piano man must do, they follow him like a grazing herd, their spiritual nourishment dependent on two songs, a brief spotlight, a whispered compliment.

Some, like Miss Jenny Trehune, have actually known the spotlight in the past. Years ago, she danced in the chorus line of Ziegfeld Follies. She later toured the country under the name of Georgia Drifting Snow, teaching the Charleston, a dance she claimed to have invented.

Once when Miss Jenny was hospitalized with a broken hip, her doctor agreed to let her attend a special MASS awards ceremony if she would promise not to drink or get out of her wheelchair. She roared into the party like a snockered wild west barmaid and insisted that the two most handsome men in the place stand beside her as she belted out her two tunes, slightly off-key as usual. The man at the piano understood. He just smiled. Some people, he said, have learned so much about music they have forgotten what music is about.

Larry Williams almost always smiles when his singers sing. There is lots of room on his face for his smile. There is no hair on his head and his eyebrows are almost too fair to be seen in bar light. A tuft of white beard hangs like a little cloud from his chin. Otherwise, the smile can use almost the entire face, and does. The smile is important. It reassures the bar community that the man at the piano is happy, that all is right in their world of illusion.

As the strains of "Misty" fade into the hum of the crowd a tall, graying accountant picks up the sound of the opening bar from one of "his" songs, adjusts his cowboy hat and moves to the microphone on the little stage in front of the musicians. That's the way it works at the Dover bar, which in appearance resembles every other shopping mall watering hole. Listeners and non-regulars sit farthest away from the stage on the side of a horseshoe-shaped bar or in one of the booths with Formica-topped tables and vinyl cushions along a wall. Regulars sit at stools arranged along the curvature of the piano or at booths near the entrance, where there is a little more light, making it easy for Larry to spot them. There is no set order of appearance, but Larry likes to alternate them by sexes. There is seldom an introduction by name, but rather the opening bar of a favorite song, which alerts the singer to move away from his companions to the stage.

The accountant sings "Your Cheatin' Heart" and "Luckenbach, Texas" and then is replaced in the spotlight by a man who markets computer personnel to corporations. He wears blue shorts and a blue shirt with red and orange trim. Adjusting his dark glasses with Bogart subtlety, he moves easily into his own private fantasy. His voice is smooth and controlled. Each word of the lyrics seems to bring a different demand to the elasticity of his face. He is working the audience. He has been there many times and likes what he can do to a crowd.

When he returns to a bar-stool, a man moves over to him and says in a tone that makes it difficult to detect if he is serious or making a joke, "You and Tom Jones have a lot in common. You sing beautifully while in obvious pain."

The specialist in computer personnel is the sole survivor of his unit in Vietnam. He has a degree in literature. His college adviser told him he was silly for thinking he could make a living with that degree. So he learned about computers. There is not much applause in computer marketing.

"I feel alive here," he says. "I love silencing a crowd. Holding them right here in my hand, you know. Total control. It feels good to have them come up to you and say, 'You should be a professional singer, man.' Sometimes I fantasize that someone will fall in love with me while I'm up on that stage. Hey, I'm just being honest."

Two female real estate agents who attend the same church are regulars. One is vivacious and into Linda Ronstadt songs. The other, a divorcee from Detroit, has children who are grown, but she is still beautiful. She seldom comes in with a date unless he, too, is a regular. Anyone else might not understand when she slips into her role. And it is the role that is important. She often sings, "I Want to Be Around to Pick Up the Pieces."

"What I do is very personal," she says. "Larry understands. I call him my sunshine. He's always got a smile and a happy thought. When I was having some problems, he telephoned me every day. He cares. He wants everybody to have a chance to be happy. You can't help but love him. Like a patient who falls in love with the doctor."

Larry's second wife did not understand. She thought there was more to this kind of thing than just friendship, more than just a sensitive man wanting to make people happy, more than just part of the job. There were arguments in the darkness and his fingers trembled as they did when he was showing 18-year-olds how to kill strangers. He left home and entered a monastery. He was looking for truth there and he found it in a silence that was louder than he had ever heard before. Now he lives in the unused portion of a plant nursery on Pharr Road. He likes it there. It is close to Monsignor Haddad and the St. John's Melkite Church. Larry is not Catholic, but he plays the organ at the church and teaches the father about plants. He does not have the desire to smoke when he is there and it does not bother him when it rains.

Larry is told there is a newcomer in the crowd who wants to make his debut. The man has sandy hair and Robert Redford eyes. He is obviously nervous. It is important that the newcomer's nerves are not transferred to the audience. It will spook them like horses in a corral with lightning all around. It will destroy the illusion.

The singer starts in the wrong key. Panic glows in his darting eyes. At the piano, Larry chants rhythmically, his lips barely disturbing, the smile. From five feet away he appears merely to be into the song, mouthing the words along with the singer. But he is coaxing the man down from the ledge of defeat. "Don't stop. Don't stop. Keep going. Listen to me. I'm with you. I'll find you."

The singer and key are reunited, and his voice booms with confidence. "Now. Now. Do it. Do it," comes the muted chant to the newcomer whose voice rises to the occasion. The sound is good. Then it is all over. There is a smiling exit, applause and whispered compliments.

By midnight the characters begin to exit. The 74-year-old man who must travel with a container of oxygen and tubes running to his nose, who imitates Maurice Chevalier when he sings "Thank Heaven for Little Girls," must not overextend himself. The man from St. Louis, who plays a horn of his own invention, wears a cowboy hat and is called Duke because he favors John Wayne, must be out and selling in the morning. The mental health worker from Rome, who says, "I have been seeing Larry for six years because he just knows when I'm funky," must drive home, fantasizing that on one such night he will be discovered. The woman who used to sing professionally in Cleveland before her son was born 19 years ago, leaves in hope of being able to get in a song at the piano bar at Joe Dale's Cajun House before calling it a night. The hooker, whose pimp allows her to come and sing one week out of every month, puts the love from the crowd into her purse and hopes it is enough to last until the next time.

By two the regulars are gone and all that remain are some waitresses who need a song to unwind from work and a few people who have simply forgotten how to sleep. Then there is time for Larry Williams to slide into a corner booth and have a couple of drinks on his own. Time to mellow out and appreciate the good feeling of having been there when friends needed him. Time to pray that God will give him good health to play the piano professionally until his last day on earth. He thinks sometimes that if it doesn't work out that way, seeing as there are no retirement benefits for piano players, he will just go on back to the monastery. He could be a big help there. He could write their music, play the organ for them and work their gardens. Just keep the fingers busy, ya know.

December, 1982

WONDER WOMAN

Long before I saw her, I heard the laughter. It was not like any laugh I had ever heard. It wasn't dainty, perhaps not even lady-like. Instead, it seemed to spring from nature, like whitewater rushing down from the hills and there was about it a sense of permanence and strength.

I was rounding the corner of Mandeville Hall at West Georgia College and the laughter drew me to its source. I saw her rocking free and natural in a big cane-backed chair, a country girl, I guessed to myself, someone who had probably spent 18 years of Sundays on rickety front porches swapping stories with neighbors and waving at passing cars. Her eyes were gorgeous, like the centers of brown-eyed Susans, and I knew at that precise moment that somehow I must impress the girl who said her name was Jackie Miller.

I'm sure she figured that since we were landlocked on the same college campus she would not be able to avoid me entirely, so we might as well learn a little more about each other. We would both be playing basketball for the West Georgia Braves we discovered. In the men's first game I scored eleven points. In her first game she scored 52. Since she is a member of the Rome-Floyd County Sports Hall of Fame, most of you already know she is a local legend. In fact, around Armuchee, where she grew up, most commonly I am referred to as "Jackie Miller's husband."

What you may not know, but perhaps have suspected, far beyond basketball and tennis she can do most things better than her husband. She can repair cars with coat hangers and fix plumbing with chewing gum. For years she raised vegetables in a garden she plowed, tilled and planted herself, pickling, canning and preserving like she was in competition with del Monte. Arthritic family dogs have lived and walked beyond their natural years thanks to her potions of herbs and magic. Two boys, one girl and one man-child have thrived on her old-fashioned mixture of understanding, forgiveness and hard labor. Once, when a date asked what sign his mother was born under, one of the boys replied, "Caution—Men at Work."

Although she is afraid of water and can barely swim, in Florida she saved the life of an *Atlanta Journal* baseball reporter's special needs son who was drowning in a hotel swimming pool. She is safe harbor for the lost, the lonely and road weary travelers. Confused divorcees depend on her to dispense country psychology at any hour of a sleepless night. Her supper table is a shrine for the down and out. They know that when they hurt, her cornbread will heal them and when they need an audience she will laugh her magic laugh.

Each time columnist Lewis Grizzard emerged from his several heart surgeries, he asked for Jackie's vegetable soup. He wrote several columns about her, including one devoted to her cornbread. Another time he wrote, "There may be a better person on God's earth than Jackie Walburn, but, then, I have never met Mother Teresa."

Valentine Day, three months prior to the start of our 49th wedding anniversary, Cupid shot an idea straight into my heart. Beginning June 8, that year, I would court Jackie Miller again for the next 12 months leading to our 50th. I would write sappy love letters. We would date and I would buy her Krystal hamburgers and a Coke. Maybe we would park and fog up the windows of an old Ford. I would reconstruct the half-dozen proposals that wore down her resistance in 1958.

It never happened. Twenty three days after Cupid left Dr. Steven Morganstern notified me that my road to rekindled romance would be paved with microscopic runaway cells.

On the days she emptied my catheter bag, on the morning she extracted the bloody tube, on the nights she lay in bed reading medical information in search of remedies for my discomfort, on the evenings she fixed my favorite meals to combat my slackened appetite, on the day she put her arms around me and let me see her cry for the first time since the cancer diagnosis, I knew that in the final moment of my life, her face would be the one I wanted to see.

Last month it was announced that married couples are now an American minority. Nevertheless, Wednesday we began the journey toward our fifty fourth anniversary. Country girl frugal, she will appreciate that I saved postage on this love letter.

June 11, 2011

THE THRILL OF THE DEAL

I t could be worse. My wife could be a dope addict, or an alcoholic slumped over a honky-tonk bar, her bright red lipstick smeared around the rim of a glass, a mound of cigarette stubs smoldering in a tin ash tray. As it is, she comes home most times without assistance. She doesn't sing as she puts the key in the lock and her breath reeks only of coffee.

If I tried to pinpoint when she began to get high on flea markets, I would say shortly after the last kid drifted off to college. When she talked in her sleep she began peppering her mumblings with the jargon of the aisles, like, "…tell you what, if that electric cord with no plug isn't gone by sundown, I'll give you 50 cents for it."

Even she agrees that if there is a rusty socket wrench or a copper tub for sale within a 25-mile radius, she will catch the aroma and run away. And it does no good to call her back. She will look back at you, judge the distance and, if she thinks you can't gain sufficient ground on her before losing your wind, will skitter away, eyes spinning wildly in anticipation. Inevitably, she would convince me to accompany her to an occasional flea market since on my behalf she often endures things for which she sees no logical point.

There is no use trying to keep up with her once she gets on point. Occasionally I may spot her hairdo bobbing up like a bubble in a bathtub of humanity, but because she primarily runs bent low to the ground, most of the time identification is best achieved by getting down on all fours and sighting through the legs of the throngs until I spot the cleats she wears for sudden cuts and quick acceleration.

Usually, while I am waiting to reconnect, I occupy myself as best I can among the special forces survival knives, eyeglass defoggers, axes, mauls, costume jewelry and T-shirts with silk-screened messages such as "Don't Mess With My Toot-Toot." If it is a really high class flea market, I can usually count on spotting an itinerant preacher standing on a van shouting Revelation into a portable sound system, and I can

123

eat up a little time watching him lay hands on a sinner or two.

One time when we visited the Cattle Barn in Rome, Georgia, a slender bearded man selling plastic Combi Chef graters and dicers for $10 was outdrawing the preacher, perhaps a metaphor for an age when miracle salads seem to hold more intrigue than miracles of the soul.

In the throes of terminal boredom, I came upon a van covered with a hand-lettered scriptural index, all of which, I came to understand, referred to biblical endorsements of the healing properties of herbs. The van belonged to Bob Steele, a large sandy-haired man with a broad Archie Bunker forehead and pale eyes. He sat beneath an aluminum canopy in a webbed garden chair and received a steady stream of the ailing. They mainly asked timidly about possible cures for swollen prostate glands, arthritis, gout, migraines and fast nerves. Men were the better customers, and they dropped an average of about $20 on the little metal folding table beside Mr. Steele.

"Herbs seem to have become a good business," I observed during a lull.

"Oh, I clear over a thousand a week just selling them myself, and I'm beginning to line up other sellers and I get a percentage from them," said the proprietor.

"How did you get into herbs?" I asked.

"Well, it's like this. I was hurt in a construction accident in Hawaii. I had so many spinal operations, sometimes the doctors would have to leave the wound open for weeks to drain. I used to look in the mirror at my spine just to have something to do. Man, I was bedridden for about 17 years. I lost my desire to live. 1 was drinking like a fish and popping pills to kill the pain. Then I heard about a herbalist over in Alabama. He got me started and now I'm feeling good and working. I'm off Social Security and making a good living. People started coming by my house just to see me cut the grass because they knowed how bad off I was before."

"Do you have any medical training?" I asked.

"No, but I get a lot of feedback from customers on what works and I learn that way. For instance, I had this 81year-old man who had lost his sex drive and I gave him some herbs and the next time I saw him he sure was smiling.

"Then I also had this preacher who got some herbs from me and he said, `Hell'—well, he didn't say hell—he said, 'that stuff really works,' and he came down and did a cable TV show on me after I helped him. Another man came to me with throat cancer and I helped him."

"Don't you face any kind of government regulations?"

"Nah. You might in the city, but not in the country. People there just figure that if it helps them, it helps them."

"Have you ever thought you might be selling false hope?"

"Over 200 people I sell to in one county have quit going to the doctor. And as far as I know, only one customer has died in the three years I been in the business. And her son told me she wouldn't take the herbs."

I asked a gray-haired customer in a silver jumpsuit if the herbs had helped him. "These things take time," he said as he pocketed his two bottles of capsules and about five dollars change from a twenty.

Having somewhat recovered from the Cattle Barn experience some 15 years ago, I tagged along to Trade Day in Summerville on a broiling Saturday in June of this year, nervously fingering the $10 bill I had pocketed should I suddenly find myself caught up in the thrill of a deal. By 10 o'clock I was dizzy and thirsty from the heat. I began to crave grape snow cones and I saw shimmering shade trees that disappeared when I ran toward them.

A man who looked like Robert De Niro was selling magic paste that keeps eyeglasses from fogging over and mine were already sweating. He offered to sell me a six pack for $3. I offered him $2. He curled his lower lip and said, "I don't need your damn money that bad, buster."

An aisle away stood a severe lady in a flowery dress, her hair pulled up in a tight bun. She stared with desire at a simulated gold ring. The man behind the display, whose jaws were so puffy he appeared constantly poised to spit watermelon seed, said, "Now, I won't tell you that ring won't turn...but I'll tell you this. It'll take a long time."

Lovely little Haley Hammonds strolls by with a basket of country pastry and trills, "Fried pies...fried pies...just a dollar," her tiny voice barely audible over the din of yapping dogs, some on leash, some for sale. She weaves her way down the aisles of "As Seen on TV" magic choppers, miracle glue and polarized sunglasses, singing her ever-hopeful refrain as shoppers barely notice her while scanning islands of straw baskets, knives, wrenches, nut drivers, ropes, pillows, socks, underwear and previously owned machinery, especially exercise bikes, most with the look of hardly used. Eventually, she would pass the hillbilly nut scratchers, Dawg, Tide and Vols trucker caps and the occasional little black fisherman statue or pogo stick. I bought a pie.

When I rendezvoused with my wife near the gospel blue grass band and rows of fresh farm produce she was negotiating for a mink jacket she would convert into fancy pillows for gifts. She walked away with the mink for a mere $20 dollars. That left enough leeway in her budget to purchase, for $5, a Kirby vacuum cleaner that sells new for hundreds of dollars. Bargain secured, she snapped open part of the housing and maneuvered a belt back on to its wheel, rendering it good as the day it left a factory. The crowd that had gathered to witness a heavyweight bargaining scrimmage applauded her triumph over the experienced dealer.

Sometimes I think her purchases, except when she buys fresh vegetables from James Henderson of Chattoogaville, are based not on need, but on the thrill of pulling off a good deal. That's not true, she says. "Lots of our friends love flea markets. I see Faye Porter there. You are so naïve if you think she shops exclusively at Lord & Taylor."

July, 2011

HONEY, I SANK THE TRUCK

I probably wouldn't tell you this story had our youngest son not sent us a photo last week. David lives in Montana, but he is Southern to the core and I remind you that the two most dangerous expressions in the Southern lexicon are "Hold my beer and watch this" and "Well, dadgummed, how hard can that be?"

The road to David's cabin on Duck Lake was impassable under a coat of winter snow so, of course, he decided to drive his truck across the frozen lake. The photo shows the upper half of his truck, the rest is somewhere beneath the ice.

David was headed to a cabin he and a Native American friend had built acting on the vision of owning a hunting/fishing lodge. It struck me as eerily similar to the vision that resulted in my own brand new pickup truck going to a watery grave.

David's mother had convinced David's father that an abandoned scout hut could be remodeled into an adorable vacation cabin. All we had to do was move it from the back lot of a Methodist Church on Shorter Avenue. She said, "Well, daddgummed, how hard can that be?"

I sometimes compare David's mother to General Patton convincing his troops it would be jolly fun to assault an enemy machine gun bunker. Well, perhaps I exaggerate. But she can be persuasive.

Her plan was simple. All we had to do, she assured me, was find a house mover with the courage to maneuver a 25-foot-wide shack over a creek and an uneven dam road bed approximately 20 feet in width and tilted, oh, about like a banked turn at Atlanta Speedway. And, all we had to do to get it that far was remove four large trees. All we had to do once that was accomplished, she assured me, was to find a careful carpenter who would remove the pine paneling board by board so we could insulate the hut, then meticulously reinstall the boards. Then all we had to do was rebuild the roof, add a screened in porch and another room. Sure, some of the exterior planks were split and rotting, but all we had to do, she assured me, was take apart, board by board, the little

127

garage next to the Scout hut and use those boards to replace the bad boards on our new cabin. I wouldn't have to lift a crowbar, she assured me.

It didn't happen exactly that way and it didn't happen right away. We found a carpenter, who said cheerily, "Why, it wouldn't take a week to get done that cabin. Onliest thing," he added, "It's deer season, so don't know when I can get to it. Go ahead and arrange for electricity, though."

I won't dwell on the battles to get electricity or a septic tank or the revelation the carpenter didn't do sheetrock ceilings and we couldn't find anyone who wanted to sand and stain the old hardwood floors. "Well, dadgummed, how hard can that be?" my wife said about the floors. She would do it herself since I had to return to work in Atlanta.

The report I got is this. About 11:30 that Sunday night (she doesn't have a pause button) she had made a trip to our barn for supplies. Returning, she parked our truck on a slight incline between the lake and the cabin and hustled inside to finish the job. When she looked outside, our truck was missing. At first she considered it stolen, but then she saw two beams of light glowing beneath the surface way out near the middle of the lake. She had left the motor running, the lights on and forgotten to pull the emergency brake.

Panicked, she ran a quarter mile for help from son-in-law, Reed Biggers. Reed placed a midnight call to Bobby Lloyd, pleading for his tow truck. Bobby did show up, but said he wasn't about to dive through a crust of ice (refer back to second paragraph for genetic connection). So, Reed called Earl Kennedy and borrowed his wet suit. He rowed a boat to the beams of light and dove through the ice, never, he thought, to catch his breath again.

The next day, I hugged David's mother. As often as she had kept the brakes on me, I figured the odds just caught up with her.

My hug calmed her down somewhat. She returned my embrace and said, "Who would have ever believed a truck could float that far?"

February, 2012

NO SUDDEN MOVES FOR ME

My absence from any of the three Celebrity Dance Challenges, including the one last weekend, startled a few readers. They saw names such as Craig Bing, Greg Cater, Lamar Clark, detective Joe Costolnick, Dr. Buford Harbin, Sammy Rich, Kit Durant, Ali Freeman and Cecil Fielder and thought perhaps I had offended the selection committee representing the Sexual Assault Center of Northwest Georgia.

I explained that word has gotten around that I am rhythm-impaired, an impediment I have tried to keep hidden, dating all the way back to my teenage years.

When I was young and in my prime, with a build variously described as "slender" or "sinewy" (or sometimes, "two ears glued on a radio antenna") I did not participate in what we called "fast dancing."

It goes without saying that a stud who could be counted on for up to 10 points a basketball game at LaGrange High School was in constant demand as a fast dance partner for scores of glandularly precocious cheerleaders at the Dallis Street Teen Club.

I turned away many a blue-eyed blonde with invented rationales I thought would soften the blow of my refusals. One of them was, "Thank you, but fast dancing is a sin."

"But you slow dance," they would plead piteously.

"That's because with bodies pressed closely together there are no sudden, animalistic moves," I would explain.

Word apparently spread that I was no easy mark, for I spent most of my high school years with few attempts to unravel the intricacies of shagging to "Work With Me Annie."

Mine is nothing if not the story of growing up in the wrong era. Just from observation, I wouldn't need rhythm to fast dance these days. It looks to me there are no programmable steps.

Recently I was reminded of the night that led me to that conclusion. Eleven days ago I attended a birthday luncheon in Smyrna for legendary political reporter Bill Shipp. My old lawyer friend, Bob Steed, was there. He and wife, Lou, a gadfly couple, once invited Jackie and me, along with AJC executive editor Jim Minter and wife, Ann, to join them for a repast of chili at their house that was lavishly decorated from the proceeds of Bob's exorbitant legal fees. From there we adjourned to a music saloon where a cult favorite named Delbert McClinton was performing. Bob explained, "Lou thinks Delbert is sexy."

Such testimony has nothing to do with the subject of fast dancing unless it explained Lou's willingness to gyrate frenetically near the bandstand with an assortment of dance partners, non of whom was her graying but game husband, who was drinking copious amounts of coffee in hopes of achieving caffeine overload.

I had a little trouble picking up on what brand of music McClinton was performing, although it was described in *Playboy* as "a swirling vortex of sound." Jim Minter, a gentleman farmer in Fayette County in his spare time, said he thought the music was familiar. "Sounds a lot like when we used to neuter the pigs. Or when the tin used to slide off the roof in a storm."

As the night wore on, our gracious host, who had offered to represent a group of young wives free of charge in their next divorce if they would dance with him, instead escorted my wife to the dance floor. She seemed to enjoy herself immensely.

But, the only person who has succeeded in coaxing me out onto a dance floor is granddaughter Anna and that at her post-graduation dance at Presbyterian College's football stadium. Over the years I had not been seen in any establishment where the music is such you can't dance to it with your beer in your hip pocket. The Presbyterian event allowed me to observe changes in fast dancing. No longer is it absolutely necessary that you move your feet, although requirements have increased for flexibility from the buttocks upward.

I must have done okay. The mother of one of Anna's girlfriends, attractive and not yet on AARP's mailing list, asked me to try out my style with her.

"Thank you," I said, "But it just turned five minutes after midnight and today is a Baptist holiday."

August, 2013

LIVE, LAUGH AND LOVE

I almost missed the wedding. That would have been embarrassing since it was my wedding. My groomsmen thought it would be a fine thing to go on over to Pleasant Valley North Baptist Church without waking me from the nap I was taking as an antidote to the jitters. They did set the alarm clock to ring at 2:30 p.m. 30 minutes prior to the ceremony. I jumped out of bed, shaved, shined my shoes, poured half a bottle of Vitalis on my hair, flung my white dinner jacket around my shoulders and gunned my '57 Ford toward the church.

The bride's father, T.G. Miller, and the preacher, Rev. Harry Sutton, peered from windows as I screeched into the parking lot and darted through a door behind the baptismal pool.

With calm restored, at the reception we served three-layer white cake, sherbet and ginger ale punch, mints and assorted salted nuts. We were just as married as the woman I saw recently on Dr. Phil's television show who had budgeted $100,000 for her wedding.

Jackie was leaving a really good job at Kraft here in Rome, but I was making only $45 per week as a sportswriter while finishing up school at LaGrange College. Ever practical, she had paid in advance for a wedding night room at Callaway Gardens. Along about Cedartown she asked, "How much money did you bring with you?"

"Well, I don't have any left," I replied. "You have any money?"

"I have $10," she said.

The $10 bought a honeymoon dinner of two hamburger steaks at the Heart of LaGrange Restaurant. We arrived at Callaway Gardens just before dark. They didn't have the famous butterfly exhibit in those days, so we went straight to our room. Left with slightly more than a dollar after breakfast, we decided to move on to our garage apartment in LaGrange, since we could do the same thing there we were doing where we were.

Later that day the notion struck we should seek nourishment. We drove to the grocery store at Skeeter Flats and with the remaining change bought a loaf of bread and some sliced bologna. As we were driving home I noticed a game in progress at the Callaway Mills baseball field.

"Well, whatta ya know, my team is playing," I said. I swear I didn't know it. It so happened my Elm City Slickers were tied with Hillside. It was headed toward extra innings and there was panic in the air. Our left fielder, Jimmy Fred Bowles, had to leave to operate the movie projector at LaGrange Theater downtown. I couldn't in good conscience turn down pleas for me to suit up. I grounded out meekly my first time up—understandable under the circumstances. But, in the 13th inning I hit a triple and scored the winning run.

That evening I had a choice. I could heat my bologna sandwich on the stove or use the steam coming out of my young wife's ears.

Today, fifty five years will have passed since our wedding. Who knows what excitement awaits? On our golden landmark of fifty years I said, "Why don't we take off and spend the night at Callaway Gardens?"

I quickly amended that to Barnsley Gardens. I even paid for dinner: salad, two six-ounce filets, a glass of blush and one of Chardonnay and we split a slice of really good Key lime pie. We strolled the garden grounds while a full moon turned the ruins of the famous Barnsley mansion into a romantic silhouette. We started laughing as we recalled our foibles, which were, as they are today, mainly mine. I reminded her that her capacity for laughter, almost as much as the most gorgeous brown eyes I've ever seen, was what drew me to her that first day of school at West Georgia College.

As was appropriate for a fiftieth anniversary curtain call, the night erupted with thrashing and moaning in bed. In fact, the thrashing and moaning woke her. She said, "What in the world are you doing?"

I didn't want to spoil the mood of a perfect day, but couldn't help gasping, "I've got the mother of all cramps in my right calf muscle!"

We both laughed.

I said it then and I say it today on our 55th anniversary. I love that woman.

June, 2013

WHY HOME BUILDERS HAVE CALLER I.D.

The thought occurred to me that John Shahan, Charles Greene, Keith Argo, Tommy Dean, Wayne Christian and Nathan Tucker might identify with a letter I once received from a fellow building contractor. Over the past several decades those mentioned have worked with the Walburns on projects ranging from home repair to home remodeling to home building; in short, all the things husbands finds fascinating as long as someone else is doing it.

Years ago when three fourths of America suddenly wanted to build a home in metro Atlanta, my wife and I decided to build in rural Cobb County. Unfortunately, builders were really hard to come by in those boom years.

Frustrated beyond all measure Jackie met a likeable old boy at a little country store called The Hitchin' Post. He was bright and fun to talk to, and most of all he agreed to build us a house. We were young and naive in those days and labored under the impression all home builders trained under Frank Lloyd Wright.

We discovered the contractor was of a notion one built a house the way one might seek salvation, that is, it was something to occupy an entire lifetime and must be pursued on faith.

Our contrasting philosophies resulted in the Walburns living with three children for two months in a 20-foot-long camper because we had to vacate our previous home. Then we lived in the basement of the unfinished house for six weeks, during which time my boss continually complained that my dusty clothes made a bad impression on clients.

Eventually, whenever the builder came around to check progress, he took to wearing a pistol. He said it was for snakes, but I knew he believed Jackie had developed homicidal tendencies.

More than a decade passed and I had recovered enough to write a lighthearted column about the experience. Shortly afterwards I received a letter from the builder. He apologized for thinking my wife was capable of murder, but was not convinced that she did not possess powers of the occult. As evidence, he cited travails that dogged those who labored on our house.

"Jess, the framing contractor, suffered a stroke not long ago. When I visited him, most of our conversation was about working on your house. When I left he was both laughing and crying. Shortly thereafter he died.

"Charlie, the rock mason, has joined Jess, as his wife called me recently about the Social Security he had forgotten to pay for 40 years. I'll always remember his frustration when Jackie tried to change his pattern of laying rock by demanding he reposition a 200-pound stone in the chimney 250 times.

"The sheetrockers disappeared the day Jackie complained about covering the electrical boxes and I haven't seen them since. I'm told one of them later fell from a scaffold while trying to look down the blouse of a homeowner's braless wife and cut himself real bad with his own knife. His partner became an alcoholic.

"One of the supervisors on your house came to see me a few years ago. He had left his wife and children and was living somewhere in the Smokey Mountains with a tribe of Indians. While he was in town he stole my trash masher.

"The painter, well, he became an ordained Baptist minister. He was just never the same after Jackie came out that morning holding laundry bags over the stone foundation to keep overspray from settling on the rocks. He must have sent Jackie to the paint store 10 times that day because she made him nervous by standing under his ladder.

"I haven't kept up with the plumber since one of his helpers accidentally set one of my houses on fire, costing me $20,000 out of pocket. One of my bankers was involved in some sort of deal that attracted the involvement of the FBI. Also, my attorney's wife left him.

"Believe it or not, Lee, the builder came out smelling like a rose. He lost everything but his humor. His wife took her tennis balls and left him and his 11-year-old son with whatever fell off the truck. Overnight I was forced to change careers and become Mr. Mom. The experience taught me a great deal of admiration, sympathy and understanding for all the Jackies of the world, and believe me there are not many left."

True, and that may explain why the local contractors I named all have caller I.D. on their cell phones.

December, 2012

BANISHED FROM THE GARDEN OF IDLENESS

If there is a major regret in my life, it is that somewhere along the way I drifted away from a devotion to idleness, the way one drifts away from active involvement in his church. I say without brag, there was a time when I was as indolent as the best of them. I was predisposed toward daydreaming since my father, Mr. Bud, was recognized throughout LaGrange, Ga. for his ability to consume large amounts of time with nothing doing.

There was a time when I thought I would mature into a man people could admire in that regard, convinced, as a budding teller of stories, that imagination blossoms brightest in a garden of idleness. Most writers agree there is a strong case to be made that stargazing, when perfected, allows us to expel any concern for that which must be done. A day of building castles in air is as chargeable to the plus side of our account as an afternoon with actual hammer and nail.

Admittedly, idleness is not for everyone. Women don't seem to get it at all. Wives consider idleness the devil's workshop, an old axiom that has personal relevance since my wife was raised in one of those families that revere sweat. There is no denying that marriage to the former Jackie Miller has rendered me unnaturally responsible at times. I could not have imagined such a dramatic transformation while growing up blissfully carefree and it illustrates the triumph of environmental influence over genetics.

Opposites, indeed, do attract. My wife's endurance is such her pulse rate wouldn't rise above 60 beats a minute in a triathlon. She recognizes no Fair Labor Law that says eight hours constitutes a normal work day. Acquaintances take bizarre delight in praising her abnormal reservoir of energy, knowing full well my guilt grows like kudzu in the fields of community commentary. "Saw Jackie out hoeing the garden," John Porter says. "Saw Jackie painting the barn," Keith Tressel says. "Saw Jackie feeding those 5,000 hungry folks with them two fishes and a loaf of bread," Bill Campbell says.

I've told you before, but I'll tell it again, once in the casual silliness of introductory conversation a young lady asked one of our sons what sign he was born under and he replied, "Men Working."

When we purchased a home and some pastoral acres in Floyd County it had the appearance of a vale where a man with a literary bent could lose himself in idleness. A little spring-fed pond was just one of the bucolic delights. Naturally, Jackie immediately wanted to double the size of the pond. We hired experienced lake builders, Jacob Richardson and a helper whose full name, as far as I could ever determine, was just George.

George drove the bulldozer and it was he who discovered why the pond was small in the first place. The rest of the property was as much rock as clay. This discouraged my wife not the least. She began to envision an Eden of rock walls and waterfalls. She directed George on transfer of giant boulders, she with wildly swinging arm signals and shouts, something of a cross between a maniacal football coach and Richard Prior's passionate direction of the Rome Symphony.

After hours of this demolition rhapsody, George brought his bulldozer to an abrupt stop and deployed to firm ground. "George!" the woman shouted with concern, "are you out of gas?"

"No, 'mam, I believe I'm just about out of George."

As an enhancement to the project she hired Decathur Miller and conscripted me to clear the privet hedges and briars around what we were now calling, "the lake." We began work early on a Saturday morning and at 7 o'clock in the evening Decathur and I were still hacking and chopping and, shall we say, muttering under our breath while attempting nothing more ambitious than to just keep up with the project manager's personal work pace.

Finally, Decathur leaned wearily on his rake and moaned, "Lord God, Mr. Lee, make her stop."

If there is a book in the self-help section of Barnes & Noble on the correlation between idleness and success I haven't seen it. America honors nose to the grindstone and our house is ground zero for nose grinding. But, I'll bet if somebody came up with 200 pages of theory on indolence as the key to wealth, it would have an audience at least equal to those diet books promising effortless weight loss.

October, 2011

life in
different colors

THE COUNTERFEIT ESCORT

The day after his son's funeral, Daddy King arrived at the Braves game with a white stranger. That's when panic struck.

Riots had erupted in 126 cities. The death count had reached 46 after the murder of Dr. Martin Luther King Jr., in Memphis had ignited a racial explosion. But the social fabric held in Atlanta and an emotional funeral service was completed at Ebenezer Baptist Church while the nation watched on television and considered the fragility of our brotherhood.

I was public relations director of the Atlanta Braves. We had postponed the opening game of the 1968 season out of respect, fear and common sense. By the next afternoon, a baseball game seemed more a sigh of relief than a ritual of spring. About 4 o'clock, a man purporting to be a friend of Dr. Martin Luther King Sr. reached me on the telephone and said that Daddy King wanted to throw out the first ball as a tribute to his son.

The impossibility of such an eventuality left me momentarily unable to breathe. I managed to stammer, "Well, we would be honored. Have me paged when you arrive."

Regaining my wits, I decided it was a cruel joke. But, about an hour before game time, I heard the page, "Lee Walburn, Dr. Martin Luther King Sr. is here to see you."

I sprinted for the lobby. There sat Daddy King with the biggest, toughest-looking white man in Atlanta. Dr. King's normally round, reassuring face was eroded. His eyes were red and he appeared to be lightly sedated and unsteady. For the second time, I panicked. Unclear what to do, I called our Stadium Club director, Gene Sammon, and demanded he clear a table for three, no questions asked.

The three visitors and I had just exited the Braves' club level offices when an elevator door opened. Out stepped Mayor Ivan Allen Jr. and his wife, Louise. The blood drained from his face. I understood immediately that I was not the only person in a state of shock. "Where are you going?" he asked, trying to make an important question appear casual. I made sure he understood we would be in the Stadium Club.

It dawned on me that Mayor Allen was actually scheduled to throw out the first ball. I told the two men with me we couldn't dare offend Mayor Allen by denying him that privilege, but we would have a nice meal. It would also give me a chance to pray.

When we had ordered dinner, I excused myself on the pretense of needing to visit the rest room. I was hunting a telephone to seek help. As I rounded a corner, two plainclothes detectives suddenly appeared, lifted me off the floor and pinned me against a wall. Mayor Allen yelled at them, "No, No. You've got the wrong one."

I practically fled into the arms of the mayor. I mumbled, "What is going on?"

He told me. The man with Daddy King, he said, had been under surveillance by law enforcement agencies. He was thought to be dangerous. Mayor Allen told me the guy had an amazing talent for infiltration. At the funeral he had worn a bright yellow sport coat and had been observed showing prominent visitors like Vice President Hubert Humphrey and Gov. George Romney to their seats. Later that day, at a ceremony on the Morehouse quadrangle, security forces observed him escorting Nelson Rockefeller and his party, most people assuming he was a personal bodyguard. Police Capt. Morris Redding had checked out the impostor and although his record scared Redding and Allen, they thought he was no longer their problem-until he was seen with Daddy King.

Mayor Allen said they didn't know what to think in this situation. They were paranoid over the possibility that harm to the elder King would throw America into a race war that many thought had been narrowly avoided in the previous few days. I was told that I must stay with my guests until a plan had been formulated.

We decided that I would convince them to accompany me to one of the VIP booths, which were enclosed in glass, providing the perfect spot for monitoring us. Once there, I tried hard to carry on a conversation, although Dr. King now seemed so tired and disoriented that he was saying nothing. At one point the other man said to me, "See that little bag Dr. King has? I think he has a gun in there. That doesn't bother me."

It bothered me. I excused myself. I pleaded with one of the detectives, "Both of these men may have guns. I'm not going back in there." They informed me that I would go back in there. I did, but when I emerged the second time, with sweat dripping from me, they moved in and separated the two.

The big white man evidently had done nothing illegal that could be proved, so he was soon released. A few weeks later, a city official said he saw on network television that the Secret Service had apprehended a man who was trying to slip into the White House to talk to the president. He said it was Daddy King's counterfeit escort.

After we had regained our composure that night and had transported Dr. King Sr. back to the offices, I asked him what in the world, with everybody's nerves stretched to the limit, was he doing at the game with this white man. His old eyes grew moist. He explained that the stranger had come by the house and told him he was expected to throw out the first ball. So he went with him.

"The family," he mumbled, "doesn't want anyone to think we blame all white people for this. My son wanted us to love each other."

Twenty-five years have passed and that hasn't happened. And there remains no acceptable, unqualified answer to the wrenching question by another black man, battered and bewildered, who cried on national television, "Can't we all get along?" Instead, we wait, uneasily, for the lighting of the next match.

April, 1993

DAVID DUKE IS RUNNING FOR PRESIDENT?

Maybe I wasn't paying attention. Maybe I was concentrating too hard on reporting the story at hand. At any rate, it never occurred to me the day I met David Duke at a Klan rally on a chicken farm in Forsyth County that I was in the presence of presidential material. Perhaps I missed such intimations of immortality because of the distractions of both nature and man.

Rain? You would have thought Noah was a Klansman. Mud? Duke's white bucks that bottomed off natty blue slacks and gray trench coat were turning orange. Danger? Well, a 300-pound man got into a fistfight with a shrimp about the size of Coach Herman Stiles on Evening Shade over who had the authority to beat up journalists. Specifically, me.

I walked in the storm with Duke to an old chicken house in the pasture where he was to be the featured speaker. Seventy or 80 people were waiting, including Virgil Griffin, the brooding Klan chief from North Carolina; Don Black, his handsome counterpart from Alabama; David Holland of Georgia, who sat quietly holding hands with his girlfriend; and lawyer Richard Barrett, a hyperactive orator from Mississippi who seemed in need of a quick dose of Ritalin. In other words, if you were Klan, Forsyth County in 1987 was the place to be seen.

Barrett was already prancing on a makeshift stage, his inflections those of what we used to call a "suck-back" preacher, one whose style is dependent on an ability to vacuum in huge gulps of air on just the right syllables.

"If Christianity can be born in a manger, justice can be reborn in a chicken house," he stormed.

David Duke lowered his head as if trying to hide his laughter inside the trench coat when Barrett continued, "A newsman said recently I reminded him of Martin Luther King 'in that you are out on the cutting edge of social change.' "

"I may never get to speak," Duke offered *sotto voce*. As Barrett's monologue began to activate the wet, chilled audience, Duke shook his head and said, "This is just like the 1920s."

Finally, Duke was introduced. Almost as if embarrassed by the histrionics of Barrett, he began to speak in a modulated tone. He seemed detached, like a road show entertainer who has been in too many cities in too many days. At times he lost his train of thought and apologized to the audience.

Duke made the obligatory attacks on the press, "Why is there no outrage in the media for discrimination against us, but attempts to make us feel guilty for being white? We are dissidents. And we are being persecuted."

The incongruity of his vocabulary and that of his contemporaries was so remarkable, I was left to wonder how his message would be picked up and translated into the jargon of those who really know how to speak the language of hate; those who spent lots of time coining epithets like the timeless reference to Martin Luther Coon.

In time, since Duke is running for President of the United States, his message has found its way to a larger audience than those huddled in the chicken house. There are growing numbers of low-income, uneducated whites who feel they really don't have a part in anything. They feel shut out and they want to belong, to be heard. Nobody listens to them, just as nobody listens to the poor, uneducated blacks, so they join these groups and they follow the first well-dressed, blue-eyed, educated spokesman who can make hatred sound so reasonable, so justified.

The real problem comes as those messages seep down to a primitive level of psychological functioning and poison those who share traits of personal failure and low self-esteem.

A former Klansman, C.P. Ellis, once explained it to Studs Terkel: "I worked my butt off and just never seemed to break even. I had some real great ideas about this nation. They say to abide by the law, go to church, do right and live for the Lord, and everything'll work out. But it didn't work out. It just kept getting worse...I didn't know who to blame. Hate in America is hard to do because you can't see it to hate it. You got to have somethin' to look at to hate."

The David Dukes show them where to look.

February, 1992

MAKE A JOYFUL NOISE

Unable to sleep, I was just lying on a narrow, uncomfortable cot in the corner of the room. A sliver of light from the bathroom had flattened, yellowish, against a wall, and I could see a lady leaning low over the hospital bed. Her face was as round as a black moon, her pupils so dark that in the pale glow all that could be seen was the crescent of white around them. Her mouth was wide and full of white teeth. Her voice, low and loving, made a song of her words, like a mother comforting a child.

"You gone be awe-rite. Oh, yeah. Don' you fret now. I be rite here. You the man that make a joyful noise. I gone get you well."

The nurse took a damp rag and laid it on the forehead of the man who lay in the hospital bed. She rubbed it across his parched lips. The man, whom I called Daddy, but most of the town called Mr. Bud, placed his hand on the hand of the nurse called Mrs. Robinson and said hoarsely, "When I leave here, I'm taking you with me."

I could hear him sniffling because when his heart was full, his eyes would spill over. And in the middle of the night in a room in the West Georgia Medical Center, I knew he was thinking that human kindness does not come in colors.

When I first started writing this piece, Daddy had been home for a few days and was inching toward his 70th birthday on July 31. But we had to readmit him to the hospital on Father's Day, and eight days later he died.

While he was home for the last time, a black family moved into the house next door, and four grandchildren circled noisily around their grandparents' new home.

"I give him two weeks before he has them down here with him," my mother said.

My daddy grew up in a different era, one in which small-town boys, who were out of school and into cotton mills by the time they were 14, didn't learn all the correct words in dealing with people of a different

144

race. But he always knew there was something fundamentally askew in hatred, especially where it concerned children.

I remember one time when a little black boy showed up at the YMCA where my daddy worked. It was over 90 degrees that day and he let the youngster come inside to drink a Coca-Cola. Later his supervisor reprimanded him: "I think you know better than that."

"Then dammit, when the next little kid shows up, let me hear you explain to him why he can't have a Co-Cola when he's thirsty," Daddy said.

Children were always Mr. Bud's weakness. He treasured the newspaper clippings of his own youth when he was a player of games—a pitcher, a boxer, a wrestler. He was also a player of music: accordion, steel guitar, dulcimer, autoharp, and harmonica. He never quite understood why anybody would want to grow up and leave all that behind.

When he was in his late 60s and had already been operated on for cancer, he entered a jog for health and officials were astounded to see him finish the race alongside some much younger people, although he stumbled at the finish line and cut his knee. He considered it a fine joke that as soon as he topped the hill out of sight of the starting line, he had caught a ride with a friend to within a couple blocks of the finish.

The staid, serious world of grown-ups just didn't appeal to him. Grown-ups keep growing older, and eventually they contract illnesses that need to be treated by doctors. He would do anything to avoid a trip to the doctor. To throw people off track that he was suffering he would arise early in the morning, whistling and talking foolishness that jarred the heads of sluggish sleepyheads. Dr. Mark Whitehead Jr. had to do everything but give him a lollipop to conduct every examination.

Daddy did not like it, either, when the doctor had to talk about the seriousness of his illness. When Dr. Whitehead tried to tell him what was wrong and what he must do as treatment, he played the part of the clown, figuring that a good joke was worth two pills any day. The doctor's hair was whiter every time I saw him.

Once while under Dr. Whitehead's care, and already missing his testicles due to surgery and now experiencing the discomfort of wisdom teeth arguing inside his gums, he said to the doctor, "Doc, do you believe in reincarnation?"

Thinking his patient was making a serious inquiry about the afterlife, Dr. Whitehead attempted to explain his beliefs. Then he asked, "Why are you asking?"

"Because," said Daddy, " I believe my nuts are trying to come back as teeth."

I wish I had a nickel for every time I heard my mother say, "Bud, you're just like a little kid."

Such attributes were not lost on the youth of the neighborhood, either. There was a boy who lived nearby who used to rap on the door until my mother answered it.

"Can Mr. Bud come out and play?" he would ask.

When my daddy ambled to the door, the child would plead, "Come on, Mr. Bud, let's walk some trails."

Lord, it would be great to see him grin and hear him say one more time, "Let's go, pal."

July, 1984

FORGIVE, DON'T FORGET

All the pictures in Lena Dorsey's mind are memories. Congestive heart failure, diabetes and various maladies stole her sight twelve years ago. She spends most of her days sitting in a big stuffed chair, her legs wrapped for warmth, some gospel music softly playing in another room of her home in Bean Creek. In her memories, the Nacoochee Valley is the most beautiful place in the world, her neighbor's garden is her garden and nobody has convinced her to hate the past or weep about today.

There is plenty she could hate. People do hate atrocities and indignities of the past. There is plenty about today she could weep for. People do weep over their afflictions and the indignities of neglect. She says that's not the way it is in Bean Creek. Nobody in Bean Creek hates, she insists. Not the Dorseys, the Nicelys, the Lowerys, the Trammels, or any of the 25-30 families that live there. Perhaps, she says, it's because their slice of Nachoochee Valley was isolated for so long from outside influences, they haven't reacted typically to historical exploitation, nor even contemporary neglect.

Every resident of Bean Creek descends from slaves first brought there in 1822. Everything being relative, a distinct cultural stratification remains through several generations of share croppers and laborers, yet 68-year-old Lena Dorsey says "I would never want to live anywhere but White County." It's the best place in the world to live, she insists, even though neighbors have been dying too young from suspicious causes, and even though they have to walk all the way to the Missionary Baptist Church for a bucket of water that still must be boiled. They don't even hate Tom Slick. The developer now owns the baseball field that for 101 years has been rivaled only by the church as Bean Creek's heartbeat. But, they do want it back.

Caroline Crittenden is determined to get that ball field back from Tom Slick. She has heard the memories in Lena Dorsey's mind. She has heard about the ball field, about the time Bean Creek beat a team from

147

Royston with a player named Ty Cobb, how Zell Miller, a man that would become a U.S. Senator, used to come down with the team from Young Harris and from the same bucket sip cool water, or whatever stronger might be in the bucket. She has heard about the community baseball team. The men who came home from World War II were so proud of their service they named the Bean Creek team The Valley Vets. They knew they were first class soldiers even if they were considered second class southerners.

Caroline Crittenden might never have heard Lena Dorsey create mind pictures of the past or comprehended the higher truths of that history if it hadn't been for Sierra Nicole Nicely. If it hadn't been for Sierra Nicole, Caroline might not have quit her teaching job to devote almost obsessive attention to both the history and the future of Bean Creek. If she had not become Bean Creek's diminutive white crusader, others there might die too soon. The ball field, scratched out of hills and hardwoods 101 years ago, is not suited for development of houses and if not returned to the community, would likely become no more recognizable than any scrub pine that struggles up from the gritty dirt where home plate used to be.

Caroline was standing one day near the doorway of the museum in what was the old Nacoochee school house. Sierra Nicole, a high school junior from Bean Creek, had intensely studied the exhibits of local history and culture. She walked up to the white woman and said, "There's nothing here that speaks to me about my people. I'd like to know what they have contributed to this valley."

Although it's difficult to find a plot of land in the lush Nacoochee-Sautee territory that isn't on a historical registry, Bean Creek has been gerrymandered out of the same past Caroline married into. She is wife of the great grandson of E.P. Williams, whose father brought the first 18 slaves to Nacoochee Valley from North Carolina. She is herself descended from a prominent slave owner in Charleston. Her legacy and that of Sierra Nicole collided head on. A teacher, she challenged Sierra Nicole to reconstruct her people's history as a school project. She volunteered her help. That led to Lena Dorsey and resulted in *Reflections From Bean Creek*, a photographic retrospective on the walls of the museum in the school that for most of the institution's history, did not allow the black people in the pictures to attend classes.

In meeting the people who would become instrumental to Sierra Nicole's project, Caroline heard about deaths and illness in eight contiguous houses in the community. She met Andy Allen, whose daughter died at 16 of an infection in her heart. Andy, who 35 years after segregated schools were declared unconstitutional helped integrate school buses in White County, works four jobs. She has become Caroline's activist cohort even though she suffers from sarcoidosis, an affliction characterized by lesions in the lungs, bones and skin.

Intuitively, Caroline suspected contaminated water as the often lethal culprit. She also understands the sluggish pace of government. Once she became suspicious of the wells and springs she fast tracked around the red tape. A team from the University of Georgia environmental lab tested the water sources and found toxic levels of E Coli, mercury residue from old gold mines and levels of lead 38 times the safety level. Caroline worked with the Regional Development Center to submit a grant on behalf of White County that on September 17, 2004, resulted in a promise of $500,000 for a satellite water system for Bean Creek. In the meantime the local water authority has brought in a portable 500-gallon military water tank that is parked at the Missionary Baptist Church. The KKK sometimes leaves pamphlets there.

With the water situation safer, if not solved, Caroline has teamed with craftsman Randy Stiles to restore the only slave cabin left in White County. They want to register the 150-year-old shack historically, to surround it with the cooling vats, iron pots, fruit trees and gardens of long ago and rocks from the wall where E.P. Williams stood to read the Emancipation Proclamation when he freed his slaves in 1865. They believe that if they build it, people will come because the history of slavery in north Georgia is not a tale that has been told often or well.

Perhaps when the tales are finally told, people will understand why bitterness is such an unfamiliar emotion in Bean Creek. Zell Miller understands already. In his book, *The Mountains Within Me*, he recalls, "One of the biggest games of the season for Young Harris was the Bean Creek Negroes. It usually would be played on July 4. And people would come from miles around. This was before Jackie Robinson broke the race barrier in professional sports and neither they nor we realized that we were doing anything unusual in mixing the races on an athletic field. We had great times and became fast friends. We were drinking from the same dipper while there were still white and colored signs up throughout the South on water fountains and rest rooms. We were feasting on barbecued chicken together…15 years before sit-ins resulted in integration of lunch counters."

But even though that ball field was as much the heart of Bean Creek as the baptismal stream, they never owned it. It belonged to L.D. Hardman and Tom Slick bought it from one of his descendants, Cynthia Randolph of Gainesville. "We didn't know its history. That was a big surprise," Tom Slick says. It was just another parcel that would become part of his Nacoochee Village, an 850-acre development offering lots costing up to $200,000.

Currently, the only access to the project is off Bean Creek Road. That means property taxes will eventually escalate for the families who reportedly average about $15,000 annual income. There once was a similar history-rich black community in Atlanta near the Lenox Marta station. It evaporated from the heat of development and no trace of its existence remains. Lena Dorsey is not so blind that she can't see a similar fate for her community.

That makes the ball field as important to memory as the slave cabin, she thinks. When Caroline Crittenden pleaded with Tom Slick to turn over the 3.5 acre plot to Friends of Bean Creek, she said he offered her an option to buy at $20,000 an acre. She counter-offered at $7,200. Finally, she accepted a one-year option for one dollar to acquire the land at a price to be determined by an appraiser.

"I don't doubt someone with a strong interest in history will come up with the money," Tom Slick says. "Preservation isn't something we do."

Bean Creek has permission to hold a fund-raising game at the ball field on August 13. Last year about 200 showed up for the 100th anniversary celebration. Lena Dorsey says unless they get back their ball field, August 13 will be their final baseball game. And that, at last, may represent the ultimate test of Bean Creek's unfathomable forgiveness.

August, 2005

A GOOD AND HONORABLE MAN

On Wednesday, May 9, 1979, mourners gathered at St. Paul of the Cross Catholic Church in west Atlanta. They came from throughout the country, most of them from the family of professional baseball, many with names already indelibly writ in the sport's history books, some to be enshrined eventually in the Hall of Fame at Cooperstown. The man whose life we had come to honor was 42 and not broadly recognized by the general public.

Bill Lucas died too young to be remembered for accomplishments in terms of records. But, he had lived long enough for Florida A&M coach Jake Gaither to gather his emotions and call him "one of God's great men." That was reason enough for most of us to be there, for he was loved more as a good and honorable man than as general manager of the Atlanta Braves.

I don't recall any speakers mentioning that Bill Lucas was the first African-American to be named general manager of a major league sports franchise. It would have been natural to do so since America was only eleven years distant from the assassination of Dr. Martin Luther King Jr. But, Lucas had advanced so meritoriously into his position that to mention he was black or a pioneer might have diminished what he earned purely with baseball savvy and reliability. Instead, we regretted he had passed far too soon to fulfill promise of becoming one of baseball's brightest leaders.

Lucas' boss, Ted Turner, famously color blind, but stunningly inappropriate as a speaker, rendered an eulogy peppered with clichés. "... now Bill is the general manager of a team that has Babe Ruth, Ty Cobb and Lou Gehrig..." Fortunately, twenty three year old Dale Murphy restored dignity with thoughts about how Lucas, first as farm director and later as general manager, had become a father figure, a symbol of what it means to be a professional baseball player. "Bill's dream was for this organization to be a success. It is our sacred honor to be chosen to fulfill his dream."

By the time Turner promoted Lucas to general manager as the season ended in September, 1976, the new director of player personnel had spent almost 20 years in the Braves organization, six of them as a minor league player. Lucas had the slender build of a middle infielder, the speed and guts of a base stealer and a respectable .273 batting average. However, a serious leg injury at Triple A suddenly left him better suited for mentoring. In 1965, as the Braves served a one-year injunction that prevented the team from moving to Atlanta from Milwaukee, vice president Dick Cecil convinced Lucas, a graduate of Florida A&M, to join the front office in a community relations role.

The Braves' arrival in Atlanta required sensitivity to the city's complex racial environment. Cecil knew Lucas would bring crucial perspective to the relationship, as would his former minor league teammate Paul Snyder. Years later, Snyder reflected on Lucas' 2006 induction into the Atlanta Braves Hall of Fame: "A number of places in the Texas League where we were playing in 1962, Luke couldn't sleep in the same hotel we did. He couldn't eat in the same place we did. Lots of nights we had to bring food down to him in the bus. A lot of nights he'd sleep in a boarded-up hotel downtown. He just buttoned his lip and played his heart out."

When I joined the Braves front office prior to the 1966 season Cecil, Lucas, Snyder, Jack Carlin and Ernie Johnson had already planted baseball's unique seeds of emotional unity in a city where previously relationships were forged mainly from mutual economic interests.

Those men initiated the Braves Good Neighbor program in under-served areas, providing athletic fields, equipment, leadership and what-ever else was needed to underscore the Braves' appreciation for their welcome. Lucas helped Cecil bring the same attitude to building a workforce for Atlanta-Fulton County Stadium. He systematically hired one African-American for every white person selected.

Lucas remained low-key, but resolutely sensitive to inequality over his 14 years in the executive suite. In the summer of 1972, my last season with the Braves, Atlanta hosted major league baseball's All-Star Game. Gender fairness had yet to chip away at baseball's chauvinistic armor. Lucas was on his way to one of the glamorous event parties when he met up with Susan Hope, wife of promotions director, Bob Hope. She had been turned away at the door of the all-male event.

Lucas, took her arm and said, "Let's go have a drink." When Susan explained she wasn't allowed, Bill said, "Look, my people weren't allowed to enter nice places for years, either. Come on, someone's got to be the first woman to integrate baseball." And, so they did.

When Lucas was elevated from director of minor league operations to general manager in September, 1976 the team had completed two of the most disastrous seasons in Brave history, losing 194 games. The dream Murphy had remarked at Lucas' memorial service would have to wait a little longer until many of the players Lucas signed and nurtured grew up and won the Western Division championship in 1982. He has been recognized in that connection far too infrequently. Nor is it commonly remarked that in 1978, a year after taking over as general manager, Lucas hired Bobby Cox to manage the Braves. He chose Cox from a list of candidates that included New York Yankee coaches Yogi Berra and Dick Howser, ex-Yankee second baseman Bobby Richardson and, former St. Louis Cardinal manager Red Schoendienst. Hank Aaron's younger brother, Tommy, was lightly considered as was pitcher Phil Niekro. The 1977 team had been so devoid of hope Niekro volunteered to serve as player/manager.

By 1978, strain of maneuvering through minefields strewn with Turner's quixotic decisions began to exhaust Lucas. Increasingly, he had to defend his reputation for iron-clad integrity. After Lucas and Phil Niekro verbally agreed to terms of a new contract, Turner balked and offered Niekro substantially less. Niekro asked to be traded, but finally signed for three years at $200,000 annually.

That same year Lucas drafted U. of Arizona third baseman Bob Horner. Horner became an instant star. The National League writers named him Rookie of the Year. In spring 1979 Lucas once again found himself in the middle of a salary dispute. Horner's agent, Bucky Woy, claimed that Turner wanted to pay Horner some $83,000 less than he made his first year if signing bonus were included. Woy publicly called Bill Lucas a liar, saying Lucas had offered a suitable contract earlier. Lucas' whole life had been characterized by integrity and the charges created public turmoil that devastated him.

Bob Hope recalled that early on May 1 he overheard Turner and Lucas embroiled in "a verbal brawl" over how the deal with Hoy was progressing. After work that day the weary Lucas went home to watch a televised Braves game, Phil Niekro winning his 200th game in Pittsburgh. Lucas telephoned congratulations and told the pitcher to have a celebration on the Braves tab. Shortly after midnight Lucas collapsed. On May 5 he died without gaining consciousness, victim of a massive cerebral hemorrhage.

Four days later, hundreds gathered to celebrate the life of a man who would never become widely remembered as a picturesque national figure; pioneering, after all, isn't always about writing your own script. It might be said, in fact, that Bill Lucas' brief life was almost a one-act play. But, every play has to have an opening line. In baseball, one was written for Bill.

In a broader, lengthier script about Atlanta, the star of Lucas' widow, Rubye , would eventually rise as her husband's would have. She would be elected to the board of directors of Turner Broadcasting in 1981. (She was one of only six directors formerly approving the sale of Turner Broadcasting Systems to Time Warner in 1996). She would become president of the William D. Lucas Fund that sends deserving students to college. She would raise funds for the NAACP and United Negro College Fund. On May 17, 2010 she would serve on the star-clustered host committee for "A Conversation with a Living Legend," honoring Sen. Sam Nunn.

For the first time in too many years I chatted with Rubye at the 2009 reunion of the original Atlanta Braves front office family, a gathering appropriately arranged at Manuel's Tavern. Rubye was radiantly beautiful and smiling on that wonderful night when old friends moved about through handshakes and hugs, trying to fit missing pieces back into a mosaic of memories. There was little doubt Bill would be proud of the woman who remains so proud of him, a man who had epitomized the very change he wanted to see in the world.

MAY, 2011

THE RESTAURANT TIME FORGOT

When I moved to Atlanta in the 1960s, the Hollywood version of the Old South, the romanticized Gone with the Wind version, the happy black folk Uncle Remus version, was slowly beginning to fade. Nevertheless, a phosphorous glow lingered from symbols that vaunted a regional reluctance to forget the past. Of course, in a city boasting it was too busy to hate (truth in advertising be damned), burgeoning commercial opportunities meant businesses would gradually grow hesitant to reflect reverence for "the old ways." For example, the *Atlanta Journal-Constitution* eliminated its long-standing Dixie Living section, and only in the newspaper's archives can be found the braggadocios motto, "Covers Dixie Like the Dew." In political arenas, flags flaunting the stars and bars that in 1960 might have helped elect a candidate were, by 1990, more likely to defeat one.

At the midpoint of the last century, restaurants became targets for headline-grabbing protests and for legal action. Yet, well into the late 1960s, quite a number of Atlanta eateries remained slow to realize that symbols of discrimination could attract social lightning bolts as well as legal storms. Many establishments freed up their diner stools and booths—if not their consciences—as sit-ins transitioned into sit-downs. The names of some of Atlanta's most popular restaurants might well have been subtitled, "Forgit, Hell!" There was Johnny Reb's, Mammy's Shanty, Lickskillet Farm, Pittypat's Porch, and of course, Aunt Fanny's Cabin.

Yes, I ate at every one of them. I first visited Aunt Fanny's in 1966, the year the Braves moved from Milwaukee to Atlanta and hired me as press and promotions director. A man named Harvey Hester owned the restaurant. He was a garrulous charlatan, Falstaffian in girth, and a longtime friend of Donald Davidson, the Braves' traveling secretary. Donald was not my boss technically, but I was a newcomer to both major league baseball and big expense accounts and I was easily influenced regarding the distribution of the team's entertainment dollars. Donald measured exactly forty-eight inches tall and taxed his tiny kidneys by seldom drinking from a glass that wasn't filled with Cutty Sark. His tongue sponsored a range of vulgarities that sometimes led to near physicality in bars and restaurants—one of the reasons he encouraged my company in his entourage. Naturally, the major league world considered Donald an irascible, lovable, and relatively harmless icon.

I remark Donald's influence in this showering of the Braves' expense funds on Aunt Fanny's Cabin, not as a personal mea culpa—I've never favored ignorance and weak backbone as a disclaimer—but as example of my hindsight awareness of mixed messages that pervaded an era diffused with irony. In corporate philosophy and in fact, the Braves, led by GM John McHale and aides Dick Cecil and Bill Lucas, built an admirable record for affirmative action in the front office and in the community. I recall with pride the Braves' enlightened view of their institutional responsibility in race relations, although I really can't remember if I personally felt any pangs of discomfort during the visits to Aunt Fanny's. Perhaps we...I...considered the restaurant a caricature, as far-fetched from actual culture norms as Amos and Andy on television.

In general, Atlanta...I... had not fully realized just how deeply symbols can penetrate hearts and minds. And that mind-set was not exclusively Southern. Aunty Fanny's owner, Harvey Hester, apparently knew or was known by the majority of America's celebrities judging by the autographed photos that covered the walls of his restaurant.

In reconsideration, the best that can be said for Aunt Fanny's is that it served the best fried chicken I've ever tasted, and perhaps that was the main reason even the more liberal of its clientele were able to reconcile digestion with the glorification of the South's legacy of slavery.

Hester had concocted a totally humbug legend that his establishment was named for a former slave famous for her cooking, who had lived past the age of 100 in the very same cabin that housed the restaurant. Guests were greeted by a small boy who poked his head through a blackboard with the menu chalked on it. In sing-song he would warble, "Wekummmrn to Aunt Fanny's Cab beeeen! Wot'll it be, fokes?" At some point in the evening black waitresses in period gowns gathered around the piano and sang haunting gospels. They shook jars and claimed they were collecting money for their church; white folks were more apt to turn loose change to the church than in tips to African American performers.

Today, almost all of the Atlanta restaurants that sold customers a South that Hollywood myths created are gone with the wind. Mammy's Shanty shocked native Atlantans and conventioneers by closing in 1971. No longer would we savor Willie B. Borders's chicken shortcake (a marriage of cream, milk, chicken fat, pepper, pimento, mushrooms, and chicken served over hot egg bread slices). One by one, other establishments with Old South themes collapsed. Aunt Fanny's shuttered in 1994.

Not long ago, while engaging a friend in intellectual sparring over the merits of fried chicken, we began to rank Atlanta's restaurants in term of the South's favorite dish. I raised my verbal flag for Watershed in Decatur. A number of other restaurants—Quinones, Sweet Lowdown—have in the last decade championed Southern cooking with a sense of culinary heritage absent a sense of cultural nostalgia. I was admittedly startled when my friend said, "But have you eaten at Pittypat's Porch lately?"

No punster could pass up such an opening and I replied, "Frankly, my dear, I didn't know Pittypat's was still in business, or even more frankly, if anyone gives a damn."

But it is indeed alive and vigorous. In 1967 A.J.Anthony abandoned his plans to open a pasta restaurant and introduced Pittypat's Porch, blatantly themed on *Gone with the Wind*. The book and movie towered above all others when the world thought about Atlanta (if it thought about Atlanta at all prior to the 1996 Olympics).

The evocation of Pittypat's Porch stimulated whatever nerve in me always seems to respond to incongruity. Hearing that, after four decades, it was indeed very much in business, I immediately reserved a table for four. And so it was I discovered that the restaurant, virtually unchanged in appearance from its 1967 inauguration, remains at what was once 25 Cain Street but is now 25 Andrew Young International Boulevard. Those who don't comprehend the irony of the address may also miss the discord of the theme.

Anthony named the restaurant after Aunt Pittypat Hamilton, portrayed lovingly in Margaret Mitchell's book and more memorably in the 1939 movie as a gracious hostess and gifted cook, though prone to faint in shock at Scarlett's socially irresponsible attitude. Then as now, Pittypat's Porch lacks street level appeal, though once inside, a customer steps up to a gigantic front porch supposedly epitomizing those that wrapped around plantation mansions. A greeter, African American, sits beneath a portrait of Aunt Pittypat's porcelain-smooth face.

Artwork reminders of "the way it was" cover the porch's perimeter walls. A painting of a Cake Walk calls attention to the blithe spirit of colorfully garbed, dancing, thigh-slappin' black men. As I walked the circumference of the porch, I saw a portrait of Robert E. Lee and other legends of The War of Northern Aggression, as well as Prissy, who famously didn't know nothin' bout birthin' babies, plus a variety of movie-gilded stereotypes.

On the stairs descending to the dining room, we passed a wall crowded with photos of recognizable faces inside plain, dark frames: Governor Lester Maddox, Representative John Lewis, and Mayor Maynard Jackson, to mention a portion of the paradoxical museum.

We were appointed seats next to a table occupied by an African American lady and two young men. A few minutes later, five black women took their seats at another table, and within half an hour, the number of African American diners reached fifteen. I counted white customers. Thirteen. That included the four in my party.

As the family at the nearby table was preparing to leave, I introduced myself and asked, "Did you like your meal?"

"Oh, yes," the woman replied. "Is this your restaurant?"

"No, just curious," I said. "I apologize for such a personal question, but does the theme, the decor of this restaurant offend you?"

"I really had not thought about it," she said. "I thought it would be a good idea to get some real Southern cooking. We don't have it in Los Angeles."

"I sorta thought about it," said the teenager, who was enrolling the next day at Morehouse College, a citadel of African American leadership.

Somewhat surprised by the answers, I moved over to the table of five ladies. Our server had volunteered the information that most of the clientele is from out of town, but these women said they lived in Atlanta. I asked the question I had presented to the visitors from Los Angeles.

"Offended?" one responded with a laugh. "That stuff is so long ago.

We come here because the fried chicken is great."

Those diners apparently come to Pittypat's Porch because…because they can…because they have the choice to express righteous anger at insensitivity—or to just turn a cheek that is munching on some mighty good fried chicken in a restaurant that time forgot.

February, 2008

PASSING THE TORCH OF WHITE SUPREMACY

(The appearance of robed and hooded white racists in Forsyth County and at other rallies and public events in Georgia and around the South had drawn renewed attention to various forms of the Ku Klux Klan). In 1987 I was given access to the inside workings of the Klan and I wrote a series of stories for the *Atlanta Journal-Consitution*. Here is one of my stories exploring the minds and motives of those involved in the group and the extent of its energy at the time.)

I n the period of evening that is neither dark nor light, David Holland and Amy Smith strolled through a pasture in Bethlehem, Ga., handsome young people holding hands and favoring each other with shy glances.

Clad in crisply pressed military fatigues, his black hair swept fashionably away from a sturdy round face and blue eyes, Holland quietly and efficiently supervised the deployment of a flatbed truck on a knoll overlooking the gathering crowd. Occasionally, he would break away to mediate a dispute between nervous security forces and me, making sure that I and a photographer had freedom of movement without damaging the egos of the camouflage-clad minions of the Southern White Knights, who seemed to feel that somebody should be required to stand inside the square plot they had meticulously laid out with ribbon and sticks.

While others spoke from the stage of the truck, Holland retreated unobtrusively to the rear of the audience, leaning with Amy against a white Ford XL of ancient vintage. Then, after old-line racist J.B. Stoner had finished a 45-minute tirade against "communists, queers, government, Jews and niggers," it was David Holland's turn at the microphone.

Suddenly, his reserved persona was transformed. His eyes widened.

A vein near a Y-shape scar on the right side of his neck engorged with blood. In the glow of incandescent bulbs that encompassed the truck, the blue of his eyes seemed almost phosphorescent. The voice that had been soft and polite deepened, and rage seemed to leap like a blaze from his lips into the slender speakers on the ground.

"Brothers and sisters," he screamed, "Forsyth County, Georgia, was the greatest white revolution in 20 years, since those great noble Klansmen knocked those niggers off the bridge in Selma, Alabama. Say white power!"

"White power!" came the echo from the crowd.

"White power!" Holland screamed again.

Right arms shot forth in open-palm salute, and again they returned the lead of the Grand Dragon of the Southern White Knights. "White power!" they yelled. "White power! White power! White power!" until the chant dissolved back into the cascading words of their fervent leader.

Thus, in a Bethlehem pasture, the newest version of one of the oldest dramas in the United States was played out: How people who hold hands on weekends and barbecue in the back yard on Tuesdays, who sell fence posts and fix cars and paint houses, who quote the Bible for justification of their beliefs and pledge allegiance to the flag for inspiration, search for salvation and solutions in the Ku Klux Klan, an organization that in the consciousness of mainstream America has come to symbolize white activist hatred and violence.

The image of hooded, night-riding, cross-lighting avengers has become a part of American fact and folklore since it was created by a coterie of restless Confederate veterans answering the call of Gen. Nathan Bedford Forrest in 1865. Their prominence has been cyclical, swelling into the millions in the early decades of this century and fading periodically into near obscurity.

But in all those years, they have never become defunct. As predictable as the effect of sun and rain on dormant weeds, there has always come along some conflict of attitudes and actions that has caused them to suddenly spring forth from seemingly fallow fields.

Such a catalyst, admit admirers and detractors, came in the recent "brotherhood marches" in all-white Forsyth County. When thousands of blacks and whites banded together to make a modern statement against racial apartness in that North Georgia county, the backlash was so immediate and intense that, overnight, the enrollment of the Klan swelled with hundreds of disgruntled white people. Among them were women, as well as children, being prepared for the perpetuation of the tenets of white superiority.

Today, there is new visibility for and curiosity about a movement that is known generically as the Ku Klux Klan, but which has come to encompass camouflage paramilitary garb as well as traditional white sheets and tall cone hats. It is a movement so fragmented and competitive that about the only consistency in its beliefs is the argument that the government, in its zeal to assist black Americans and patronize "business- controlling Jews," has overlooked the need for help, understanding and opportunity for the white working class.

In contrast to its heritage, the modern Klan purports to be strictly a political movement, ensuring its legality. Yet, the GBI, the FBI, the state patrol and local police often ring courthouse steps and pastures in greater numbers than rallying Klan members.

Bill Padgett, the agent in charge of the GBI's anti-terrorism task force, says the surveillance is necessary, that there is among the membership too much fascination with the past, when the Klan dominated many political arenas, and vigilante enforcement of their own brand of justice was feared and unopposed by citizens.

"If they were not not monitored," said Padgett, "violence would erupt. If left unmonitored, no telling how big they would be."

As recently as February, the reality of Klan violence received public exposure when a federal jury awarded a Mobile, Ala., family $7 million in damages against an Alabama Klan group and six past and present members for the 1981 slaying of a black teenager whose body was left hanging in a tree.

Charles Wittenstein, regional counsel for the Anti-Defamation League (ADL), estimates that for every Klansman there are 10 Klan sympathizers in America.

As Holland spoke at the Bethlehem rally that, in addition to rekindling the flames of Forsyth County, was concocted to protest sympathy for a 13-year-old Barrow County black youth accused of killing his white principal with a fingernail file, young Randy Cash and Byron

Burger stood at rigid attention among military-clad honor guards in front of the stage. This was not their first rally, but it would be their first observation of the traditional cross lighting since they joined Holland's Southern White Knights in the wake of the two brotherhood marches in their home county. Earlier, as they sold Klan T-shirts and caps from the back of a truck, they spoke of their Klan heritage.

They remembered the lighting of crosses by their fathers as they stood in childlike fascination. Cash, a burly man with a bushy beard, reminisced about his cousin who "was bad to drink and half the time his kids didn't have shoes. The Klan took him up on a mountain and whipped his butt. He shaped up.

"My daddy told me a lot of stories about the Klan and the good they did. This seemed like the time to stand up for what I believe and follow in his footsteps," Cash said.

The 32-year-old Holland, who has been a Klansman for 12 years, says that seven out of every 10 new members of the Southern White Knights join with the expectation of the Klan operating as it did before the passage of civil rights legislation in the 1960s.

"When they see we can't go out and act a damn fool, they drop out," he admitted. "I get phone calls all the time asking the Klan for assistance. Last night, a woman called me from Walton County. She has been ill, she's up in age and some people are coming down to take her land. She wanted the Klan to come down there and stop that.

"I get letters and more letters like one saying, 'I want you to come beat hell out of my daughter and her boyfriend who is black.' I'll tell them all I'm not going to violate the law for them or anybody. If I was to get arrested, they wouldn't donate 10 cents to hire a lawyer. At the first march in Forsyth, I tried to advise the crowd against violence. The second march, I stayed away. What you don't hear is that of all the people who were arrested for rock throwing or violence, not a single one was a Klansman at the time.

"Of course, back several years ago, some Klansmen went to Tallapoosa GA. and allegedly whipped the hell out of this black man and white woman who were living together, but they were drunk. If the Klan as an organization tried to do anything like that, the GBI would be right on top of it. They are not stupid people.

"And this may sound funny coming from a Klan leader, but I'm glad, in a sense, they do keep close watch. Hell, we know they know everything we are doing. They have informants within our organization and everybody else's."

Padgett, who confirmed there were no Klansmen arrested in Cumming, Ga., for specific incidents, smiled and shook his head when told of Holland's remarks. "We consider Holland perhaps the most dangerous of them all. When you talk with him, he's polite as he can be, but when he steps behind a portable PA system, that's a different matter.

"He jumps out there with that verbiage about white power and 'whitey, you need to get off your rear end.' He can really whip up a crowd. And that's one of the greatest dangers. Not so much what the leadership does themselves, but how their rhetoric can maybe flip out that one unstable person in the crowd. Holland's a powerful speaker."

Mark Mize, following Holland to the platform at the Barrow County rally and very much in the same speaking mold of the Grand Dragon, flailed his arms toward the enthralled audience and demanded hoarsely, "Will you just sit back and do nothing about our problems? What happens when Hosea Williams marches in Barrow County?"

"Shoot the mother," yelled a slender man who appeared to be in his early 30s, as if to substantiate Padgett's observation on the influence of inflammatory rhetoric.

In terms of his emergence as a leader, Holland's work as a Klan member has been a metamorphic experience. About two years ago, he broke away from James Venable's traditionalist National Knights to form the Southern White Knights. He claims to have been so shy as a student at Cross Keys High School in DeKalb County that "I never really associated with girls until I was about 17.

"I joined the Klan at 20, and, for years, I wouldn't even speak at a meeting. A few years ago, Dr. Ed Fields publisher of the racist publication, Thunderbolt, asked me to speak at a rally, and I haven't stopped since."

Some psychologists say that it is just this type of discovery of an unknown self, a new perception of individual worth, that attracts and binds many people to the ritualistic support of the Klan group.

"They gravitate to those groups because it compensates for their low self-esteem by making them feel superior to others," says Fred J. Pesetsky, a psychologist at Jackson State Prison.

In a paper prepared for the American Psychological Association, Dr. Steven Earl Salmony, research assistant at the University of North Carolina, offered the opinion that people who join the KKK appear to share common traits: aimlessness and personal failure, lack of status, low self-esteem and alienation from the social context.

"Through its rituals, the KKK provides its members with a carnival-type, good-mother group atmosphere. But the Klansmen, at these meetings, regress to a primitive, infantile level of psychological functioning, which also arouses their negative, hostile feelings toward society," the paper noted.

Others put it more succinctly. "They have an overwhelming need to be recognized."

For example, Klan security officials, some in a position of responsibility for the first time, often squabble among themselves over territory and assignments. On the day following the Winder, Ga., rally, at a Forsyth County Defense League rally in a chicken house in Headsville, a broad-shouldered guard and a small, leathery chain-smoker got into a shoving and cussing match over who had the right to throw a newspaperman off the property.

The little man whipped out a hand-lettered piece of cardboard on which "Security Chief" was written, and that settled the issue. He pounded on the reporter's car and shouted, "Out, out, out!"

Whatever their motivation for joining, according to Holland, after an initial burst of enthusiasm, the fire goes out for many who never advance beyond menial tasks. "The Klan is just like any other organization," he said. "There is just a handful of people who are going to do anything, anyhow. Most just want to stand around and talk. I hate to say that, but it's true."

But, for the dedicated workers such as Holland and Daniel Carver, the newly appointed Grand Dragon of the Invisible Empire in Georgia, the rise to leadership can be swift. And there seems to be a common thread among the leadership who have ascended the ladder recently in Georgia. For most, there is a specific racial incident from the past that has kept the flame burning beneath their basic convictions on a variety of issues such as race, abortion, drugs and homosexuality.

Holland was involved in a shop-class brawl with black students at Cross Keys High. He said they had irritated him with "T-shirts that said 'Black and Proud' and all that foolishness. They were yapping all the time, and some of us whites got tired of it, and we had a big fight."

Carver says that his sister was killed in 1980 in Houston by black assailants who were never caught. Padgett says the GBI has not found any evidence that such an incident ever happened.

Last March, Holland was fired from AT&T, an action he claims was triggered by the corporation's opposition to his Klan activities, which resulted in several unexcused absences. He said the company "often allows blacks to have pep rallies there."

Carver's predecessor from Jonesboro, Ga., Ed Stephens, resigned, he says, to move to Forsyth County with the intent of running for public office within the next two years. Stephens remembers days at Walter F. George High School in Atlanta when "blacks took my lunch money away from me, until a cousin who was on the football team helped me stop that."

Three years ago, Stephens was fired at an electrical shop. He says his boss told him, "Ed, I'd love to keep you, but because of minorities, I've got to keep Robert who was black.

"I got a job at a new company, and, a few weeks later, Robert showed up there. I took him aside and said, ain't ever leaving my job again because of my color.' Shortly thereafter, he left."

Economics plays a big part in modern enrollment in the Klan, says Holland. "Every time the economy gets bad, the Klan grows. Every time somebody loses a job to a black he says, 'I'm going to join the Klan.'"

Of the speakers who followed Holland to the stage in Bethlehem, almost all spoke of oppression of poor whites, of a society that wipes its feet on the backs of the down and out. Mark Mize, a Barrow County resident, spoke of the difficulties of the farmer and how the government was more interested in blacks and Jews than the hard-working tillers of the land.

A procession of speakers, some practiced, some not, followed as the gloaming turned into a dark chilling night. One, a local person who did not give his name, became so overcome that for almost 30 gurgling seconds, he seemed to be choking on his own emotions. The crowds broke the silence with cheers and applause for his intensity.

The last speaker was Darlene Carver, whose husband Daniel is barred from wearing robes or appearing at Klan rallies because of a 1986 conviction in Gainesville, Ga., for "terroristic threats." Before darkness, he was seen across the road, idling beside a policeman who accompanied him every inch of his visit in Barrow County.

"Friends," Mrs. Carver began, "I'm here tonight on behalf of Daniel Carver, the new Grand Dragon of the Invisible Empire, who can not be here because of court order. But his heart and soul and his family is here."

Mrs. Carver is a dedicated member of the Klan, and her four children are members of the Klan Youth Corps in Hall County. According to her husband, the offspring distribute literature clandestinely and make periodic reports on offensive activities in the schools. Like a diminutive petitioner for the PTA, Mrs. Carver urged the mothers in the crowd to get involved with their children and their schools. "When your child has a problem at school, you should go there and help straighten it out. And you don't have to kill the principal with a fingernail file to do it," she said.

The crowd cheered and moved forward as she continued her litany. Although she claimed nothing more than status as an adoring wife, she held them spellbound. When she repeatedly asked that they dig into their pockets for money, the assemblage of about 300 people filled Crisco cans with their dollars and their loose change.

When Mrs. Carver finished, Holland mounted the stage for the final time and said the hour had arrived for the lighting of the cross. A blond woman with a patch of freckles across her nose jerked at the sleeve of her husband and pleaded, "Come on, now, or we ain't gone get no torch."

Cigarette lighters and matches ignited the nodules of diesel-soaked burlap at the end of long wooden staffs. Soon, a circle of fire was formed around the cross. A phalanx of Klansmen touched the base of the cross with their torches. Slowly the flames licked at the stem, then steadily devoured the oil as it ascended toward the juncture of the vertical and horizontal limbs.

"Lower your torches…" Holland began to intone the ritual instructions over the microphone.

"Raise your torches…"

Obediently, the Klan followed the chant. By the light of the flames, shadows darted across faces rigid with half-smiles and transfixed eyes. And the voice of David Holland boomed through a night that, except for his commands, had grown almost reverently silent.

March, 1987

life in the family

A FATHER AS A WORK OF FICTION

In time, every son becomes his father's unauthorized biographer. In some dim corner of a son's mind where he remembers what never happened and discards inconvenient truths, he rearranges the paragraphs of his old man's life. He reunites broken pieces of praise and blame until they fit a newly crafted remembrance, reinforcing common events until they become uncommon. Finally, the father becomes not biography but an extraordinary invention, a remarkable work of purest fiction tailored to the son's subconscious requirements for heroes and villains.

Each Fathers' Day I apparently can't resist rewriting Bud Walburn, the compulsion like some unavoidable law of nature, as if fruit is obliged to explain seed. My friend Joe McDade is Irish, so naturally he understands. We sometimes swap tangled memories.

In one version my dad is the great athlete, which he obviously was. I have held his trophies. I have seen the medal he won as a regional wrestling champion. I have read newspapers regaling his lightning fists and the fights he won as a small-time professional boxer. His old baseball coach once told me, "Bud Walburn was the best curve ball pitcher that ever spit between two shoes." Maybe it wasn't an exaggeration. He was offered a baseball scholarship to Oglethorpe University, but instead dropped out of school and went to work in a cotton mill.

I never saw him when he was that young, when those who followed games spoke his name with appreciation. In the geography of grownup life I remember Daddy more like a neutral country. He neither attacked life nor resisted. He was neither hero nor villain. He was willing to give a full day's work for his pay, but he could come down with a bad back if there was any heavy lifting to be done around our house. He didn't go to church regularly, but neither did he cuss much. He didn't put up a fuss when my mother warned him she would take me and what was left of his paycheck home to Alabama if he ever drank liquor again. His only act of rebellion that I ever heard about was when

170

my son-in-law, Reed Biggers, discovered Daddy grinning like a possum and holding up a Budweiser can in symbolic defiance shortly before he went into the hospital for the last time.

Daddy's obituary was unencumbered by credits of material accomplishment but pastor Max McCord, who knew us both so well, said at the funeral it would be unfair to blame Mr. Bud for my array of character defects. There had to be reasons, he said, a good portion of LaGrange, Georgia was engulfed in gloom at Daddy's passing.

Others seemed to see into him better than his own son, especially the village kids. He had left the mills to work at the Callaway YMCA for many years and it was routine for one or more of the children to knock on his front door and say when my Mama opened it, "Miz Walburn, can Mr. Bud come out and play?" He always did, even when he had a catheter strapped to his thigh in those latter days.

I think most sons see in their father either what they hope they themselves will become or what they fear they have become. Author Pat Conroy has said, " I think I have held my father as accountable for what he did as any child ever has." Perhaps it was another way of saying he holds his father accountable for who Pat is, that Don Conroy's physical violence became the literary violence that has rendered his son unable to explore other emotions with equal brilliance.

Ironically, one of Pat's best friends, Terry Kay, reinvented his father exactly the opposite way in *To Dance With the White Dog*. The two friends are joined at the heart but disconnected by one of the most profound themes in literature.

I've heard it said that the way a person dies tells the story of how he lived better than any written tale. On his deathbed Daddy said to me, "I just hope you know how much I love you." He was too far gone to define it further, and that and his pocket watch is what I have left. My consolation is that the watch still keeps good time, that love is timeless and that even as I continue to reinvent him, he will remain, as he was, a good man. Anything else I ever write about him is needlessly of my own invention.

June, 2012

THE LOST SUPPER

Saturday night supper was a big deal in the cotton mill village where I grew up. It was the only time I was guaranteed to see my parents together, because they often worked different shifts at the mill. And usually there would be cousins to play with, because most Saturdays several generations and several branches of the family gathered at the home of Aunt Lil and Uncle Ollie. Aunt Lil was a marvelous cook and prepared the meal for everybody not in jail for drinking and fighting.

Aunt Lil cooked on a wood stove. Food tastes different on a wood stove. Her biscuits were the size of cat heads, brown and crispy on the bottom, darker on top and fluffy in the middle. Her fried chicken wasn't greasy and had the taste that can only be produced from being cooked in black iron skillets. Her mashed potatoes were white clouds of comfort. I always used my spoon to make a bed in the potatoes for the creamy little English peas, and I continue the practice today. I never recall that the dessert was other than thick, rich banana pudding.

Sometimes when we would get the call to come bail some kin out of jail, I would think, why in the world would anyone rather drink liquor than eat? Till this day I have never heard of anyone being arrested for driving under the influence of banana pudding.

Saturday nights were different in my wife's family in that the Millers were consistently less rowdy. But the idea of the family meal was the same—three or four generations together, solid, indestructible, gossipy, caring, sharing.

I count as a blessing that my brood still looks to the Saturday night get-together as cherished ritual. Fortunately, it has been significantly influenced by the kinder, gentler Miller temperament. A Saturday night without a hog-wallowing supper has become like Christmas without presents, so we try not to miss many weekends eating together. One of my daughter's friends regularly checks the supper schedule at our house, intrigued as much by the food as the phenomenon of three generations of family that actually enjoy each other's company. And just as the kitchen table is the reservoir from which my wife and I draw many of our childhood memories, I trust that so it is with my sons and daughter, and so it shall be with theirs.

I sometimes wonder if the destruction of the family unit in this country can't be traced to whenever the family meal ceased to be ritually important. Drive around on any weekend night and you'll see that every restaurant and fast-food joint is packed. Can't be that many families dining together at home. And those that do usually don't congregate at the table, but disperse to various TV sets with a tray of food.

The demise of the family meal shortchanges the oral histories of families, especially in the stories that are told over and over for a healthy chuckle. Like the time my granddaughter Anna got the winds. She said, as only a child could, "Mom, I've got the bottom hiccups." When she's big enough to lovingly embarrass, we'll haul out that story at just the right time.

There's so much guilt associated with eating these days that it is almost impossible to prepare a meal that appeals to everyone. The ones that eat for taste fight with the ones who want low calories and no fat, thanks to all the nutritional education that is without question beneficial but, frankly, aggravates our temptation gene to stressful levels.

Whatever the reasons for the disappearance of Saturday night supper, I can't point to a single positive thing about the phenomenon. Love, especially parental love, requires physical presence. Nothing provides a better example of what is now labeled "quality time" than dining together—at home. It's during those unpredictable moments that something grabs at the heart that couldn't have occurred otherwise. There comes a brief moment when a memory happens and a generational bond becomes strong as steel.

March, 1997

UNCLE FRANK

For a long time I've wanted to tell you about Uncle Frank. I've held off because he wasn't quite sure if he had an unpaid debt to society, and, well, you know the memories of some of those old-time Southern sheriffs.

Uncle Frank died this year in Detroit, so I guess he won't have any objections now. I doubt if anybody wants to chase him into his new territory.

As you might have surmised already, Uncle Frank was once a purveyor of untaxed whiskey in a dry county. He bought in Columbus, and he sold in Troup County, and he delivered right to the door. Sometimes so many pint bottles were strapped inside his trouser legs, he sounded like wind chimes when he walked.

His profession was one of pragmatism as much as choice. The mills weren't running regularly, and Uncle Frank had a boy who wanted to go to college. He had a mother living with his family, and he had a slew of relatives who, at varying times, depended on him. Whatever else he may have registered on the debit side of life—and there was plenty— it would be impossible for me not to remember him warmly.

There was that time when my own father was unable to work because of a bum back, and Mama was getting about three days a week at the mill. I remember that spring was when I was graduating to a baseball league where they used big folks' gloves and spiked shoes. I was unable to register for a team because I had none of the necessary equipment.

The day before sign-up, I came home from school, my head full of excuses I was preparing for my friends, and there on the front porch of our shotgun mill house was a pair of spikes in my size and a baseball glove. Nobody ever said who left them there, but I knew.

The year his son graduated from college and that economic burden was eased, Uncle Frank gave up the midnight runs from Columbus and moved to Detroit.

My daddy always said his brother was a genius, and if he wasn't, he must have been close. When Uncle Frank was in grammar school, he made many trips to the principal's office for disciplinary rebukes. The headmaster was usually delighted because the two of them sat and worked crossword puzzles for the rest of the day. His father was rigidly opposed to the reading of popular novels, but Uncle Frank built a false top in a closet and, hidden away, read every novel he could acquire. He was a world-class domino player, although my Uncle Foxy would never concede such a thing.

In Detroit, a large department store sued Uncle Frank over some difference of opinion on debt. The store had an army of lawyers, but they were routed in the courtroom by the seventh-grade dropout who defended himself.

Uncle Frank weighed about 127 pounds, but 120 of that was temper and the other seven pounds were fists. He was an outstanding professional boxer back in the days when $50 was a headliner fee. Sometimes, when the occasion demanded, he blithely switched from pro to amateur again.

In fact, he went all the way to the finals of a state amateur competition. As he walked cockily to the center of the ring for the last bout, the referee that night did a double take and said, "Hey, don't I know you from somewhere?"

"You ought to, you SOB," said Uncle Frank. "I whipped your ass five years ago in Columbus."

Thus ended a brief, but impressive, amateur career.

Outside the ring, he would have waded through Hades just to fight a buzz saw. My daddy said he saw Uncle Frank throw a bigger man into the millpond in a dispute over territorial rights to a young lady who worked in the spinning room. My cousin Bill told me that one time he was at a beer joint with Uncle Frank when a man with a complaint similar to the one left floating in the pond stuck a knife through their car window and placed it against the accused's jugular. Uncle Frank grabbed the blade of the knife with one hand, pulled the guy in through the window and knocked him cold with one punch.

My Daddy said of him—too often after he got into that period when old men like to tell tales—"Oh, I seen Frank get whipped, all right, but I never seen him get hit first."

Uncle Frank always said he wasn't going to die because by the time he got old, somebody would develop an alternative. I knew better than to argue with him, even though I felt certain he wasn't right on this one.

June, 1986

WHY I LIED TO MAMA

When my friend was growing up in Shannon village, he never heard his mother curse. Not once. When she was old she began to call him unspeakable names and use words like son of a bitch and bastard. He told me it crushed his heart like nothing before or since.

Because he had confided his pain, I was better prepared when my mother accused me of stealing her money and when she scalded my ears with profanity. The tirades started after I made an appointment for her with a local neurologist. She accused me afterwards of trying to have her committed to "the lunatic asylum."

The doctor struck me as someone who had seen the signs so many times he had lost his capacity for patience and compassion. He was not amused by Mama's sense of humor, which, strangely enough, wasn't completely smothered by the plaque buildup in her brain. He began a brusk diagnostic routine:

"Mrs. Walburn, tell me the name of the president of the United States."

Silence.

"Mrs. Walburn, tell me what month it is."

Silence.

"Mrs. Walburn, look at the clock. Tell me what time it is."

Silence

"Mrs. Walburn, I'm counting to 100, can you tell me what number comes after 50?"

She finally spoke. "Whoever you are, you don't know a damned thing, do you?"

To check her balance he asked her to walk to the door. When she turned the door knob she looked back, grinned and kept right on going. Fortunately, she was not faster than her son.

The doctor aros quickly from his chair as a signal to end the appointment. He wrote a prescription after I appealed, "isn't there something you can do?" He said I ought to find a senior care home for her.

I had as difficult a time as Mama accepting that as last resort. At 91 my mother appeared to be genetically programmed for a run of at least 100 years. She was physically strong, but in the months following the appointment her cognitive powers continued to diminish. On the mornings I made sure she swallowed her Aricept and Cerefolin medications I would encounter increasingly unusual situations. One day she took a full bottle of milk of magnesia, the results not confined to one room. She complained of a choir singing Christmas Carols all night at Garland Hubbard's house across the pasture.

Dr. Rob Puckett, her primary physician, advised me to make sure she bathed and wore clean underwear every day to prevent urinary infections. The only way I could convince her to hand me yesterday's pair for washing was to remind her that Dr. Puckett ordered it. Growing increasingly petulant, one morning she said, "I'm tired of this. I just don't understand why Dr. Puckett collects old women's dirty drawers."

Mama began to object to "that woman you are staying with." She told me she didn't understand why I didn't come live with her. I said, "Well, Mama, if I did that who would Jackie live with?"

"She ought to be able to find somebody," Mama said.

One of my coping mechanisms was remembering how to lie, a technique that from childhood seemed to spare Mama unnecessary worry about me. When my brother and I finally managed to enroll her in a constant care facility, the only way I could settler her down was to tell her I had bought the place and needed her to help run it.

"Where did you get enough money to do that?" she asked.

Caught off guard I said, "From Daddy."

"Your daddy didn't have any money."

"He had a second job working for the government," I lied.

"He never told me that."

"He couldn't. He worked for the Secret Service."

I make no apologies for my artful deceptions. It's part of the loving circle of life. My Mama lied to me lots of times and I understand now why she did.

"When you grow up you can do things your way," she would say.

"You are perfect the way you are," she said.

"Everything happens for a reason," she said.

Mama was 98 last Monday. I visited her at the dementia ward.

When it came time to leave I hugged her and told her I loved her. And I remembered the biggest lie she ever told me:

"Big boys don't cry."

August, 2013

THE HOUSE THAT CHOSE US

The lamp light in the living room window begins to glow about midnight on Saturday nights. My wife and I have decided the mysterious illumination is a reminder that we are as much caretakers as owners of this old house.

Until last year the house sat where it was built 104 years ago on a knoll overlooking a dirt road that later welcomed asphalt to an avenue of stately homes. In time all but one surrendered beauty and serenity to bulldozers and razing arson of developers. One by one the homes vanished, replaced by pockets of commerce, but this old house sat there on that knoll like the Alamo. Louise Hoge, the owner, answered each sales solicitation the same way. "I was born in this house and I'm going to die in it." She missed only by about six months when at age 98 she needed special care.

A few months before her death and the sprouting of "For Sale" signs, my wife and I drove along Shorter Avenue in Rome and I said to her, "You can't see it well because of the trees, but I adore that house on the hill." She smiled and said, "I think it's time to tell you, I've had a secret love affair with that house for years."

Shortly after "Sold" appeared, the city's master gardeners began to transfer the estate's magnificent plant life to new homes. One of them, our friend, Peg Arey, called to tell about her haul of plants and said the house was scheduled for destruction to make way for a parking lot. A few days later, in a board meeting for a cancer patient retreat founded by Dr. Matt Mumber, I sat next to Dan Sweitzer, an official with the purchasing company. Almost in jest, I asked, "May I have that old house on Shorter Avenue?"

In response to the unanticipated affirmative answer, in some respects, I was like the dog that had been chasing the same car and after catching it wondered, "What do I do now?" The first thing that occurred to me was to call my wife. "You know that house on Shorter Avenue you have been fantasizing over? It's yours."

The *Rome News-Tribune* chronicled on its front page the process of slicing the house into movable top and bottom portions and loading the pieces onto the massive steel drays belonging to W.A. Womack Movers. It is a nerve-testing profession Mr. Womack has plied since 1968, something he would have never aspired to, he says, if it hadn't been for his friends Jack Daniel and Bud. To our surprise, news that the house was to be saved triggered emotions ranging from relief to outright joy in this northwest Georgia town. We were unaware that Mrs. Hoge's house claimed a corner of so many tender memories.

Everyone in Floyd County who plinks the keys of a piano received instruction from Mrs. Hoge in one of the rear rooms of this old house, we were told--apparently with only mild exaggeration. Once we had moved it 15 miles north to our lake site in Armuchee, not many days passed without someone paying a sentimental visit. Some shed respectful tears, as did two of Mrs. Hoge's children who had driven into town from Augusta and Kennesaw to pay final respects, unaware their old home would live on.

At times, as we inventoried all the happenstances surrounding this adventure, we have wondered if we chose the house or were somehow chosen. How else to explain our unspoken dual fascination with the house, the serendipitous call from Peg and the meeting with Dan--and, later, the puzzling Saturday night lamp light? Other events that otherwise might seem insignificant, have grown in proportion to our willingness to believe our own imaginations. For example, the restoration contractor we thought would be a perfect match was in jail, we were told. We had no time to pursue the particulars of his incarceration, but were fortunate that his circumstance led us instead to Wayne Christian and Barry Nelson, who had as much bravado as experience, plus forgiving natures that worked around my temperamental outbursts and the weather. With the house barely stitched after the chain saw surgery necessary to separate the halves, on July 14, 2004, tornadoes struck both south and north of Shorter Avenue. It was as if the storm had split and spared the house.

After that, our imagination interpreted every unusual incident as a manifestation of destiny. The event that validated our conviction came when the contractors began to disengage a kitchen connected to the house by a breezeway. As was the norm in days before air conditioning and firewalls, the kitchens in that era were usually located away from the main structure for both comfort and safety. Once all parts were settled at the lake site, workers pried away a large sheet of plywood where the breezeway had joined the kitchen to the house. Behind the cover they found layers of old *Atlanta Journals* that had been used for insulation.

I noticed immediately the date on the pages: September 27, 1962. I said to my wife, "I was working at the *Journal* in those days." We carefully separated the yellowed, fragile pages into two stacks. I saw bylines by my friends Jim Minter, Terry Kay, Furman Bisher, and Gregory Favre. "Guess Mrs. Hoge thought my stories weren't worth saving," I said. We looked through the sheets once more without finding anything by me.

The next day my sister-in-law, Cheryl Holland, came by to inspect construction progress and I was telling her the story of the bylines and how disappointed I was not to find myself among them. She looked down at the stack and said, "Well, isn't that your name?" Overnight, my story about the Atlanta Crackers had appeared right on top of the stack. Later, behind the wall on the other side of the kitchen we discovered two more of my stories, one of them about the impending firing of the Cracker manager, Joe Schultz, the first real scoop of my newspaper career. "My name has been on this house for 42 years," I said. "I guess it has been waiting."

The restorative process, though replete with such delightful surprises, was not without a conflict of ideas. But in the end, we made no changes to the exterior. Inside, we abandoned most thoughts of modernization, but did add a kitchen to the ground floor. After considerable debate, my wife and I finally agreed on colors for the interior. Workers began to scrape away layers of paint lapped on top of each other over the years. When they reached the bottom layer we discovered that we had chosen exactly the same two hues as the original.

And so, when the lamp light glows on Saturday nights, we just say, "Oh, cut it out Mrs. Hoge. We are just as happy to be here as you are."

November, 2005

Goodbye To A Good Neighbor

As I write this, it is still early spring. From the distance, the redbud and peach trees along the driveway at Hodge Podge Lodge seem delicate as pink mist. The apple trees in the pasture next door will be blossoming soon if we don't experience a late cold snap like last year's.

I have been standing alone on the front porch, gazing out across the pasture that contains a solitary, scraggly old horse. But I know that the face I am looking for will not appear again, except in my mind, and for a moment I play Sambo back in my thoughts like some old movie with every line and every scene memorized.

We had no real claim to Sambo, except his name, which we gave to him before we discovered that his owner simply called him "Dawg." He was legendary even before we met him; neighbors warned us about the heavily muscled liver-and-white pointer with yellow eyes who bit first and asked questions later.

Nobody had lived at Hodge Podge for quite a while. It sat near a path the dog had worn as he hiked the bank of the river from which came much of his food. At the first notice of us settling in his territory, he stood at the edge of the pasture, baring his white teeth and snarling.

As the days of that first summer went by, Sambo advanced closer and closer to the cabin. Finally, he was eating dog food and table scraps my wife placed just outside the door. Within a month he became a member of the family.

At first he took it upon himself to protect us, even when we didn't need it. He was pure hell on our own dogs, not to mention relatives and friends who learned to sit in their cars and honk the horn until we rescued them.

By the end of summer, however, Sambo had become a pal to everyone. He lay contentedly in the sun while visitors stepped over him or petted him and helped spoil him. A powerful swimmer, he took to following our johnboat on fishing trips. He knew that eventually his enthusiasm would be rewarded by a seat in the front of the boat while we drifted the banks in search of bass and bream. On float trips down to the Highway 140 bridge, he and his friend, Black Puppy, had their own rubber tubes. We have pictures of them bobbing along like teenagers.

Eventually Sambo took up with another Hodge Podge visitor named Miss Puppy. She was as sweet and innocent as your first girl friend and all the dogs on Old Dalton Road were mad about her. One by one they came calling, and Sambo fought them all, including a mastiff almost twice his size.

The two suitors tore at each other until they were both bloody, exhausted casualties and, frankly, Sambo got the worst of the wounds. But when he limped off into the woods, Miss Puppy was at his side, preferring that her first litter be sired by her gallant protector rather than by the red bully who thought he could just swagger in like the leader of some motorcycle gang and demand her affection.

In time we came to love Sambo so much that even before we put the key in the lock we began to look for him. He never failed to make coming back an event. Down he would come off a nearby hill, out across the pasture he would bound. You could see the smile on his face from a hundred yards away. On the porch, amid the soothing summer night sounds, he had a way of placing his head on your lap and hugging you.

One weekend, just before Thanksgiving, Sambo didn't come around. Night fell and my family stood on the porch in the darkness. We shivered in the cold air blowing off the river. We listened to dogs barking in the distance.

"That's Sambo's bark," said my wife. "I think maybe it's deer season and they've got him penned up. You know how he likes to run Turkey Mountain Ridge. They just don't want some hunter mistaking him for a deer."

When Sambo didn't show up the next weekend, we went to the edge of the pasture and called him. Down the hill and across the pasture, Black Puppy walked slowly. When he finally stood before us, we knew from the look in his eyes he was trying to tell us of a great sadness that had gripped his life.

My wife immediately got into the car and went to see her cousin who lives nearby. He said Sambo had been killed by a car as he went with his real master to pick up the mail down by the road.

Now we have reopened Hodge Podge for the spring, but there is a lingering emptiness from a subtraction that no addition can ever rectify. I have seen my wife and children standing at various times on the porch, looking out across the pasture. Nobody says a word. But I know what they are thinking. I know the feeling in their hearts.

April, 1984

LITTLE ORPHAN ANGEL

Maybe dogs pass the word around. Maybe they have an underground network. Maybe dogs just know about the Walburns.

It was a lazy summer day. My son, Steve, and my son-in-law, Reed Biggers, were driving around, listening to Willie Nelson on the stereo. Steve, said to Reed, "Let's take the long way home so we can finish listening to the album."

So they headed over Dunnaway Gap, a dirt washboard of a road over Johns Mountain. As they were slowly winding down the back side of the ridge near where thoughtless rednecks have raised a carbuncle of beer cans, moldy mattresses, fast food wrappers and decaying refuse, Steve moaned and said to Reed, "Oh, my God, stop the car, but don't look."

She had climbed out of the trash heap, scrambling over a berm on her short legs, limping on sore feet until she stood in front of the car with an attitude that said, "You gotta help me or you gotta run over me." She limped around to the side of the car and pirouetted like a tiny ballerina, no bigger than the fairies that danced through your childhood dreams. Then she placed her paws on the side of the door.

She was bald from mid-back to the jagged claws of her back feet. The hairless half of her was raw and red from frantic gnawing and clawing in her attempts to find relief from the fleas and ticks that mercilessly assaulted her. On the west side of the mountain, clouds dark as the heart of the bastard who had dumped her were poised to cross the Alabama line into Georgia, leaving no doubt she would not survive the next thunderstorm.

In the back of Reed's vehicle, Steve located a cloth gurney used for transporting hospital patients who must be moved gently. He wrapped the little hitchhiker in it as Reed activated the cell phone. He managed to locate my grandson, Corey. "Go find Nana, quick," Reed instructed. He knew my wife planned to attend a Memorial Day service at Rome's Myrtle Hill Cemetery where America's symbolic Known Soldier from

186

World War I is buried and where a commemorative brick similar to those placed in Centennial Park bore the name of her late brother, Raburn. "Don't let her leave 'til we get home," Reed implored.

Nana's bag of healing tricks is a source of constant amusement, but when a situation is no longer a joking matter, she is our go-to guy. As word began to spread, old and young family members began to gather for a viewing. Steve's "Oh, my God!" became a recurring echo.

The newcomer was so filthy even the most compassionate of us didn't want to touch her. We put her in a pen in the back yard and stood around studying her as if she were from outer space. Button eyes, brown as daisy centers, are set above a flat nose that was barely visible through her stinking white hair. One tooth appeared to be missing from the under-bite typical of the Pekinese breed.

My granddaughter Colby said, "She looks like an angel." And though it was difficult to determine at the time how the bedraggled orphan could have possibly inspired such a thought, another granddaughter, Anna, said, "I am naming her Angel." And that was that.

Later in that evening, after Nana had executed the fleas and picked off the ticks, she bathed Angel, applied the obligatory tea tree oil (healer of all ills), cut the matting from her remaining hair and fed her liquids. Steve came back in from the lake where he had been fishing and a strange look came over him when we said, "She has been named Angel."

"You know what was playing on the stereo when I saw her?" he said. "'Angel Flying Too Close to the 'Ground.'" In my pocket was a silver angel given to me a couple of weeks earlier by an artist, Wayland Moore, survivor of a heart attack. The string of coincidences made her new name so amusingly appropriate that we laughed.

We took Angel to the vet the next day. He said she was very sick, but there was an excellent chance she would recover her health and her hair as long as we kept her absent of fleas, to which she was allergic. Slowly, over the next month, she began to heal. One day as I cradled her in my arms, both of us relishing the thought of a noonday nap in my easy chair, I scratched her tummy and she licked me a kiss. I couldn't think of a reasonable reason not to fall in love.

September, 2001

BRIDGING THE GENERATION GAP

In the darkest, stillest hours of night the ringing of a telephone always sends an electric shock of terror through me as I brace for bad news. There is a surrealistic moment when time becomes a slow-motion movie and my heart seems to stop.

"Mr. Walburn, this is the Cobb County police. Do you have a green Toyota truck, license plate GKD 846?" "Yes."

"Do you have a son named David?"

"Yes."

"Mr. Walburn, he has been frog gigging in a private pond. Would you speak him about it?"

I promise to discipline him as if police had caught him robbing First National Bank, when in truth, what I want to do was gather him into my arms and hug him and thank God he is alright.

The smothering fear of something happening to your children is the most common of all emotions, a trait shared by humans and beasts of the field. And once your 16-year-old has put his or her hands around the steering wheel of a car, every siren in the night, every tire that screeches on asphalt causes you to prick your ears like an animal in the woods and you pray for the mythical day when the child is mature and cautious in judgment. You fight, often unsuccessfully, not to think the unthinkable. You silently run through self-pitying parental clichés about insensitive children.

It was 10 minutes before midnight in November when I received the call that told me our mutual friend had just lost a son in an automobile accident. Neither of us could talk for awhile and outside the bedroom window I could hear rain slashing angrily at everything in its path and I knew the night had dealt heartache again.

In the darkness I sat on the edge of the bed, struggling for control of my thoughts. I switched on the night-light and began to dress.

"Are you going now?" my wife said. "It's 30 miles away. I'm afraid for you to go in this weather. Are you sure it's best to go tonight?"

"I don't know," I replied.

"I understand," she said. "I will go with you." She did understand. Fourteen years before she lost her younger brother in a wreck. When we received the terrible news by telephone, we floated temporarily in a vacuum of disbelief. The automatic reflex was to get into our car immediately and drive in numbed silence toward the people we loved and wanted more than anything simply to touch and weep with. We had hoped never to encounter such grief again but now we would.

The father and mother were in their living room when we arrived. It was still that interlude when you hope you will awaken and the absurd dream will have ended. There was nothing to say. There never is. An embrace, and "I love you."

As we held on to each other, my friend said simply, "The worst thing that could happen has happened."

In less than a week many of the same mourners would gather at the graveside of another friend's son, also a victim of a car wreck. And every father and mother there shared the hollow grief and the unspeakable dread. Each knew the nights would never be the same again. Perhaps they thought, as I did, if only the children understood. Understood what? Are their parents simply articulating self-pity?

Exactly seven days after the second funeral I was awakened from a snooze on the couch by the sound of David's voice. My mind raced. He is supposed to be in school in Tifton. He is in the middle of final exams. I glanced at a clock. It was almost midnight. David's eyes were red from travel. Both he and his roommate, Mike, were obviously tired and shaken.

"Jimmy's father died today," David said.

Jimmy is their friend. He had not returned to school the day before and they knew something was wrong. When they received his phone call their fears were confirmed.

"David," I said in the unthinking way of fathers, "if the funeral is not until day after tomorrow wouldn't it have been better to finish your exams tomorrow morning and then come home?"

He looked at me sadly and said as I once said, "I don't know."

January, 1983

THE SCARS THAT LAST

At The Cracker Barrel, we couldn't avoid hearing chatter from the family eating nearby. They wore rummage sale clothes and looked to be more in need of a bar of soap than a meal. The waitress approached them, grinned and said, "You don't remember me, do you?"

The two adults stared at her and said they reckoned they didn't. The waitress told them her name and reminded them she used to live next door in Tennessee when she was growing up. They began to chat and one of the customers asked what ever happened to her sister?

"Oh, she's living here. She's got four kids, but she's trying to give one of them away," the waitress said as casually as if she had been trying to place a litter of puppies.

"Why, we'll take him," said the woman. "That's how we got these here two."

The waitress wrote the address of her sister on a napkin with a stubby pencil.

That happened more than a year ago, but nearly every day there is a new story about child abuse in the newspaper. I often wonder if that anonymous young boy was lifted from a horrible situation to a better one, or if somewhere he is being beaten or starved when he isn't being ignored. I wish I had thought to get the tag number of the family's car.

Child abuse is almost always conducted by cowards behind closed doors, but the children always wear expressions of torment that can't be disguised, even when their bruises are hidden by clothes or beneath the surface of their minds.

An old hound my mother calls Dumbo recently started hanging around her yard. He eats the scraps she leaves for him, but he won't come close enough for anyone to pet him. If a hand is raised even in the most nonthreatening gesture, he whines and runs away. No matter how good anybody treats him, he obviously will never trust humans enough to be touched. If it can happen to a beaten dog, can it be otherwise that the children of abuse will grow up the same way?

When my daddy died about a year ago, I received a letter from a lady who lives in Atlanta, but grew up in my hometown. And if I had harbored any misgivings about the contributions my father made in his plain, unambitious life, I was forced to bury them with the man known back home as Bud.

"Without him," the letter said, "my childhood would have been very drab, indeed. The only happy memories I have of being a small child revolve around him. When I remember my own daddy, all I think of is being told to shut up or being slapped so hard I could see stars. He never took me anywhere, never threw a ball to me, never even spoke to me except to scold and I never remember him touching me except in anger.

"I'm not looking for sympathy, I just wanted you to understand how much Bud meant to my childhood. I remember his making and flying kites on a windy day. Bud would get newspapers, flour, water and sticks and let me tie the tail together with pieces he had ripped from rags. I would let the kites get away in the wind, and I can still remember Bud running after them and bringing them back. He used to take me through the back alley to the store and buy me ice cream and candy. He took me and my brother to the movies. He tried to teach me to play the electric guitar. I can still see the guitar in my lap with picks on my right hand and the bar in my left as I tried to play 'Birmingham Jail.'

"When I was about 10 years old, I made too much noise one day and Daddy gave me the worst beating of my life. I had blue welts on my legs and back for two weeks. I can remember how angry Bud was and he raised hell with Daddy. Then he took me around to all my uncles and showed them. It was the last beating I ever got from my daddy.

"What I'm trying to tell you is how very special your daddy will always be to me. Not because of anything he ever said to let me know he cared, but because of all the caring things he did to make a lonely, unwanted little girl's life so much brighter than it would have been otherwise. Lee, all this happened before you were born, but they are still clear to me."

May the little boy who was given away in a roadside restaurant find his own caring Bud.

August, 1985

A LOVE SONG

When J.J. appeared on the porch of the Turn in the River Inn, walking out into the sweet Montana air on the arm of her father, Tim Torgerson picked up his guitar and began to strum the bridal march. David, who had been squinting distractedly at the distant mountains, turned to watch the slow procession across the green grass, down the rock steps, past his friends sitting there, some misty with remembrance, some alert in naive anticipation. J.J. looked at David and smiled.

There are moments, you know, when even the familiar is transformed into the mystical. And when J.J. smiled, David's eyes widened as if he had suddenly been visited by some great truth. He began to weep. Then he began to sob. J.J. handed him her handkerchief. Pastor Brad Brittsan read a passage from Ecclesiastes, "…Two are better than one…for if they fall, the one will lift up his fellow.…if two lie together, then they have heat.…But how can one be warm alone?" Then he talked about for better and for worse and in sickness and in health, and by then the bride was crying too.

Pastor Brad paused in the ceremony and David picked up his own guitar. He said to their friends, "I would like to sing the first song I wrote for J.J." And as he sang, Pastor Brad's lips began to tremble, and his eyes were fixed the way eyes are when accosted by a powerful memory. I was startled that tears falling on grass made sounds, but perhaps over the years I had just forgotten. From all around tears fell on grass like a natural song.

Pastor Brad took a deep breath before concluding the ceremony and said, "Folks, I believe they really mean it."

I suppose it is not all that uncommon to hear guests remark, "That was the most beautiful wedding I've ever seen." Liz Hackman whispered to me, "Your son is special." I thanked her, of course, and showed admirable restraint by not elaborating.

Somehow, the comments did not seem gratuitous this time. Many of the women appeared to be under some sort of spell, and it seemed that without an additional spoken word they were drawn down toward the cold, clear Whitefish River, where one by one they began to walk into the water, some in their wedding clothes, some with their clothes left scattered on the bank.

There is something overwhelming about realizing your son has a gift. David's gift of music will not make him rich; perhaps his obsessive love for music will, in fact, keep him poor. But his poetry and music have the power to make people laugh and cry and go wading in cold rivers.

October, 1995

life isn't always fair

GOOD MEN DESERVE MORE THAN 'BEFORE LONG'

Too many times I've waited too long. Too many times I said I would visit "soon" only to have "soon" turn into "before long" and "before long" into "let me check my calendar."

I have attended too many memorials for too many good men and wished I had been there two weeks earlier. John Willis, who edited my column in this newspaper, was one of those good men. I had not seen him during the month before his death, but I had spoken with him over the telephone and said we will have to do lunch before long. But we didn't.

Several months prior to that I had promised Fred Abston I would attend the next Fifth Sunday singing with him at West Union Baptist Church. But I didn't. I attended his funeral there. A good man deserved better than my "next time."

In many ways another friend, Gerry Chatham, was like John Willis and Fred Abston, the kind of men who love being part of the show without being the show. They give a honest day's work for their pay, coach your kid's recreation league basketball team during the week, teach a church class on Sunday. They have gentle hearts. They are like cheerleaders for the success and salvation of others. Cheerleaders should not die waiting for a visit from those they cheer.

Gerry's wife called on a Friday in January and said he needed more than the doctors and the chemotherapy and the blood donations and the prayers. He needed to see friends. I said I would visit on Monday. I knew it could not be "soon," it could not be "before long." It had to be an irrevocable Monday.

To find the right building at Northside Hospital in Atlanta I walked a maze within a maze. I asked a woman at a desk in the third building I visited if Gerry Chatham was in Room 450 and she said there was no room 450 in that ward, nor a Gerry Chatham for that matter.

She offered no further assistance. As I wandered through the halls a nurse noticed my bewilderment and when I described the nature of my friend's illness she personally escorted me to the correct wing and a set of double doors.

Another nurse told me that before I could go through a second set of double doors I would have to wash my hands, don a special gown and sterile booties. At the door to Gerry's room I was told to change from the special gown to another type of sterile apparel. Each new cautionary instruction magnified the seriousness of Gerry's weakened immune system.

I arrived thirty minutes late, but he grinned and said he was glad to see me. That's the way it is with good men. They really are glad to see you. We rekindled oft-told tales...the time Dolly Parton visited us at our public relations firm...the times we played on Lewis Grizzard's slow pitch softball team...the time in Peachtree City when the umpire threatened to toss Gerry from the game because he insisted on smoking his pipe while playing third base. A man of principle, Gerry reasoned he should be able to smoke on third if Walburn was allowed to chew tobacco at shortstop.

I said I would be back to see him soon, but this time it was the leukemia that caused me to lie. His son, Scott, sent messages saying Gerry had became too weak to receive visitors anymore. Two days later in Atlanta I met Jim Minter, Terry Kay and David Cleghorn. Along with Gerry we represented most of what's left of The Bisher Boys, Furman Bisher's early sports staff at the *Atlanta Journal*. Clumsily we recorded video messages to Gerry. Terry miraculously figured out a way to install it all on YouTube. Jim's message was truest of all. He said, "Gerry, if you had been here this would have been a lot better organized."

By then, Gerry had slept for several days and nights. A day after the video was recorded Gerry awoke. Scott hastily booted up his laptop and played our messages.

Scott told us at the memorial that Gerry had smiled, signaled thumbs up and said, "Great!" He went back to sleep and did not wake up again.

I like to think he passed away proud that The Bisher Boys had met another deadline.

March, 2013

TWO KINDS OF HEROES

Norman Akers owns a black dog named "Blue." He says he named him after his battered old truck although the truck is black. He wears combat boots and his pants are tucked inside foot soldier–style. His long hair, the color of soiled sand, parts in the middle over piercing blue eyes and is pulled tightly away from a round face by a rubber band at the juncture of a pigtail.

When Norman Akers graduated from high school in Missouri, he volunteered to fight in Vietnam. He had never seen his father, but his mother said he had been in the Navy. He figured his old man must have been a hero and when he was a child, Norman's favorite TV show was called Combat.

When Company B, 3rd Battalion, 39th Infantry, 9th Division was set afire in Tan An by intense mortar and rocket attack, Norman said it felt kind of like he had a role on the TV show. The citation he was presented along with the Silver Star for heroism stated that after personally extinguishing a raging inferno, "despite the constant danger of exploding munitions and the ever present torrent of enemy rounds ... grabbing an M-60 machine gun and running some 300 meters through the killing zone, he then mounted a burning bunker and began returning fire in the insurgent force. Although the bunker was constantly receiving rocket and small arms fire, Private Akers continued to place suppressive fire on the Viet Cong until all of their weapons were silenced."

A citation for one of several other medals says that when a claymore mine exploded, wounding several men in his platoon, "Private Akers carried a wounded comrade 300 meters through a deluge of enemy fire to an evacuation site, then went back and aided other wounded men." Norman was wounded in the leg, had his rifle shot out of his hands and his hat shot off his head.

In Florida, where he was hitchhiking after the protesters in Oakland spat on him and called him "baby killer," he tried to trade his Silver Star for a bowl of chili and a cup of coffee. The owner of the diner ordered him to leave. He tried picking fruit, but other workers kept stealing his baskets when he wasn't looking. Since then he has more or less been a carpenter. Eventually he settled in Atlanta.

In high school, he and a friend had sometimes hitchhiked from Missouri to the hippie strip that is now midtown, because "I liked all that free love." It was fun then. But when he reached Atlanta again, everything everywhere was different than before he went to Vietnam and got addicted to marijuana and beer. To entertain himself, he bought a black Ninja outfit. Lots of nights he would smear his face and hands with black makeup and creep through some woods in Kennesaw, trying to see if he could be invisible.

Norman Akers has no home now. He has two ex-wives and a son. He has served time for abandonment. He carries his military citations in a briefcase in the black truck. "My son is proud of me for being a hero," he told me one night as he poured concrete at a friend's house. "That's all he's got to be proud of me for." His face and body quivered as if an electrical current was passing through.

The new president of the United States is about the same age as Norman Akers. There's lots about their backgrounds that is similar. Neither ever saw his father. Each was somewhat poor. Both apparently liked girls a great deal and it seemed to cause them considerable trouble.

Both tried pot. One said he didn't inhale. The other says he still likes it when he's with his buddies. Norman supported the war in Vietnam. As you know, the new president did not.

Had he gone on to college, who knows, Norman says, he might have even protested the war. "College students are made aware of what is going on in the world. They are taught to question things. You learn to think like you are taught, at that age.

"College took President Clinton and taught him to see the world one way. The Army took me and taught me to think, another. They took me as a baby and taught me to be a man. But when you come back to society, you're less than a man because if people screw you, you can't do anything. Too much red tape. There you could fight it out and feel like a man. What somebody took from you, you could take back. In our society, if somebody can lie and cheat and steal and beat you out of something, he feels like he's the hero. And you can't do a thing about it."

Norman Akers is now being treated at "a place for people who have lost everything, but want to get back into the flow."

If Norman Akers hadn't gone to war, would he be different? On the other hand, had Bill Clinton fought in Vietnam, would he be the same? Would he have become president of the United States? Or would he be creeping through the woods at night trying to be invisible? Would his entire sense of worth be found inside a battered briefcase? Would he not be able to resist when his buddies pass him the bottle? Would he have a black dog named "Blue?"

January, 1998

WHEN MAMA STOPPED READING

I knew Mama's life had changed forever the year she stopped reading. There was no test a doctor could conduct, no prescription he could write that would tell me so clearly.

Mama's house was filled with books, overrun by books, books stored on the back porch, books stored in the well house, books on the headboard of her bed, books in the bathroom. She read them all: good books, trashy books, expensive books, paperbacks from discount stores, books from the library.

My Daddy used to say, "Myrtle, what would the neighbors think if they knew you sat reading all those books?" Sometimes Mama's choice of words could be found in her more robust novels. She would invariably reply, "Bud, I don't give a damn what people think." And she didn't. Hers was a lifetime of being in charge.

She was as beautiful as a princess, but she wasn't a fairytale mother. She had a right hook and I saw her use it more than once. I was ten years old when one of my friends said, "Your mama is 'bout the prettiest woman I've ever seen. But, I hear tell, don't mess with her."

Mama was 62 the year a serial rapist terrorized LaGrange. A neighbor managed to telephone that a man was trying to break in to her apartment. Mama bolted out her front door, taking it partially off the hinges. She chased the rapist down railroad tracks and through a briar patch. Policemen said when they caught up with him he was fleeing like the hounds of hell were nipping at his heels. An officer rebuked Mama for such a foolhardy act. She said, simply, "Well, the s.o.b. made me mad."

Shortly after Mama stopped reading, she began to hear a choir at Garland Hubbard's house singing Jingle Bells. It angered her, as did the monkeys that surrounded her house. She insisted someone had been writing on the walls of her bedroom. She had scrapped away a moon-sized portion. I asked her what the writings said and she snapped, "I can't read every blasted language in the world."

"Mama," I said, "The wall is just the way Jackie painted it."

"Well, she did a crappy job," she replied, as always jabbing for the final word, even if it meant downgrading the wife she had always loved.

She began periodically to pack a bag, stuff her purse and take off walking on those days when I had to run back to my house or conduct some business. Sometimes Harold Pierce or his son would see her walking along the fence row in front of John and Faye Porter's house and bring her back before she reached Highway 27. I would ask, "Where were you going, Mama?" She would reply, "Home."

Repeatedly wakened by a night sitter's telephone call I would drive over to reason with Mama. It became impossible to convince her she was already home. I would take her to my car, drive for a half hour and then turn back into the driveway. She would smile and say, "Well, here we are at the old Glory Hole."

All my life she has referred to me by my knickname, "Mose." As she became more and more agitated by my care giving, she concluded that I was two persons. Mose, as always, could do no wrong. When her sitter tried to convince her that Mose would never leave her on the back doorstep of a strange house, she replied, "No, but that Lee would."

It was Lee who called his brother, Rick, and said "The time has come. Mama needs to be in assisted living." That lasted less than a month. We agreed to transfer her to the dementia ward and eventually moved her to Avalon Health and Rehab in Newnan near Rick's home.

She seems at peace now. Well, as long as nobody messes with her. "We love Miss Myrtle," the nurses say. "She's different." Only once has she managed to fool the alarm system. Nurses saw her wandering around outside. "We knew not to grab her," a nurse told me. "I said, 'Miss Myrtle, what you doin' out here?'"

"Walking," Mama said, then added, "How do you get back in this place? It's hot as hell out here."

She will turn 96 next Friday. I will buy her something red and I will say, "Happy birthday, Mama."

If she thinks it is Lee speaking she may not reply. If she thinks it is Mose, she will say, "Lord, you have just made my day."

August, 2011

STRANGE THINGS, WAR MEMORIES

Curious what you remember about war. I was just a child when World War II began. The earliest thing I recall is bedcovers pulled up around my shoulders and static from a Philco radio, the crackling voice of Gabriel Heater saying, "Ah, there's good news tonight. Our boys in Europe..."

And I remember that President Franklin Roosevelt died before the war was over, and heartbroken cotton millers wept softly as they sat on their front porches. Shortly afterward, there was something about a new and terrible bomb. There was a lot of noise downtown—horns, people forming a V with their fingers and yelling. My Uncle Ollie came home from Europe then. He had been a mail clerk. He showed me medals he claimed were his Purple Hearts.

When the Korean War began, I was in high school. One Saturday night at the LaGrange Theater, I saw an older boy named Charlie. He had been drafted. He was a tall, handsome fellow with dark hair. That night at the theater, he was crying inconsolably. A couple of his buddies held him by the shoulders and told him to get hold of himself.

"I'm going to die in Korea," he cried.

Charlie left for boot camp the next Monday. I remember, when the war was over, I saw him again. He said he had been in a mental hospital for a while.

Nobody wanted to call the next war a war. The official name for the killing fields of Vietnam was "conflict."

I could have been there. I wasn't too old. But, I had three children and I was not drafted. I remember nights in front of the television set. War viewed firsthand was riveting. I remember a feeling in my stomach like motion sickness and later, the impression that networks look at war like sports programming. Just keeping score.

I was working for the Atlanta Braves then. A college student named Joe Champion worked there part time. I remember how great he was in our touch football games. One day I missed Joe and I asked the vice president of the Braves, Dick Cecil, where he was. Dick replied that the kid had been drafted. Later, we heard that Joe had been killed in Vietnam, and we had a little bronze plaque made for a wall at the stadium. Yesterday I found Joe's name on the Moving Wall Vietnam memorial in Woodruff Park. I tried to remember his face, but I couldn't.

When the permanent version of the wall was being constructed in Washington I opposed it as being too somber, and lacking in drama. It spoke nothing of war, I said. I was wrong. I know now that as long as that wall stands with the names of the dead inscribed, it will keep me remembering and wondering about war. It will make me remember that I do not understand war, in part, because I have not fought in one. Perhaps only those on the wall really understand.

Nevertheless, over the last few days I couldn't help but have new and personal thoughts about war, though it's not called war anymore. I have wondered what I will eventually retain about the "retaliatory action" against Libya? If the names on the moving wall could come down and materialize in the forms of the heroes they represent, what would they suggest I remember about this new and different conflict?

Perhaps they would suggest I remember, instead of specifics, essential truths, that attacking Americans in airports and cafes is no less an act of war than bombing Pearl Harbor; that, as Conrad Adenauer said, "an infallible method of conciliating a tiger is to allow oneself to be devoured."

Or, perhaps the names on the wall would say, "What difference does it make to the dead?"

What if they said that personally, all they recall about war is how a bullet pierced their skull and how, strangely, for a microsecond, they could almost smell their mother's fried chicken cooking back home?

"Curious what you remember about war," they might say.

April, 1986

THE BOY WHO CAME IN FROM THE COLD

Sometimes Anita Beaty glances out the window of the van and sees the woman. She wears the ragged, motley ensemble of the homeless, and her brown hair is long and stringy, matted with grease and dirt. She clutches a filthy infant to her hip.

Anita's stomach tightens as she realizes how much the child of the streets resembles Donnie, the boy sitting beside her in the van. Anita watches Donnie's face for any sign that he recognizes the woman and prays that she and her husband, Jim, will choose the right words if Donnie demands to know if the beggar is his real mother.

Somewhere in the dreams that once caused Donnie to wake screaming several times a night, he has already come to the conclusion he is adopted. Anita and Jim had agonized over how they would eventually tell the child.

The nightmares told him instead.

Recently, he put his arms around Anita and Jim and said, "You're not my first mother and father, but you're my real mother and father. My first mother took me into cold water, but you took me to a warm place."

Donnie is 8 now. When Anita and Jim first saw him, they were working as volunteers at The Open Door, a haven for the homeless on Ponce de Leon Avenue. Donnie was 14 months old and could not walk because he had been strapped so often into a makeshift stroller. He had a cold and hacking cough. His diaper needed changing, but his mother didn't have another. When they brought Donnie a peanut butter and jam sandwich, he instinctively gave half of it to Anita, who was holding him.

Another volunteer told Anita, "Why, he is a legend, that baby. He has been living in the streets since he came out of Grady Hospital."

She told Anita how the boy was brought to The Open Door by a man and a woman. The temperature outside was 9 degrees.

The ambulance workers summoned from Grady could find no pulse in the hands and feet of the child at first. After treatment, he and his mother vanished again.

Thoughts of the boy haunted the Beatys. Anita began to drive the streets looking for the boy. When she occasionally spotted him with his mother, she would chase after them, imploring the mother to come into a shelter.

In March 1985, Anita received a call from a caseworker. "Remember the baby you've been so interested in? He is sitting in my desk drawer right now. We just don't have a place for him. Would you consider taking him until we can find a foster home?"

The Beatys already had six children. Jim, a professor at Georgia State, took a summer off to be with Donnie. The child had virtually no vocabulary. The doctor who discovered the boy's terrible ear infection told Anita, "If you had a similar affliction, you would need morphine to stand the pain."

Donnie's habits, nurtured on the streets, amazed the Beatys. Whenever they changed his diapers, it was like tapping into a slot machine. They began to understand why his eyes seemed to always cast downward. He was looking for loose change that he had been trained to store in his diaper. He couldn't pass a trash can without rummaging through it. The first word the new family heard him say was "money."

But when I saw Donnie, when he was 4, the past seemed successfully buried. He had just that week asked Anita, as they were riding in the family car, "Mother, would you please play some Mozart on the radio?"

Four years later, he has grown brighter and more inquisitive. Not long ago, he asked Anita, "Why did you take me away from my mother?" To Anita's amazement, he has dredged from his memory an extremely accurate description of the woman with stringy brown hair and ragged clothes.

"I just haven't had the nerve to tell him everything," says Anita. "One day soon, he'll put it all together, and I dread it. Sometimes I think he already knows and is trying to spare us.

"Not long ago, he wanted to talk about his mother. 'I would like to go see her,' he said. When I asked him why, he said, 'I just want to tell her I love her.'"

January, 1992

THE INVISIBLE PEOPLE

He was standing as still as a wooden Indian, his face a weathered piece of walnut lined with deep crevices that had cracked open from too much exposure to rain and wind and sun. As I drew near, he tried to step from the street to the curb and, as if melting, he slowly sank into the pavement right in front of me.

He was lying there shaking and dangerously close to being struck by one of the cars streaming by the Henry Grady statue on Marietta Street. Another man and I dragged him back onto the sidewalk. I asked a passerby to go inside the *Atlanta Journal-Constitution* building to call for help.

I don't know who summoned the ambulance, but before it arrived I asked the man if he needed anything. His eyes had the distant stare of someone gazing hard into his vaguely remembered past. He said, "I want to go home."

There was no home, except in the thoughts that sometimes caught on the wind of memory and blew like scrap paper down the back alleys of his mind. Merely in the struggle to remember he was as close to home as he had been in a long time.

Atlanta's city government is considering actions that would move the homeless like this man out of sight, lest those with money in their pockets get the impression downtown Atlanta is not Disney World. But Atlanta is still Southern, and Southerners—rich or poor—are supposed to have some place to go home to.

Some people of the streets manage to spend their days in shelters; others materialize on the avenues like scruffy ghosts. A woman layered in ragged clothing pushes at the refuse of an alley trash can with slow patient prospecting. A man in a found trucker's cap tries to keep his hand still long enough to light the inch-long butt of a cigarette. A businessman hurrying to an early meeting passes without really being aware of them. At times the homeless must long to be looked at in some fleeting moment of acknowledgement that they are not invisible.

206

Within the street people there seems to be a primal instinct to live that supersedes their destitution. I look at them and wonder, what is it that keeps the human spirit alive in a body that is always too hot or too cold, a stomach that is always too hungry, a hand that clutches a bottle always too empty? What happens when they long for love and reach to touch someone with skin like peeling paint and the breath of decaying food and twice-tasted whiskey? Do they fantasize about perfume or fancy cologne?

Maybe, like the man in the street, more than anything they just want to go home. I wanted to know. One bitterly cold October, I volunteered to live among them. On a Tuesday I layered my body in old clothes, emptied my wallet of comforting credit cards and all money except $6. I simply dropped out of a world of virtual guarantees—firm beds, adequate food, regular pay and soft familiar touches in the night.

The first night a wet wind furiously swept paper scraps through the corridors of downtown and miniature whirlwinds of grit stung my eyes. About 1 a.m., in an alcove across from Grady Hospital where I had bedded down, I awoke suddenly, perhaps sensing the presence of the man who had softly reached inside my tattered coat.

As I struggled across the threshold that separates deep sleep from alertness, he ran. I could not stop shivering. I slipped inside the Grady emergency room. A policeman shook me awake and banished me to the street that seemed colder after the brief reminder of warmth.

I thought of a vent that blew warm air near the *Atlanta Journal-Constitution* building, where I worked as a writer. I spread a sheet of cardboard there. Two white men drove their van up onto the sidewalk as if to run over me. I got up, stored my cardboard in a crevice and walked hunched, hands in pockets, until the church that served grits and coffee let the street people in.

Next morning I saw a man, he may have been as old as 40, it was hard to tell. He wore a cotton shirt, a thin sport coat assembled perhaps a decade ago, and loose-fitting trousers. The cold front that moved in after the rain had congealed the morning temperature at 41. The wind had taken the chill factor lower and the night had sucked all the stored warmth from the pavement. The man was beyond the point where his fragile mind could control his shaking body. Mucus ran from his nose. He sat on his cold, red hands until The Open Door soup kitchen began serving breakfast to a small portion of Atlanta's estimated 6,000 homeless men and women. He took his bowl of grits, a single sausage patty and a cup of coffee to a concrete bench and began to eat rapidly. His shaking hands caused globs of the grits to spill from the spoon, but he was careful that the plastic bowl was always in the right place, lest a bite be wasted.

By my third night on the streets I noticed that my own hands were trembling, that my shoulders ached from lack of sleep and that my mind seemed incapable of thought more complex than anticipating the openings in the skyline where the rising sun might warm me, or remembering vaguely a breaker against the wind, some indentation in the walls of city concrete created by architects for aesthetics, not for some weary person without a home or hope.

It was not yet 8:15, but already I was thinking about lunch, soup and perhaps a sandwich and some overripe fruit at St. Luke's Episcopal Church. And in my wretchedness, I had almost forgotten that I was merely acting.

I looked for the man I had seen shivering in the cold. I wanted to leave my sweater with him. He was gone. I searched for a man named Al "Gypsy" Smith. I had met him the day before at Samaritan House, a day refuge for the homeless on Peachtree Street. I thought Al might remember the man and hold the sweater for him at the shelter, where he assisted director Joe Houston. Although Al had been in Woodruff Park early the night before during a rally for the homeless I could not find him. I found out that Al had been killed as he slept at the shelter, where he lived. Someone broke in, beat him to death.

The night of the rally, I was trying to sleep on a small piece of cardboard that fit into a corner of the entrance to the Fulton County health building. A black man, wearing a denim jacket, blue jeans and no socks, asked if he could lie down under the ragged blanket that covered me. It soon became apparent that the blanket would not work for two people and the newcomer had added an aroma of dried sweat.

"Tell you what, man, if you will let me have a little more cardboard, you can have my blanket," I said.

He readily agreed and despite a gimpy knee injured when he was knocked to the ground for trying to throw hot chili on a television reporter, he bounded happily across the street toward the state hospital, the blanket flowing from his shoulders.

The next morning, in the line for hot grits in Woodruff Park, he said it was the first night he had been warm in a week. "I be wearin' this blanket in heaven," he said. He hugged me. The blanket already stank.

Had I not relinquished the blanket voluntarily, chances are the man would have removed it with practiced hands the first time my head dropped into light sleep. On the streets at night you rest, but never sleep in deep conventional unconsciousness, for awakening is to find yourself without something you went to sleep with.

A man named Eddie told me, as we talked about dangers on the streets, that he had been robbed four times by people he knew. A couple of times he was beaten. He did not have the assailants arrested.

"They were all new to the streets," he said. "They took what they needed to survive. After they learned where to find things they stopped stealing. They just did what they had to do.

"Street people don't really do all the things we blamed for," he said. "As long as we got somethin' to eat and we warm, we not gone cause no trouble."

He waved his hands at the office buildings. "They's people in there who do things I wouldn't do, but they look down on us like we are animals. They don't know what is in my heart. There's no violence or disrespect there."

Anger and violence, nevertheless, are always either a real or implied presence among the homeless. Often that is the only means known to resolve problems. The conflicts can be as inventive and non-physical as childlike arguments that are designed as mere filler in boring days where minutes seem like years, or they can erupt as suddenly as summer lightning.

One morning in the grits line at Butler Street CME Church I accidentally stumbled into a black man in front of me.

"Excuse me," I said quickly.

His response, impacted by the way he spit out "white man," was immediate and required an anatomically impossible act on my part.

At the end of one of two long tables in the room, a man endlessly chanted an obscenity about sex organs. The man beside him told him to shut up. When he did not, the man suddenly grabbed the chanter by the throat and choked him for a few seconds before sitting back down.

A representative of The Open Door moved quickly to sooth frayed tempers and to lay out the consequences of a repeat performance. Most of the diners never missed a stroke from grits bowl to mouth.

The Open Door, directed by the Rev. Ed Loring, laid out plans for a rally of the homeless in Woodruff Park. Word circulated through the street network about the free chili and blankets to be distributed. About 200 were expected. More than 600 showed up, not all of them homeless, but rather toughs from housing projects. It was there that the dynamics of the street became exemplified in their most dangerous form.

When a van arrived with covered dishes that appeared to be more substantial than the usual Styrofoam cups of chili, a crowd pressed close. Several began shoving and using a familiar epithet. A man named Alan, who had become part of my buddy system for the night, had seen such a scene before. He moved with the quickness of an animal and bolted from the throng with a plate of nutritious food lifted high over his head. He wound up giving it to an old man who stared at it with ravenous eyes. Alan had another cup of chili instead.

I left and found a grate that was pouring lukewarm air from the side of a building. I huddled below the grate and tried to sleep. Drivers in vans and cars frequently blew their horns to frighten me and some drove toward me as if to plow me under. About midnight I gave up and went back to the park.

Just as I arrived I saw on the far side of the park a flurry of activity near the van where blankets were to be distributed. A slender man was running past the Trust Company Bank building. He was pursued by a throng.

A short man, obviously too well-fed and in too good condition to be a street person, closed the gap and tackled his prey like a lion on a wounded giraffe. Quickly the mob was on the fallen man, pummeling him with their fists and kicking him in the ribs. By the time I could get there it was over. It was said he tried to break in line.

Ed Loring stood in the middle of the crowd and said that because of the disturbance blankets would not be passed out. Many of the street people dropped their heads in shame and understanding. There were only a few protests.

I headed for the Fulton County health building where I had previously spent a night. I already had become a creature of habit. Because I gave my blanket away, my clothes by 3 a.m. were no match for the cold. I had planned to wait until 4 o'clock before playing my trump, but the discomfort dictated otherwise.

I explained to some companions how, one by one, we would drop into the emergency room at Grady, where I had discovered that street people sometimes trade confrontation with security officers for a few minutes of warmth.

This time I lasted 45 minutes before being told, "You can't sleep here. You will have to leave."

Outside the entrance a young white man approached a police officer and said, "Arrest me."

"What have you done?" asked the policeman.

"I have to get to jail somehow. I don't want to cause trouble if I don't have to, but I can't take the cold any longer."

As they talked we slipped one at a time into the room. This time we made it until 5 a.m. Food was only 2 1/2 hours away and we would stay warm if we kept moving.

Loring was still in the park the next morning, shifting his feet to maintain body heat, talking and listening with obvious compassion to knots of homeless men and a few women. The grits breakfast in the park was scheduled for 7:30. About 6, three policemen told Loring politely to have upright those sleeping on the grass and benches, before the business community began to report to work. Shortly thereafter a representative of Mayor Andy Young's office arrived to survey the scene and word spread that the mayor would appear to address the homeless.

By 8:15 the street people had been fed and Young had not appeared. They began to drift in search of sunshine or maybe a few minutes in the warm downtown Atlanta library before being discovered and dispersed.

I looked to see if a particular fast-food restaurant had opened for the day. I wanted desperately to go to the bathroom and remembered the previous night when I had gone there to urinate because there are no public restrooms on the streets of Atlanta. An employee blocked my path. "You can't use our bathrooms unless you are a customer," he said.

I felt the meanness rising inside me and sensed no great amount of regret for my anger. "You can't use this bathroom," he repeated. I replied, "Then I'll piss on your floor, and if you don't get out of my way

I'll piss on you."

He called the police. I used his bathroom quickly and ran.

After I had eluded the police, in an alley I picked up a large piece of cardboard. It would make a fine mattress for the night. Or at least until the night chill began to seep like ice water into my hips and feet, and I would be forced to con my way into a warm room or simply walk to keep from freezing.

Walking and waiting, walking and waiting; waiting for the first ray of the sun, the most believable symbol that I had somehow made it through another night on the streets.

October, 1986

*life
as
a
game*

THE MEANEST MAN OUT HERE

I have coached midget football. I have yelled at eight year olds and longed for a knife to cut out my tongue when the tears rolled softly over their round cheeks. I have scouted the opposition with modern video tape equipment and have reported with glee that the nine-year-old at right linebacker would crumble if we kept the pressure on him.

I have listened to mothers trade insults and spit venomous cliches that would blend more naturally with a backdrop of strafing planes and exploding grenades. I have known mothers who have traded the ultimate favor for special consideration for their sons. I have helped raise funds to send nine-year old all-stars to far away places and to buy trophies that left their competitive urges sated and jaded by the time they reached junior high school. I have stayed awake until 2 a.m. designing complicated football plays with the maniacal intensity of a deranged scientist.

The most memorable product of such late night brain scorchers was a play called the "27 Slide." The play was rather simple in design, but was replete with options to take advantage of the amazing instincts of our fleet halfback (every son of a coach is a fleet halfback for whom special plays must be designed to take advantage of his amazing instincts.)

Success of the famous "27 Slide" depended significantly on the ability of our nine-year-old halfback to read the defense. In other words, if the opposing end was taken wide by our wingback's block, the halfback was to slide inside; if the end played tight, the halfback was to use his speed to get outside for what we imaginatively referred to as "large chunks of real estate."

One Saturday we were playing the Packers. The Packers had a big, tough end who was stubbornly disinclined to be blocked inside or outside. He simply marked off his turf and each time the fleet halfback with amazing instincts attempted to slide either way, the big, tough end methodically reached out, lifted him off the ground and appeared to be shaking change out of the runner's pockets.

In the fourth quarter we were behind, 6-0. Not quite in desperation, but with salty beads of concern forming on my brow, I turned to Tim, who, despite his choir boy countenance, was the toughest kid in the neighborhood. "Tim," I began as I placed my arm coachingly on his shoulders. "Tim, this is the biggest game of the year for us. It won't take much to win. All we need is one guy with enough chittlins to go in and throw one good block on that end. Will you do it, Tim? Will you go in there and do it?"

Tim looked up at me, his eyes steely cold and without panic.

"No," he said.

"No?"

"You gotta be crazy, Coach. Look at the size of that guy!"

Having put the situation into perspective, Tim returned to the bench to draw stick figures in the mud that his spilled Gatorade had made.

It has been many years now since I last coached a midget football team. I had started because of my sons and I quit for the same reasons; first because of what I did TO one of my sons and second, because of what one of my sons did FOR me.

Like many a father concerned lest his son get a late start and thus be deprived of a professional career 15 years later, I allowed, even encouraged, my oldest son to strap on a tiny jock and oversized shoulder pads when he was eight years old (some start at six). I was astonished to realize that my eyes were stinging with tears when he took the first football ever laid in his belly by a quarterback and ran 64 yards for a touchdown. It turned out to be a good team and the coach was right when he told the players that if they dedicated themselves they could go unbeaten. He laid down the training rules: eat right, plenty of sleep and no missed practices. "Most of all," he said, "you have to protect yourself on the field by protecting yourself off the field." That meant no dangerous recreation such as roller skating or bike riding.

My son, developing a pattern of freak injuries that was later to be perfected in high school, was the first to wreck his bike. Wrecked it on the day of our biggest game. His shoulders were raw meat from tip to tip.

I fumed. "I can't believe you did this."

He said nothing, as I recall. He went to his room, put on his uniform and reported for the game. He played the entire contest. When the game was over his T-shirt was soaked with blood and when it was removed it peeled little pieces of flesh from the shoulders.

The next year, when he was nine, he took a blow on the elbow and it swelled to the size of a cantaloupe. But because he was a fleet-footed halfback with amazing instincts he was asked to "suck it up and play." He did. He also played a couple more games in pain. When the season ended he looked up at me with steely eyes and without panic he said, "I am not going to play this game again."

By the time the next season rolled around, he had changed his mind, as kids will do. Perhaps it was because I would not be coaching him, having decided that his younger brother should not be deprived of the same personal attention.

Amazingly, the first time his younger brother touched the football in a game, he swept right end and ran all the way for a touchdown. It won the game, 6-0. As history was later to reveal, it was the only taste of victory. Thirty-point defeats became the norm.

One Saturday we were playing the Cardinals, undefeated and un-scored upon. We had a little red-head named Bubba who was a star at no position, but would try to play anywhere he was needed. His father was of the same mold. He would lime off the field, man the yard mark-ers or carry the water bucket; anything to be involved.

Bubba was sitting on the right end of the bench as the Cardinals per-functorily marched through our defense and with ease registered their first touchdown. Bubba looked up at me. With steely eyes and without panic, he said, "Well, looks like we are gonna get clobbered again."

Suddenly he viewed his rear end going over his head from the force of a backhand to the helmet from his enraged father.

"You get up and don't ever let me hear you say anything like that again," he screamed. "We can win this game."

We, of course, were clobbered again, Bubba having, quite early, put the situation into proper perspective.

The following week at practice, I, as assistant-coach-in-charge-of-morale, decided that oratory might accomplish what plays designed to take advantage of the amazing instincts of our fleet halfback had not. I had recently discovered, in *Boys' Life*, an article by professional football player, Calvin Hill. In addition to being a player of consummate skill, Hill was deeply religious. In the article he pointed out that off the field one had to walk with God, but on the football field, it was necessary to be physical, yes, even MEAN.

At the conclusion of practice that day I gathered the squad together near the south end of the field, placing myself between the sweaty little band of losers and the anxious parents who assembled outside the chainlink fence to witness whatever evangelistic miracle was about to occur in the lives of their children.

I shared the insight of Calvin Hill and beseeched each player to dedicate himself to new pinnacles of meanness on that gridiron: every boy a Buford Pusser; every boy a Big John; every boy a Man. The air became pregnant with silence when I finished. I thought I saw a father clinch his fist in determination; and was that a hearty thumbs up from another that I caught out of the corner of my eye?"

"All right," I said as I sucked in a loud breath for effect. "I'm going to count to three and then I want to hear it. I want to hear it from every last one of you who isn't going to be a loser anymore. I want to hear it from every last one of you who thinks he's the MEANEST man out here!"

"All right. One…Two…Three…WHO'S THE MEANEST MAN OUT HERE!?"

The air was still pregnant with silence.

"All right, I'm going to ask you one more time. One…Two… Three…WHO'S THE MEANEST MAN OUT HERE!?"

The air remained still and silent as 36 little round eyeballs stared incredulously ahead.

"All right. You're going to regret this. I'm going to run you 'till your tongues hang out. You'll be doing Oklahoma drills 'till you think you are part of a demolition derby. You'll scrimmage 'till you beg for mercy. And…and that's just the best part of what is going to happen to you unless you tell me who is the MEANEST MAN out here!"

In the back row Doug, the right end, timidly raised his hand for permission to speak.

"All right, Doug. Let's have it, Baby. WHO'S THE MEANEST MAN OUT HERE!?"

He looked up at me with steely eyes and without panic he said, "You are, Coach."

Having had the situation put into perspective there was nothing to do but wait for the next game. The contest turned out to be particularly heartbreaking. With three minutes left in the game we had a chance to close the gap to 42-6 and blew it.

But at the sound of the final whistle the kids quickly congratulated the winners and then, laughing and plotting what to do for fun that day, joyously dove for the big galvanized tub with the icy Gatorade and Cokes. With unrestrained happiness they reaped the post-game rewards as parents, their faces sagging with fatigue and disappointment, gathered nearby, murmuring under their breaths.

"How can we ever win," I heard one grumble, "when the only play we have is for a coach's son to run out toward the end and get tackled?"

The Head Coach approached the grimy group of urchins as they splashed and laughed and drank of the cooling beverages, His face was taunt and red. The veins in his neck were swollen. His eyes bulged. His voice was breaking with rage.

"Just look at you!" he shouted. "Just look at you. No wonder you lose. All…all you are interested in is getting it over with and slopping up the Gatorade. You just don't care. Do you? Does anybody on this team care?"

My eight year old, who had once questioned if he were truly fast enough to be a halfback, popped the top on another cold Gatorade and slowly pivoted in his squatting position and faced the Head Coach. He looked up at him with steely eyes and without panic. With the patience of a patriarch and the wisdom of a sage, he said, "Now, Coach, I want you to know that I do care. But this ain't nothing but a game for little boys to play and enjoy."

Having had the situation put into perspective, parents silently began to gather up their muddy little warriors and trudge toward the station wagons in the dusty parking lot. I reached down and offered my son a hand and he scrambled to his feet. I knew at that precise moment that I, along with the famous "27 Slide," had retired forever.

September, 1979

PHIL NIEKRO AND ELWOOD'S BIG DAY

By the time Phil Niekro had pitched 5,404 major league innings and won 318 games he was 48 years old. AARP and The Scooter Store were already scouting the most popular pitcher in Atlanta Braves history. Laid back and fan friendly then, laid back and fan friendly now, the Braves' goodwill ambassador visits our town Monday. He comes as Rome Braves GM Mike Dunn's special guest for the annual Hot Stove celebration at The Forum.

I find it quite amusing that Phil was born on April Fools Day. What an appropriate date for a Hall of Fame pitcher whose dipsy-doodle knuckleball was the major league's ultimate magic trick for 24 years. One frustrated hitter described the experience, "...like trying to eat Jello with chop sticks."

Such entertaining quotes and anecdotes about Phil abound in baseball anthologies. But, I would like to offer you a tale I haven't seen written, one saying more about Phil's character than his accomplishments. It's a long-winding story that helps explain a gigantic jar of marbles Phil displays in the foyer of his home at Lake Lanier. Telling it may stir memories for anyone who grew up in Celanese, Pepperell or any cotton mill village where yards were not mowed so much as swept, the dirt beneath chinaberry trees broom-whisked smooth for cut throat marbles games of keepsies and ringers.

Phil grew up in Blaine, Ohio, a coal mining town where yards looked a lot like those around Rome. His neighbor and best friend was John Havlichek, a future NBA Hall of Famer. Their mutual pal was Elwood. Phil and John, as athletes usually are, were the most popular kids at school. Elwood, who was mentally challenged, was sometimes teased or, more frequently, ignored. Except by Phil and John.

Like most mill village kids, Phil never turned down a challenge at a marbles circle. He had the spirit, John and Elwood had most of the good steelies and taws. It made an effective alliance. What Phil and John knew, and most schoolmates didn't, Elwood was one heck of a

219

shooter. So, the two star athletes concocted a grand plan to elevate Elwood's status. They organized a series of marbles tournaments calculating that, with deft planning, Elwood would reach the finals. In a perfect ending to a perfect plot, Elwood did take down the two coolest guys in town. For one bright shining moment he reigned as the marbles prince of Blaine, Ohio.

Oh, about that jar loaded with multicolored taws, cat's eyes, agates, plunkers and pee wees. There's more to it than just Elwood. On Mothers Day,1994, blessed by wife Nancy and sister Phyllis, Phil agreed to manage the Colorado Silver Bullets, first all-female professional baseball team in 50 years. The ladies played all comers, in ballparks ranging from those in small towns to Candlestick in San Francisco and venerable Fenway in Boston. They even toured Taiwan.

Although the Bullets eventually played baseball with surprising skill and fervor, Phil says it took some adjustments early on. A pitcher starting her first game fired just eight pitches before signaling for a coach to visit the mound. Phil's brother Joe was the pitching coach and fearing she had hurt her arm, he trotted out to assess the problem. She said to Joe, "Next time you come out to the mound could you bring me a cup of lemonade?"

The Silver Bullets would, after a fashion, learn to play the game like men. In Albany, Georgia, summer of '97, they showed they could brawl like them. After an Americus Traveler's pitcher hit Kim Braatz-Voisard with a pitch he made the mistake of laughing at her. She balled her fists and led her bench clearing teammates on a fury-filled charge toward a bewildered Greg Dominy. A newspaper reporter noted, "She was on him like a mama dog on a pork chop."

In due time, Silver Bullets players learned the story of Phil's boyhood passion for marbles. As players sprinted out to shake the manager's hand during pregame introductions each would leave a shiny marble in his palm. It took a jar as big as the one in the foyer at Lake Lanier to hold three years' accumulation of marbles. It took a heart as big as Phil's to carry a one-day rainbow for Elwood.

January, 2011

SATCHEL MIGHT BE GAINING ON US

Frankly, I thought he might have "passed"—as Leroy (Satchel) Paige described death. That a decade had passed without a single headline about this ancient of ancients probably meant something that had been gaining on him had finally caught him.

Nevertheless, there he was in a newspaper photograph, mugging for publicity on a soon-to-be-released movie about his life. It was unnecessary to read the caption to know it was him. Purple ropes of veins hugged the contours of his bony neck. The heavy lidded eyes appeared wise and bewildered at the same time. The lips gave an impression of perpetually pursed to cool soup.

Depending on which lie one chooses, Satch would now be 74 (or 79); he doesn't look it, just as he never looked 44 (or 49) or 54 (or 59). Despite a lifelong argument with a disputin' stomach and a clinic of minor ailments, Paige has always been considered a medical marvel, a geriatric anomaly once studied in amazement by a team of international physicians. Paige even ventured, after the anatomical inquisition, "Maybe I'll live forever."

Paige, in fact, may have already lived forever. Nobody, even his Momma, has been able to pinpoint his exact age. It was once great sport to speculate about his beginning point because he was known be well past 40 (or 45) when he became an American League rookie pitcher in 1948. Nobody really cared and just settled on Satchel Paige as the greatest pitcher of all time. If not the greatest, he certainly threw the fastest ball to ever to leave a human hand. That much was agreed upon by other legendary fast ballers, such as Dizzy Dean and Bob Feller.

Long before black baseball players were allowed in the major leagues, Satch used to whip Dean, Feller and touring major leaguers as regularly as Monday wash. In one exhibition he struck out Rogers Hornsby five times. He fanned Charley Gehringer three times in a game, Jimmy Fox three times in another. In fact, perhaps the greatest baseball game ever played was not even played in the major leagues. It was a 13-inning masterpiece in 1934 in Hollywood, California. Paige was opposed by Dizzy Dean, who was coming off a 30-win season for the St. Louis Cardinals. Dizzy allowed just one run and fanned 15. Satchel shut out the Dean All-Stars and fanned 17.

There is no doubt Paige pitched more games of organized baseball than any player ever. Only 179 were consummated in the major leagues, but he pitched over 2,500 times as a professional. Most came in the old Negro Major League, Latin America, and exhibition tours in the United States. He won over 2,000 times and pitched 100 no-hitters. His promotional billboards proclaimed, in advance of his appearances, "Satchel Paige, World's Greatest Pitcher, Guaranteed To Strike Out The First Nine Men."

His assortment of pitches boggled the mind. He featured the "two-hump blooper," a tantalizing slow pitch; "the barber," a fastball designed to shave the whiskers off any batter who dared dig in too forcefully; "Little Tom," a medium fastball for ordinary hitters; "Long Tom," his terrifying fastball; and the famous "hesitation pitch," where Paige's right arm seemed to stop in mid-throw before delivering to the confused hitter.

The first pitch for which he was paid was thrown in 1926 for the Chattanooga Black Lookouts, his last was thrown 39 years later in 1965 when he shut out the Boston Red Sox for three innings-that is, if you don't count the exhibition he pitched for the Braves before the final game of the 1968 season. He retired in order Junior Gilliam, Wayne Causey, Ken Boyer, Gil Garrido, Don Drysdale and Hank Aaron.

"If they wouldn't bunt on me, I could pitch nine against them guys," he said as he pulled on a cigarette in the cool of the dressing room.

For years I had heard Clint (Scrap Iron) Courtney, who was a coach when I worked in the Braves front office, claim that when he caught Paige for the old St. Louis Browns in the early Fifties, Satch could throw seven out of ten pitches for strikes using a chewing gum wrapper as home plate. The night of the exhibition I saw him do it, despite the fact his eyesight was so bad by then his glasses looked like the bottoms of Coke bottles. His myopia was so severe that only a few nights before, when he exited Atlanta Stadium, he mistook a police car for a taxi. He squeezed his six foot, four inch, 170-pound frame into the rear seat and smiled at the policeman, "Marriott, please, driver."

Paige never got into a regular season game with the Braves, although he had been signed, ostensibly, as a player. Owner Bill Bartholomay had read in *Sports Illustrated* that Paige needed 158 days to qualify for the minimum five-year pension. He dispatched Bill Lucas to Kansas City to track down the legend and to sign him for the Braves. The following year the Braves officially designated Paige as a "trainer," although most of his healing consisted of regaling the young players with legends and lies before taking a snooze during the regular game.

Ralph Garr, naive and fresh from the Richmond farm team, would tag along after Paige like a puppy. Paige would tell Garr of the legendary black stars such as Josh Gibson and Cool Poppa Bell.

"Cool Poppa, he so fast that he turn off the light switch and be in bed before it get dark," Paige would offer as warm-up. Then Paige would discourse reverently on Gibson, who, he insisted, was the greatest long-ball hitter of all time.

"Once we was playin' the Homestead Grays in the city of Pittsburgh. (Paige would roll his large round eyes to the side to make sure his fish had the bait). Josh comes up in the last of the ninth with a man on and us a run behind. Well, he hit one. The Grays waited around and waited around, but finally the empire rules it ain't comin' down. So we win.

"The next day we was disputin' the Grays in Philadelphia when here come a ball outta the sky right into the glove of the Grays' centerfielder. The empire make the only call he could make. 'You're out, boy!' he yells at Josh, 'yesterday in Pittsburgh.'"

Paige once described himself as "…a mountain of information on hunting, expensive cars, jazz, Central American dictators, quartet singing, cameras, Kansas City real estate, Missouri River catfish, Indian maidens, stomach powders, mules and other matters."

Most of all, he was an expert on women and gave free advice to younger players.

"Love," said Paige, "is a proposition I wouldn't advise you to mess with, as regards the general run of women. You restricts yourself to one or two lady friends and you gonna be all right. But you expand to include the field and you bound to get cut up."

"Myself," he would add with dismay, "I'm a passel of scars. Oh, I seen some terrible, terrible times."

When asked, Paige sometimes admitted to being married; at others, he would deny it totally. Yet, he regularly left a ticket at the Will Call gate for "Mrs. Paige" and a different woman would pick it up each time. Bill Veeck, owner of the Cleveland Indians, once asked him about this curious phenomenon.

"Well," Satch said, "it's like this. I'm not married, but I am in great demand."

And now they are making a movie about Satchel Paige's life. I can't help but wonder if he will be playing himself. Why shouldn't he? After all, he doesn't look 74 (or 79). None other than Leroy Paige wrote the most famous recipe for long life ever composed. I'm sure he would be glad to share it again:

How To Stay Young

1. Avoid fried meats which angry up the blood.

2. If your stomach disputes you, lie down and pacify it with cool thoughts.

3. Keep the juices flowing by jangling around gently as you move.

4. Go very light on the carrying on in society. The social ramble ain't restful.

5. Avoid running at all times.

6. Don't look back. Something might be gaining on you.

September, 1980

FIELD OF GREED

When the social commentator Jacques Barzun wrote in the 1950s, "Whoever wants to know the heart and mind of America had better learn baseball," the passage probably read more like poetry than prophesy. But now it is April, 1995, and neither the month nor the game is bringing that old sense of optimism.

Instead, Barzun's words fall hard and cold, like blossoms victimized by an unseasonable frost, distressingly accurate as a modern American analogy. It is now conceivable you could be beaten, bloodied and robbed by the poor, the desperate, and the uneducated on the way to watch the selfish, the arrogant and the marginally talented perform indifferently, their wails of victimization souring in your ears. You may try to convince your son that it is still the greatest game in the world, but secretly you wish you could vote out of office the owners who tax you $25 for a molded plastic seat and $20 for cold hot dogs and warm beer and flat soft drinks in order to make enough money to stay even with fat-cat rival team owners who have no fiscal self-discipline and are so out of touch with the average American, they think every complaint can be solved with a promise of financial restraint while contemptuously elevating personal lines of revenue.

There is no simplicity left in this beautifully simple game. Only contradictions. The player who smugly allows union representatives to negotiate the most astounding benefits in the history of collective bargaining sees nothing unseemly about hiring an agent to finagle an individual contract that would embarrass evan a rock star and mystify the most lavishly compensated corporate CEO. Amazingly, baseball has managed to fashion an order in which the most indulgent aspects of socialism and capitalism have melded into a "have your cake and eat it too" system. It would be even easier to vilify the players were it not for their employers, who, without extremism on the part of the athletes, would probably opt for something resembling benevolent despotism, or as it was called in the old days, the plantation.

Just as there is no simplicity remaining, there is no innocence. Mayo Smith, a former major league manager, observed of the players of his era, "Open up a ballplayer's head and you know what you'd find? A lot of little broads and a jazz band." Open up a ballplayer's head today and you would find a lot of little accountants and his own record label.

And because baseball has lost its simplicity and its innocence, it has lost more than just its character. It has lost its characters. Once it was the best of all games because it did not suffer from the "hurrying sickness" that infects other sports vulnerable to a ticking clock. There was a time when a major league baseball clubhouse was like a little town of its own, with its drunks and fighters, its spendthrifts and tightwads, its soft hearts and soft-heads. There were those who kept the peace and those who disrupted it. And each knew each.

All that was back when players arrived at the clubhouse more than 30 minutes before game time because there was nowhere else they would rather be, nobody else they would rather be with. I think that is why the standard of play on the field was so superior to that of today. Each knew each. And it was reflected in the beautifully sweaty synchronization of their work/play.

You know what I really miss? I miss the stories. There are no great stories in baseball anymore. Only sound bites, even in the newspaper. The reporters who used to spend time in the clubhouse and in the dugout discovering those stories are now somewhere else doing their own radio shows, infinitely more interested in improving their inflection than their inspection of the clubhouse culture.

The malapropisms of that jester Casey Stengel would go unrecorded today. No more dugout soliloquies, for there would be no appreciative audience of writers scribbling furiously on their notepads. No "Alright, everyone line up alphabetically according to height." No "Being with a woman all night never hurt no professional baseball player. It's staying up all night looking for a woman that does him in." No "The secret of managing is to keep the guys who hate you away from the guys who are undecided." No Casey Stengel, in fact. The players would not allow a genius masquerading as a clown to lead them.

That is the particularly disgusting thing about baseball, as it is in the country per se, this loss of respect for authority figures. Between the pushing of the owners and the pulling of the players, the manager has become little more than a wishbone.

"The worst thing," said former manager Gene Mauch, "is the day you realize you want to win more than your players do."

It is April, 1995. I look at baseball with more cynicism than I ever thought possible. I look at baseball and, just as Barzun foretold, I understand the heart and mind of America.

April, 1995

WORLD'S SMALLEST GIANT

O n my first road trip after joining the Atlanta Braves as publicist in 1966, Donald Davidson clearly established the rules.

"Walburn, you room with me," Donald announced. "I need somebody who can reach the bleeping towels when I take a shower."

I was the tallest roommate he had ever had and all of a sudden he felt secure. As traveling secretary for the Braves, he had had his problems with hotels. They were just not built for a man 48 inches tall, whose job was to move an army of baseball players smoothly and efficiently all over the United States.

I've been told that long ago in Cincinnati, when the team arrived at two in the morning at the Netherland Hilton, Donald entered the same elevator as pitchers Warren Spahn and Lew Burdette, who were on the 11th floor. Donald was on the 26th. When the lift stopped at 11, the diminutive traveling secretary told the players to punch 26.

"Punch it yourself," Spahn said as he and Burdette exited laughing. Donald was forced to retreat to the lobby and wait impatiently for a bellboy to punch 26. He solved that problem, as he did many others, by moving the team. I lost count at 25 the number of hotels he vacated in a snit. Once in Tampa during spring training, he moved us in the middle of the night. Henry Aaron said that if we had been singing, it would have looked like a civil rights march.

Donald was born with the temper of a Doberman and a sense of being big. He used to wander into our room at about three or four in the morning after half dozen Cutty's and water and, as a matter of routine, thrust his stubby, muscular arms under the mattress and dump me on the floor just for fun. That finally ended one night in Pittsburgh when, in uncontrollable rage, I tried to lock him inside his own suitcase.

He was not above an old-fashioned brawl. Before a Braves exhibition game in Sarasota, Dodger general manager Buzzie Bavasi took aside the keeper of the press gate and warned him that a midget from Ringling

Brothers circus had fake baseball credentials and would try to crash the game.

"Aha," said the elderly attendant when Davidson strolled up. "I know all about you and you ain't getting in."

If Donald didn't invent profanity, he at least elevated it to an art form, and he verbally pummeled the old gatekeeper. Exasperated, the guard lashed out and knocked off Donald's glasses. Donald kicked him on the shins. Bavasi and the Braves' Birdie Tebbetts, who had been hiding behind a post, rushed out and grabbed the furious old man, who then took a swing at Tebbetts.

"Thank God you picked on an 80-year-old man," Tebbetts said. "I might have gotten killed."

It might be successfully argued that Donald Davidson is the most popular non-player in the history of the game. He wasn't even 10 when he first became a part of the old Boston Braves. He was involved in a skirmish in front of the ball park when catcher Ray Mueller, seeing that he was the smallest kid in the fray, rescued him and took him around for autographs. Manager Bill McKechnie allowed him to sit on the bench during the game, which the Braves won. From that day until he finished high school, Donald was an errand boy and mascot, not only for the Braves, but for the Red Sox.

He has been personal friends with the legends of the game, from Babe Ruth to Henry Aaron. But it is among nonplaying personnel—writers, officials and the like—that he is a legend. For years, Room 129 at the Ramada Inn in West Palm Beach, where the good times rolled, was the highlight of every visit to the Braves' camp.

I suppose it was inevitable that an owner with an ego the size of Ted Turner's would, as one of his first irrational acts after buying the Braves, fire Donald. It may be the biggest heart I've ever seen broken.

Donald works for the Houston Astros now, and he's had an operation on his throat that has caused Cutty Sark stock to sink to an all-time low. I don't know how many more years he plans to give to the game, but I have a suggestion for the writers who voted him 1984's King of Baseball.

In the 1940s, Eddie Gaedel was the only midget ever to go to bat in the major leagues. That was a joke, but this is not. Donald Davidson deserves to be in Cooperstown's Hall of Fame. Nobody has ever given the game more of himself, and God knows, he won't take up much room.

April, 1985

FULL MOONS AND FOOTBALL

On Thursday and Friday nights my anxiety level rises. From my home in the valley I look toward Johns Mountain where my friend lives. If I should spot torch-wielding mobs, football team logos reflecting from trucker caps in the firelight, I could telephone Norman Arey and warn him.

Norman's sports column appears in the *Rome News-Tribune* on Thursdays and Fridays. The effect is similar to that of a full moon on werewolves. It causes fangs to lengthen and hair to sprout on the knuckles of college football fans, the level of their ferocity relative to how badly he has wounded their favorite team.

Writers of strong opinions usually divide their readers into just two camps: 1) those who hate them and 2) those who haven't quite made up their mind; people tend to vilify what they don't understand. And I would have to say, based on some 45 years of friendship, Norman Arey is misunderstood.

Movie directors tell us that villains, by definition, "must be a thing of power, must be wicked enough to excite our aversion, strong enough to arouse fear, but human enough to awaken some transient gleam of sympathy." As to the sympathetic aspect, to see Norman's sensitivity to cultural inequities find release in a colicky sports column, is to wonder how a normally gentle man conjures up enough motiveless malignancy to biweekly fill readers' hearts with rage.

This is not to say he is Floyd County's version of St. Francis of Assisi, repairing the broken wings of songbirds and cooking nutritious meals for shut-ins. But neither is he the equivalent of Austin Powers' nemesis, Dr. Evil. He does not sit atop Johns Mountain stroking Mr. Bigglesworth the cat while composing malevolent insults. Granted he manages to infuriate Georgia Bulldogs, but he is highly thought of by Stray Dogs. Especially Molly, whose worship inspires Norman toward becoming the kind of man Molly thinks he is. Stray dogs instinctively smell out a soft heart and I side with Molly's appraisal.

Some fans don't really know Norman except by his opinions. Nevertheless, they are not shy about painting him as a bad guy. His response is to hand his critics a paint brush and telling them to paint away. Most intelligent readers understand that sports columnists by job description are "pot stirrers," although foe and friend alike sometimes substitute another word for "pot" when referring to Norman's observations. It only serves to amuse him when he sees neck arteries pulsating.

Peg Arey isn't quite as entertained by those who respond psychotically to Norman's football columns. Friends restrained her when her husband was accosted by a belligerent customer at Schroeder's on Broad. I quote from Norman's account of the encounter.

"A middle-aged guy came up and said, 'I'm an Auburn fan, but lots of my friends hate your guts.'

"Hate my guts?"

'Yeah, and you bring it on yourself by writing all that bad stuff about Georgia.'"

Although I am a Dawg fan, I do not react passionately to Norman's observations, having long ago differentiated the importance between football and say, cancer. I respect that he was born with a strong opinion gene and can no more refrain from pontificating than can the Pope. That includes his assertiveness in the arena where I am more comfortable and moderately sensitive, syntax and grammar.

More than once he has publicly chastised me for saying I "loaned" a book instead of "lent" one although Mr. Webster points out either is acceptable. Except by Norman. His grammar spankings have been described by Catholic acquaintances as very Sister Mary Katherine-like in their sting.

On a boys-only trip that included noted authors, Terry Kay and Robert Coram, we were strolling down the streets of Caernarfon, Wales and Norman had commenced to advise us on this or that when a giant sea gull soared overhead.

The sea gull dumped a load of you-know-what directly on top of Norman's head. It's volume was such we first thought a housemaid had emptied a chamber pot from an open window. Although Norman might have suspected his companions had managed to rent a trained sea gull, in my memory of the event I heard the housemaid shout immediately after the bomb exploded, "Go, you Hairy Dawgs! Woof Woof!"

August, 2013

REGARDING HENRY AARON

He is easier to love as a legend than he was as Henry Louis Aaron, No. 44. Or so it seems. He's just as black as he ever was. He still speaks his mind, unafraid to jar someone's consciousness, even stoke the fires of anger. But even when, as a result, he receives a letter of disagreement, most of them don't open with Dear Nigger, anymore.

Yes, definitely. He must be easier to love now. Back then, back even on the night he hit his 715th home run in 1974, the night he broke Babe Ruth's sacrosanct record for home runs, why, the lordly commissioner of baseball attended a dinner in Cleveland as if nothing special was happening in Atlanta. The year before, when he slammed his 3,000th hit and donated the ball to the Hall of Fame, the shrine stored it in a back room instead of putting it on display.

It's easier—let's say acceptable—to adore him now. In the early days of the Braves in Atlanta, he wasn't even the most popular player on his own team. But just a few years ago a poll of young people revealed him to be second in popularity only to Michael Jordan as an American athlete. The 715th homer has been voted the greatest moment in baseball history. Hank Aaron Drive runs past the Braves' stadium, past the statue of Henry Louis Aaron in the plaza. Just two months ago, it cost the rich and famous a $500-a-plate charitable donation to eat dinner in honor of Aaron's 65th birthday. President Clinton was there. This year Major League Baseball is dedicating the entire season, the 25th anniversary of The Homer, to Hank Aaron. And on his birthday, Major League Baseball announced the creation of the Hank Aaron Award, to be presented each year to baseball's best hitter.

Ah, all that feels so good. Anniversary tributes and monuments are such nice ways to salve our consciences. These latter-day love fests are like giant erasers. Just erase the bad stuff from your memories, Hank, and we'll do the same. Come on, Hank. *Think about it.*

Think about it. Think about it. Think about it....

The kid was carrying a little duffel bag and wearing a leather jacket

234

when he knocked on the clubhouse door at the Milwaukee Braves spring training camp in Bradenton, Fla., in 1953. Joe Taylor, the clubhouse attendant, opened the door and after telling the kid to stay right where he was, went looking for the manager, Charlie Grimm. "There's a black boy out there who wants in," Taylor said to Grimm. "Says his name is Aaron." Grimm ran his finger down a list and said, "He's on the roster, let him in." Grimm took an immediate liking to the kid. He nicknamed him "Stepin Fetchit," the stage name of a shuffling, grinning Negro comedian, and the press obligingly quoted the boss man in the newspapers. Stepin Fetchit! Whoa, slap yo' knee!

Twenty-one years later, at 9:03 p.m. on a Monday in April of 1974, I look at my watch, as I had each time Henry Aaron came to bat that year, having the idea of benchmarking the exact moment of sports history. After checking my watch, I look back at the field as Henry Aaron leaves the on-deck circle at Atlanta Stadium and approaches home plate in a routine that seemed never to vary: two bats in his left hand, the blue batting helmet with the swoop of white from bill to crest in his right. Dropping one bat to the ground for the batboy to retrieve, he balances the 34-ounce Louisville Slugger against a thigh and uses both hands to place the helmet on his head. With characteristic economy of motion that some critics have consistently, maddeningly mistaken for nonchalance, he settles comfortably in the batter's box, hands held high and away from his body.

The Dodgers' pitcher, Al Downing, has already walked Aaron once without a swing. This time the first pitch bounces in the dirt. There are two Braves on base and the Dodgers lead 3-1, so Downing decides to gamble with a fastball rather than risk loading the bases with another base on balls. A split second after the decision there is a cracking sound as sharp as a rifle report and stunningly, in a moment to be recollected years later as a blurred mosaic in my mind, Henry Aaron becomes the greatest home-run hitter in major league history.

As he circles the bases with the same casual gait he's used 714 times before, nearly 54,000 of us rise from our seats like a giant ocean wave churned by a sudden gust of wind. But in that muzzy mosaic of memory I cannot honestly rid myself of the feeling that we were cheering the event more than the man.

I did not know—WE did not know then—that we admired him but

did not love him, and just how much he needed—no, deserved—that love. Another 24 years passed before I, at last, understood.

On September 8 of last year I was watching television when Mark McGwire hit his 62nd home run, breaking Roger Maris' single-season record. Oh, how America loved McGwire that night. He blew kisses to heaven and you could almost sense that God was blowing one back. McGwire leapt into the stands to hug the family of the man whose record he had broken. They wept and embraced him. The pudgy, cherubic son of Mark McGwire was enveloped by his father's blacksmith arms, and on television, with all the country dabbing moisture from their eyes, they shared a scene for the ages.

In a coincidence of scheduling, McGuire's St. Louis Cardinals were playing the Chicago Cubs. Sammy Sosa, the Cub right fielder, was almost lock step with McGwire in a dual quest to break Maris' record. He rushed in from right field to embrace his opponent and to blow his own kisses and to thump his heart in a symbol of unity—Sammy Sosa, dark as midnight, and Mark McGwire, red hair and freckles dotting the landscape of his pale white skin. Sociologically, it had everything that America wants to believe about itself.

Hank Aaron was also watching television that night. One day not long ago he and I sat in his office overlooking Turner Field, a stadium many think should bear his name. We talked about our feelings as we sat in separate living rooms watching the same event. As public relations director of the Braves from 1966 to 1972, I had seen hundreds of Hank's homers, including historically significant numbers 500, 700, 714 and 715, his first all-star homer in Detroit and even his landmark 3,000th hit. As I watched McGwire almost explode with joy, I understood the difference between then and now, and I thought, What a shame it couldn't have been that way for Hank.

As we sat in his office, Hank took a deep breath and his eyes rolled back in memory. He almost echoed my own thoughts. "You know, as I watched, I was really excited for the fans, for baseball and for McGwire. And I said to myself, if just a little bit of that had happened for me, how glorifying that would have been." But what really got to him as he watched was the boy hugging his father. He averted his eyes for a moment, as if some spectral memory was dragging heavy chains past the plate glass windows overlooking left field. "It's too bad my kids couldn't have enjoyed it like that," he said.

His young children weren't batboys for Hank's 715th home run. Only a few weeks earlier there had been a false report that his daughter, Gaile, had been kidnapped from Fisk University in Tennessee. Hank, himself, was accompanied to and from the ball park by Calvin Wardlaw, a policeman assigned to his protection after he began to receive countless death threats. How does a performer give himself to his fans, not knowing which of them might be a sniper? And it would have been a tough thing to do, this smiling, this blowing of kisses, for a man who had been reading his mail:

> Dear Nigger,
> You can hit all dem home runs over dem short fences, but you can't take dat black off yo face.

> Dear Nigger Scum,
> Niggers, Jews, Yankees, Hippies, Nigger Lovers are the scum of the Earth. Niggers are animals, not humans. Niggers do not have souls because they are animals, have strong backs and weak minds…You niggers are no good, sorry, dirty as cockroaches and a dead nigger is a good nigger.

> Dear Hank Aaron,
> Retire or die! The Atlanta Braves will be moving around the country and I'll move with them…You will die in one of those games. I'll shoot you in one of them. Will I sneak a rifle into the upper deck or a .45 in the bleachers? I don't know yet. But you know you will die unless you retire!

The U.S. Post Office estimated that Hank received 930,000 pieces of mail that year. Hank admits most of it was kind. But hundreds of the letters were not. Hank keeps them all in boxes in the attic of his home. As Jim Auchmutey wrote in 1996, "The hate mail, the death threats, the racial slurs, they're all there, boxed up like toxic waste. . . . Billye Aaron has read about how her husband goes up in the attic and digs out those letters and picks at the psychic wounds he suffered as a black man threatening a white man's legacy.…"

Sometimes over the years when I would read a comment by Hank in which he attached a racial spin to some current event, I would think, why can't he just let it go? As late as last year he voiced displeasure on ESPN's Up Close that a *USA Today* poll indicated that 75 percent of baseball fans wanted McGwire to break the record rather than Sosa. McGwire is American, Sosa from the Dominican Republic, but Hank saw it more black and white than nationalistic.

I had read about Hank's attic more than once and with each comment the attic became more metaphorical. I must admit that I approached our meeting apprehensive that I would be visiting someone who had grown into an angry old firebrand. Instead, the first sound on my tape recorder is a booming laugh that was an instant reminder of the young Henry Aaron's laugh, a laugh full of teeth and tongue and dancing eyes. Hank had just hung up the phone after talking to a lady at the Social Security office. His face, looser, rounder now, tightened with laughter as he noted, "That sure puts a lot of things in perspective."

Perhaps, in its simplest terms, Hank Aaron has achieved, if not peace of mind in his 65th year, at least an understanding of the difference between ignorance and hatred. And if he has not developed a tolerance for either, he has apparently adopted a philosophy that allows him to deal with both. Where once he blamed the South for the hate mail in 1973 and 1974, he now acknowledges that most of it came from other parts of the country, primarily the East and Midwest. Perhaps it was the stereotype of the South that claimed his anger. More accurately, how the South's history epitomized the hatred that he felt was levied specifically at him. After all, he was born black and raised in the South. He never needed to get the darker side of Southern history out of a book. But now he knows it wasn't the South per se, the South exclusively.

Where once he grew colicky over the seeming lack of respect for his accomplishments by the institutions of professional baseball, he lowers his voice almost to a whisper and runs a hand across his gray-flecked hair and says how honored he is that Major League Baseball is dedicating the 1999 season to Hank Aaron, a celebration of the 25th anniversary of home run 715. The only other player similarly honored is Jackie Robinson, the pioneer who broke the color barrier in 1947.

Where once Hank detested old-time, cigar-chomping sportswriters who seemed to view him as an intruder in the record books, he says now that he is grateful to the media who voted home run 715 the greatest moment in American sports history. And he thinks that maybe the antagonism he perceived in the old guard press wasn't exclusively racial. "Many of the writers in those old cities like New York and Cleveland and Chicago were old enough to have actually seen Babe Ruth play. I think that when you took Babe Ruth away from them you were taking away part of their own history, you know. If they gave up Ruth they gave up part of themselves."

Perhaps it simply took a new generation of media to put things in perspective, to look at the record as an athletic achievement rather than a social one, a perspective that, by his own admission, has been difficult.

And if he is not exactly reaching out, he is, at last, allowing us to reach in.

Truth is, Hank Aaron had, maybe has, every reason to be bitter. And although his emotions have evolved healthily, there are facts that can never be entirely expunged from his psyche.

His personal experiences alone would crowd the pages of an anthology of bigotry. In Aaron's spellbinding autobiography *I Had a Hammer*, his first wife, Barbara, tells of their first year in Atlanta: "We'd sit in the stands and hear Aaron being called 'nigger' and `jigaboo.' One time a guy sitting behind me was yelling about 'nigger' this and 'nigger' that. I didn't say anything, but I went out to get a hamburger and made sure I put some extra mustard on it. The next time that guy said 'nigger,' I turned around and put that hamburger right in his face."

As bad as many aspects of the major league experience were, they paled compared to what he had endured in the minor leagues. Not much is made of this part of Aaron's history. While Jackie Robinson is rightly credited with breaking the color barrier in major league baseball, he really integrated only parts of the country—big league baseball had not ventured farther south than St. Louis and Cincinnati when Robinson began playing in 1947. When Aaron was assigned to the Jacksonville Braves in 1953, he and Felix Mantilla and Horace Garner reported to a city that only six years before had canceled an exhibition game involving the Dodgers rather than permit Jackie Robinson to play on city-owned property. Such was not unusual in Southern cities

—in Birmingham, whites and blacks were forbidden by law to even play dominoes or checkers together.

Memories of that time haven't blurred and are vividly recounted in his autobiography. A guard who thought a black kid was trying to sneak into the Braves' minor league training camp barracks in Waycross shot at him. In Augusta, Garner had to ask the umpire to plead with fans in the right field stands to stop pelting him with rocks. Once, when Mantilla charged toward a white pitcher who had been trying to bean him with fastballs, Garner ran and tackled him, whispering in his ear, "You dumb son of a bitch! I know you don't speak much English, but hear what I'm telling you. You're gonna get us all killed."

Someone would get a big laugh from the crowd in almost every Sally League stadium by tossing a black cat onto the field. Back in their rooms Aaron and Garner would compare insults they had heard, such as, "The big nigger (Garner), he's got to mow the owner's lawn on Saturday. Aaron's got to feed his hogs," and "Hey, nigger, why you running? There's no watermelon out there." In one game Garner chased a foul ball at full tilt and his momentum carried him into the crowd. A little white boy was in his way. Rather than run over him Garner scooped him up in his arms at full speed. The boy's mother became hysterical, screaming, "My God! That nigger's running away with my baby!"

When the Jacksonville team traveled, the black players couldn't eat in restaurants. They picked up sacks of groceries whenever they spotted a store along the roadside. When they arrived in one of the other league cities the bus would grow quiet as all the white players exited for their hotel. Then the bus would take Aaron and Garner and Mantilla to some private home in "colored town." Sometimes it was a week before they could wash their clothes. Manager Ben Geraghty, a white man with a sad face and a hunger for liquor—a man Aaron maintains is the best manager he ever played for—would leave the hotel and come over and drink beer with the black players on their side of town. Aaron has never forgotten this simple, kind gesture.

Those events were reality. Time and social changes have dealt with reality in ways both legal and attitudinal. But as we talked in Hank's Turner Field office, it was obvious that he is still mystified about certain aspects of unreality, certain themes that take on a life of their own within the media and that through repetition are regarded as history.

Because Hank was black—its own stimulus for thoughtless indignities—and so graceful he seemed never to be burning an extra calorie, even writers who meant to compliment him seemed to always extend his real name with deprecating adjectives: Slow-talking Henry Aaron. Uncomplicated Henry Aaron. Anecdotes about his "natural ability" accumulated by the scores. The legend he still hates is the one where he steps into the batter's box during the World Series and the Yankees' catcher, Yogi Berra, looks up and says, "Hey, Hank, you holding the label on the bat wrong." Aaron supposedly replies, "I didn't come up here to read."

"Stuff like that never happened, but after a while you realize you are never going to set the record straight and you just live with it," he told me. "Natural ability" had become, in his mind, code words for "otherwise, dumb."

"They wrote so often about me having 'natural ability,' as if thinking or hard work was never a part of my game," he said. "Well, there's no such thing as a dumb hitter. You have to study things like what a pitcher likes to throw in a certain situation, learn to recognize the pitch from its release point, know what pitcher will get impatient and throw one down the middle if you wait him out.

"I've always thought the mark of a smart ball player is what he does first-to-third as a base runner and what he allows to develop with the other team's base runners when he is on defense."

In all the years I watched Aaron play, I never saw him get thrown out going first to third on a batted ball. I never saw him misjudge whether to stretch a single into a double. I never saw him throw to the wrong base or miss the cutoff man when on defense.

It was his grace, ironically, that damned him in the eyes of the unsophisticated. We used to say that he was so smooth he could steal second base and appear to walk all the way. Bob Hope, who succeeded me as public relations director, reminded me of a particular game with the Cincinnati Reds that illustrates the point. "I forget the exact year," said Bob, "but we were playing the Reds and both Aaron and Pete Rose were playing right field. Somebody hit a foul ball down toward the bullpen and Rose flew over there, hat flying, long hair bouncing and he ran full speed into the fence and tumbled over it trying to catch the

ball. The crowd just went crazy even though Rose missed it. A few innings later one of the Reds hit a foul ball to the exact same spot. Hank
glided over, just reached over the fence and caught the ball. The crowd
applauded politely because he made it look so easy."

Despite his accomplishments, Aaron never felt connected to the fans
of Atlanta. He was not an object of affection in his playing days, like
Mickey Mantle, Rose or Willie Mays. Hell, he wasn't even as popular
with Atlanta fans as Mack Jones or Rico Carty, and it perplexed him.
Jones was an outfielder raised in Atlanta, a modest talent with a major-
league mouth. Carty, who called himself "The Beeg Boy," never met a
reporter he didn't like and few he couldn't charm. Hank's shyness—he
dressed quickly after games and seldom offered a memorable remark
relative to the outcome—was interpreted as arrogance and lack of respect by some of the press. The fans, as enamored of Carty as the press
was, responded to his toothy smile and friendly waves of acknowledg-
ment when he trotted out to position in left field.

If most of his teammates were merely irritated by Carty, Hank
loathed him. He considered Carty a racist. Carty was as black as Gunga
Din, so black we couldn't photograph him in front of a dark background lest it appear to be a picture of a uniform with eyes and teeth.
Yet, Carty was wont to call the American black players "niggers." One
night on a flight to Los Angeles, Aaron heard Carty call him "a black
slick." Carty had been a boxer in the Dominican Republic, but Aaron
was all over him. Hank took a swing, missed and his fist put a hole in
the luggage rack. Neither Hank nor Carty was hurt, but pitcher Pat
Jarvis had his shirt ripped off him trying to break it up.

Truth is, the fans might have showered Aaron with affection that
exceeded what was bestowed on The Beeg Boy or any other Brave had
they only known how to reach him. At times he seemed impenetrable.
An aura of wariness surrounded him. His shoulders would noticeably
stiffen when a great play compelled of him the obligatory acknowledg-
ment of spectator applause. He was not a blower of kisses, a thumper
of heart, a pointer to heaven sharing credit with Somebody-Up-There.
A quick tip of the hat was his most explosive response. Mostly he was
polite and sincere during a post-game interview, but just slip and ask
a stupid question, and his eyes alone could level the room like a pan-
handle tornado. Reporters made to feel stupid or off limits don't often

write the kind of endearing copy that attracts the affection of fans. And Hank's straightforward answers to the press' questions about racial matters positioned him in a way that his reserved personality couldn't override.

"Where Hank got branded a certain way," said Hope, "is that if you asked him a question—and it's still true today—he'd give you an honest answer. It's not so much that he goes seeking an audience for his views, but if a reporter asks him something he'll give his viewpoint. Then the next day it always comes out like he was the one to bring it up."

There have been those who insist that Hank's second wife, Billye, widow of civil rights activist Rev. Sam Williams, turned him into a caviler, a raiser of trivial and unnecessary objections on racial themes. Actually, Hank had been outspoken even in minor league days; but without benefit of a national audience it went virtually unnoticed. The first national exposure for his views came in 1966, the year the Braves moved to Atlanta. After a day game in Chicago, he went to dinner with Roscoe Harrison, a reporter from *Jet* magazine. And, in answer to questions, Hank listed the ways baseball discriminated against blacks. Jet shelved its planned cover and replaced it with one that read, HANK AARON BLASTS RACISM IN BASEBALL. Shortly afterward a black former star, Monte Irvin, was named to a newly created position in the commissioner's office. But far from musing over the connection, coincidental or not, reporters were thereafter on point like bird dogs for any comment from Aaron that dealt with a racial theme.

The odd combination of shyness and honesty was confusing. As a result, fans generally didn't feel ownership of Aaron as a hero. To them he was a mythical mystery, to be observed with awe, but seemingly without heart-to-heart connection. Yet there were times when, if they could not adore Aaron, they at least moved him with their respect. In 1973 Aaron was closing fast on Ruth's record. Other than Maris' 61 homers in 1961, there hadn't been a major record broken in baseball in decades. There was no blueprint for how fans were supposed to react. There was no ESPN, no CNN, nothing to stimulate the hoopla. Atlanta, without the pro sports heritage of northern cities, was without a behavioral road map. If Atlanta was giddy over Aaron's move on history, they displayed it with almost British reserve. On the night

Hank hit No. 711, just three away from Ruth, he played before 1,362 fans, the smallest crowd in Atlanta Braves history. Hank was angry and exhausted. The pressure, the media attention, the death threats, the hate mail had been overwhelming. His thoughts and his emotions were scrambled. He didn't understand the lack of fan interest—even if the Braves were a fifth place team.

In the next to the final game of the season, Hank hit home run number 713. Suddenly, it dawned even on Atlantans that something memorable was afoot. They packed the stadium for the season finale against Houston.

Aaron got three hits in the final game, but no homers. Feeling the weight of self-perceived failure to achieve his goal, he took the field to start the ninth inning with shoulders slightly drooping, his eyes on the ground. As he trotted out to his position, nearly 40,000 people from the city too busy to love Hank Aaron rose and cheered so long it seemed that umpires would never be able to restart the game. Even today, as he remembers it, he is moved.

Aaron has never been one to ignore gestures, big or small, kind or cruel, whether an unanticipated warm accolade from the fans, a beer with his manager on the other side of town, or a cold shoulder. He doesn't forget the night of his 500th home run in 1968. The great Willie Mays was playing center field for that game's opponent, San Francisco. Willie had already hit his 500th home run and we asked him to have his photo made with Aaron. Willie refused. Superstars in those days didn't gladly share their turf. There was no kissy-kissy quid pro quo when it came to superstardom.

Hank was equally a protectionist. Pride was the basis of his long-term feud with Milo Hamilton, then lead broadcaster for the Braves. It all started when Milo put his foot in his golden mouth in 1967 by declaring that the Pittsburgh Pirates' Roberto Clemente was baseball's premier right fielder. We were at a Braves 400 Club luncheon when it happened. The visiting Pirates were guests of the club. Milo introduced Clemente and said that when the annual All-Star Game came around, Aaron had to play left field to make room for the flamboyant Clemente in right. To the contrary, Aaron had actually received the most votes of any outfielder in All-Star balloting. He was furious over the remarks. The next day Aaron went four-for-four with a pair of two-run homers and threw out Clemente, a spectacular base runner, trying to go from first to third on a single.

In the post-game interview he said, "When you're No. 2, you have to try harder."

The closer he came to Ruth's record, the angrier Aaron seemed to grow with everyone—the fans, the commissioner of baseball, Bowie Kuhn, even the Hall of Fame. After donating the ball used for his 3,000th hit to the hall—at their request—his pride was thunderstruck when they put it in a back room instead of displaying it immediately. And at the start of the 1974 season, he became the focus of a scorching controversy involving Kuhn.

Despite Aaron's growing antagonism toward Atlanta fans, Braves management thought it best, especially for the club's bottom line, for Aaron to break the record at home. Braves manager Eddie Mathews announced he would not play Aaron when the season opened in Cincinnati. Commissioner Kuhn intervened and ordered Mathews to play his star.

It appeared that the controversy might suddenly become moot. Tornadoes had destroyed much of the Cincinnati area the day before and weather at game time was ominous. Nevertheless, 52,154 fans packed the stadium. In the top of the first inning, with the count three balls and one strike, the Reds' Jack Billingham threw a sinking fast ball that didn't sink. The crack of the bat against the ball was almost like a movie sound effect, so sharp and penetrating it was to the ear. The ball jumped off Aaron's bat like a tee shot and just like that, Henry Louis Aaron was lock step with the ghost of George Herman Ruth. It was the first time in his career he had hit a home run on opening day. NBC television interrupted Another World to show the historic moment, prompting soap opera fans to jam the Braves' telephone lines with protests.

Commissioner Kuhn stepped in again and threatened to fine, even suspend Mathews if he did not play Aaron in the final game of the series, though Hank was still receiving death threats. On a Sunday, in Cincy, Hank played, but struck out and failed to get a hit.

Monday night in Atlanta, damp and overcast, was meteorologically discouraging to the prospects of a home run. As usual, Atlanta fans were waiting until the last minute and the Braves had not sold out the park until one hour before the 7:35 p.m. starting time. Ordinarily, that would have precluded a local telecast, but NBC, breaking precedent, waived the rule and allowed the game to be viewed in Atlanta. Commissioner Kuhn was not there. He said he had a dinner to go to in Cleveland.

At 9:03, I look at my watch. Hank enters the batter's box. The first pitch arrives, a fastball in the dirt.

I look again at 9:07. Four minutes that seem hours.

Aaron twitches slightly as Downing releases a fastball. His famous sinewy wrists whip a 34-ounce Louisville Slugger through the strike zone, following the violent torque of his hips. The rifle shot report of solid contact is familiar, but startling. The ball streaks away on a line and, at first, appears to be catch-able. Dodger left fielder Bill Buckner crouches at the base of the chain link fence, ready to leap. He jumps, but the ball flies over his head.

It is over.

What then should, could Atlanta professional baseball…America… have done? No ticker tape parades followed. No million-dollar auctions for the ball. No elaborate ceremonies presided over by the commissioner. It wasn't even the lead story in the next day's *Atlanta Constitution*. It happened. Then it was as if it had never happened at all.

The Braves didn't even bring Aaron back for another season, trading him to Milwaukee for two obscure players. The chief operating officer of the Braves, Dan Donahue, said Aaron, with a salary of $200,000, was making too much money for a player past his prime. The next spring, a preseason game against Aaron's new team was cancelled for lack of interest. After two years and 22 more homers in Milwaukee, Aaron retired with a total of 755 home runs. By then Ted Turner had bought the Braves, and there was opposition inside the organization over his plan to bring Hank into the front office. Over protests, he hired a living legend for just $50,000 a year.

Perhaps it has taken all the years to gain true perspective on Henry Aaron, and on the times. Author J. Hudson Couch had part of it right in his history of the Braves. He said that Hank Aaron was a man who played the game of baseball so well and so completely that he almost took the excitement out of watching him do it. He drove himself year after year in pursuit of an excellence even he couldn't define. "But if there is one thing that Henry Aaron accomplished, it was to somehow be able to resist all the things that try to force a man to lose hold of his dream."

Yes, perhaps it has taken all the years for us to understand what Hank Aaron understood all along. He was a black man who had broken a white man's record. And without even meaning to, he had told America more about itself than it wanted to know.

Thousands of words have since been written about the night of 715. But as the 25th anniversary, April 8, 1999, nears, I think my old sports writing colleague, Charlie Roberts, captured the most poignant summary of all. After the game he cornered Hank's dad, Herbert Aaron, and said, "Now everybody will be chasing Hank instead of the other way around. There will be fans who will be pulling for someone to break his record. How do you think Hank will deal with that?"

It was then that Herbert Aaron told Charlie about the fox.

The fox had been running from the dogs all night and finally, as he ran to the top of the hill and realized he couldn't get away, he saw the sun coming up. And when he saw that sun, he just sat down. He looked at the blazing dawn and he said, "I don't care if they do catch me now, 'cause I done set the world on fire!"

April, 1999

life bites me in the butt
(might as well laugh)

A BITING DRAMA

Thank goodness we have officially concluded the summer of my discontent, made miserable by an outright declaration of war by this state's insects against my pink flesh.

Perhaps it has been God's way of telling me I should not have laughed the day the yellow jacket got inside my wife's pants as we strolled following a leisurely lunch on Fort Mountain near Chatsworth. My neighbor, Fred Edwards, gentleman that he is, discreetly turned his head when Jackie screamed and disrobed down to her britches, but I can't say for sure what perverse gawking may have gone on among tourists. I was too busy tackling and wrestling her to the ground.

But enough about her. I started out talking about my own troubles, which began at the 125th anniversary parade in Tallapoosa in August. Right in the midst of several thousand spectators, as I purchased a Coke and a sausage biscuit, I felt a stab of indescribable pain at the juncture of my hamstring and gluteus maximus.

I threw my snack and drink to the ground and began to hop around, but I did not drop my pants. I grabbed at my trousers and tried to crush whatever was inside my clenched fist and I ran off seeking cover for an examination. Finding none, for it was a residential area, I hop-skipped toward a store that sold books about religion and convinced the owner I was in desperate need to use his back room in which to disrobe. I had bummed a chaw of Red Man tobacco from a startled parade watcher and I dabbed the time-honored remedy on the huge welt with merciful relief.

A few weeks later, as I lay sleeping at Hodge Podge Lodge on Old Dalton Road where we visited from Atlanta on weekends, I felt such a sting on my lower thigh that it awakened me. The pain quickly passed, however, and I thought no more about it until on the following week's visit I casually mentioned to Jackie that I thought perhaps I was dying, or at least was in the later stages of leg rot. She, never quick to panic whenever my health is at stake, suggested that during my next physical

I should call it to the attention of my physician. I offered that perhaps we ought to get the hell down to a doctor right then.

At the time I was not acquainted with Rome's medical community, so I presented myself before an unfamiliar doctor, who took one look and exclaimed, "Gawdamighty, damn!" He called in a second doctor and said, "Would you just look at that!"

I took his reaction to mean I might not live unless I immediately got a prescription for brown recluse spider bite filled across the street at the Big B Discount Drugs.

While my incident will be little noted or long remembered by historians, it did serve to remind me of the most famous spider bite in state history. Ol' Gene Talmadge was involved at the time in a tough race for governor and one way he ingratiated himself with the rural constituency was to stop frequently to use their outhouses.

On a July 4 near Moultrie he performed such ritual only to emerge from an outhouse screaming, "A bleep bleep black widow spider bit me on the balls!"

Talmadge's driver roared off for Moultrie and after medication the intrepid Talmadge, in great pain, delivered an hour's worth of speech in a driving rainstorm, but needed help from his friend, Hellbent Edwards, to finish.

Spider bites obviously were not then, nor are they now, an affliction to take lightly. In fact, just recently I was leaving my office when I felt a peculiar brush against my right leg. After cramming a briefcase and several books under one arm, I grabbed in the area of the sensation with my free hand. I hobbled back into the building as passersby stared and left my materials with the guard. "I think there's a spider in my pants," I said.

In the restroom a man was just coming out of a cubicle as I fought furiously against the offender inside my trousers. When I had crushed it sufficiently I reached inside my pants. I opened my hand to discover an inspection tag with the number 12 on it. As the man looked curiously at me I held up the tag sheepishly and said, "You can't be too careful. These things can be, dangerous."

October, 1985

LEWIS, RON, ZELL AND SISSY BEARD

Two days after Billy Ramsey asked me why I never write anything about my friendship with the late Lewis Grizzard, I was having breakfast with Joel Snider, Shannon Loy and Willis Potts. Willis attended high school with Lewis in Newnan, so it was sort of natural we would began swapping stories about the columnist who caused liberals and Georgia Tech football fans to gnash their teeth. It put me in the mood to fulfill Billy's request by telling about the time Lewis almost got me badly bruised.

Lewis was an admirer of country singer Don Williams. As was I, as was columnist Ron Hudspeth, as was Lt. Governor Zell Miller. We made a pact to attend a Don Williams show at Country Roads music hall. It was a good thing Zell was late and here is why.

Better you should kick Lewis' dog and insult his latest wife than to talk while he was trying to listen to Don Williams sing. I could see Lewis' knuckles pale and the veins in his neck enlarge. I knew it was just a matter of seconds until he would turn to the drunk at the next table and say, " Shut the hell up when the man is singing!"

The girls with the loud talker looked startled. They were very young and suddenly afraid. The man was kind of old, but he was not little. The barrel chest and the blacksmith arms were beginning to show fat, but overall I got the impression he might have emptied a bar or two. He rolled up his knit shirt as far as the left sleeve would go. He wanted to make sure Lewis could read the tattoo on his deltoid. It did not say, "I Love Mother."

"Okay, babe, let's go outside," said the old brawler. He began to strut in sort of a semi circle in front of our table, flexing his muscles as he moved.

"Not until I hear Don Williams sing," said Lewis, "Which is why I would like for you to shut up."

The old brawler was momentarily stunned, as if he didn't understand such a ridiculous response to his challenge from someone so skinny he resembled a cartoon stick figure with coke bottle glasses. Suddenly he switched his attention to me. "Well, what are you laughing so hard about, Sissy Beard?"

Finally the man's companions diverted his attention. Between songs Ron Hudspeth, who seemed to be shaking slightly, turned to me and asked, "Well, what WAS so blasted funny?"

"I was thinking how lucky Zell Miller is," I said. "All night long he has been rushing through meetings, trying to get here for the show. Can you imagine trying to explain how three newspaper columnists and the Lt. Governor came to be in the middle of a dance hall fist fight?"

I could just imagine Zell explaining to political reporter, Bill Shipp, "It may surprise you, but I didn't start the fight. It was Lewis."

On this night Zell had been spared guilt by association because his presence was required at a big dinner for President Jimmy Carter. Even so, Zell had carefully calculated his exit to the point he could still make it for the final show. Unfortunately, his schedule didn't parallel that of the President's important guests, some of whom wanted some additional time with the lieutenant governor whose political career was on the rise.

It was 12:30 a.m. when Zell and his party of five pulled into the parking lot. A crowd, including his three amigos, was beginning to stream out of the night club door. Zell didn't see us in the mob, but we bore witness to his pitiful lament.

He stuck his head out the auto window and said to one of the ladies that was with the man who threatened to throttle Lewis, and perhaps even Sissy Beard. "Pardon me," Zell said. "Is Don Williams through singing?"

"Why do you think we are leaving, you Dummy?" the old brawler that was with her said. Were we still inside, he might have discovered that mountain tough Zell Miller could back up his legendary temper a lot better than Lewis.

September, 2013

UNDOING IT MYSELF

Do-it-yourself is big business in this country. Although it is said some people actually derive a considerable amount of fun from hammering, sawing and bolt twisting, I have not personally entered that nirvana-like realm, which, for me, remains as mythical as the ecstasy reported by compulsive joggers.

Whenever I venture into a Home Depot or PlyMart, it is for one reason. I perceive a chance to save a lot of money by not hiring a tradesman, whose wage scales seem to rise steadily through the years, impervious to drought, famine, recession, outright depression or political upheaval.

I am reminded of the story of the physician who hired a plumber to fix the drain beneath the kitchen sink. After staring at the bill in disbelief, the customer said, "My Lord, man, I don't make this kind of money and I'm a doctor."

"I didn't either when I was a doctor," replied the plumber.

I hate to do it myself, because nothing is ever as simple as I thought it was going to be when I decided to save the money. On my last vacation, I had a modest game plan. One, I would reroof the porch of our cabin, Hodge Podge Lodge, and two, I would either repair or replace the rickety gate at the end of the driveway.

I visited a builders' supply house and sifted through the samples of roofing shingles, discovering a dark green tile that somewhat matched the old roof. I purchased roofing tar, flashing and, according to instructions, a supply of 1 ¾-inch nails.

I also asked for two 10-foot-long aluminum gates, which, when I got to my truck, I discovered were bent. So I had to go back inside and within a mere 15 additional minutes had the gates removed from the invoice.

When I got to the cabin and opened packages, I was upset to see that the shingles were not dark green but white with green flecks. I returned the shingles. The clerk was sorry, but they didn't actually have dark green shingles. They could order them, but it would take a week for delivery. Instead, I switched to gray, which actually was closer to the weathered shingles that remained on the roof. The paper work for the exchange took another 15 minutes.

In the meantime, I had decided that instead of a metal gate, I would build a new wood gate. I ordered lumber and a heavy-duty fence post, all pressure treated. After the boys out back had loaded the wood, I discovered the clerk had not specified pressure treated.

To heck with it, I groused. I had them unload the lumber and went back inside to have the invoice changed, which took 20 minutes this time, because the clerk's hand was shaking from frustration. My decision to keep the post but not the lumber tacked another five minutes on the paper work.

But at least I could begin on the roofing on the porch. After the first hammering, however, my wife noticed that the 1 ¾-inch nails were coming through the planking, causing an unsightliness she couldn't tolerate. I drove 10 miles back to the supply house for 1 ¼-inch nails.

After laying the first row of tiles, I became gripped with a fear that the first strong wind was going to rip them up, so I asked the wife to drive down to J. M. Green's for 1 ½ inch nails. I nailed one, and the tip barely showed through. Thus, the decision was made to stick with 1 ¼ inch and hope for the best.

In the meantime, our friends Linda and Fred Edwards visited. Fred had purchased an old auger bit at a Summerville flea market. It dawned on me that with this device I could bore a hole in my gate and install a wheel my wife had found, giving the old entrance new life and stability while retaining its weathered personality. Fred left his auger in my keeping.

The next day, I tried to bore the hole, but the bits were too old and dull. I set out for the hardware store. I had been very precise in my research of what the tool was called, to avoid being embarrassed by my naivete.

But when I asked the clerk for a ½-inch auger bit, she said, "I don't know if I ever seen one of them thangs."

I described the tool. "Oh yeah, we got those! Most of our customers don't know the names of what they want. But if they describe it, I know where to find it."

So finally, at a cost of less than $5, my gate had a wheel on it. But I was left to dwell on the mystery of how something so simple could get so complicated. I hope I can remember that the next time I am tempted to rail at the President just because he can't get a nuclear disarmament pact worked out in a couple of meetings.

February, 1987

A WHISTLE BLOWER'S LAMENT

Harry Musselwhite had little recourse but to accept the speeding ticket without his usual flair for drama. After all, what cop would be sympathetic to Harry's explanation that he was running late for Friday breakfast at Dirt Town Deli and first he had to pick up Jim Dixon, with whom he was car pooling. It was a humbling intrusion into euphoria occasioned by recent publication of Harry's children's book, "Martin the Guitar," a runaway best seller.

Upon his arrival at Dirt Town Deli Harry's impassioned recitation of the constabulary event elicited little sympathy for such is not a trait shared equally among our group. But the tale did generate a great deal of empathy. After all, who among us, our principles as straightforward as a scoutmaster's, has not at least once plummeted to disfavor in the eyes of motorized law enforcement?

I, myself, was once hoisted on my own petard. A petard is a small, bell-shaped bomb and loosely interpreted, the fancy phrase just means I was injured by my own cleverness, as I shall now explain.

At the time I had become incensed that drivers seemed to consider the curving road on which I lived to be a practice strip for Lemans. I had been waging something of a personal campaign to bring attention to the danger. I considered it my duty to cuss drivers as they zoomed past and like Mayberry's Ernest T. Bass I was tempted to toss pebbles at the cars. Instead, as a dutiful whistle blower, I reported on behalf of local citizenry my concern to the sheriff's department. I usually added prophesy, "If y'all don't stop all those speeders, somebody's gonna get killed." They always promised to look into it. Yeah, like I believed that.

One day when my wife was out of town, I was reduced to driving to Piggly Wiggly to pick up a frozen chicken pot pie for dinner. As I was returning and turning into my driveway I noticed I was followed by a car with blinking blue lights and a terribly obnoxious siren.

The officer got out of his car and spoke to me. "Let me see your license, please."

Without a word I showed it to him.

"Let me see your proof of insurance."

A miracle occurred. I found it.

I was steaming, but was determined to take advantage of my Miranda rights by remaining silent. My credit card holder had fallen out of my wallet during the transfer of credentials and I was having an angrily difficult time trying to get them rearranged, spilling them twice.

"Step out of the car," he said.

I did.

"How many drinks have you had?"

"Three beers over the last six months," I said truthfully, breaking my stretch of silence in the process.

"Say your ABC's"

I did and, with considerable restraint, resisted the temptation to sing ABC's the way we did as children.

"Would you mind telling me why I've been singled out for this honor?" I asked.

"Well, first of all, you were speeding. Just as you got past me you suddenly slowed and turned into this driveway leading back toward the woods. And I noticed you had a hard time getting your cards back in your wallet. And you didn't say a single word until you had to."

"I think all those things can be explained," I said. "First of all, I live here. Second, my wife, who is easily embarrassed, made me promise not to use certain words when I get upset. Last of all, I am naturally clumsy, but tell you what, turn your back, I'll drop the card carrier on the ground and let's see you get them back in the right slot the first time."

He was not in a test-taking mood. He told me I had the right to check the calibration on his radar gun. "Are you kidding?" I replied. "I need a jeweler just to set the time on my digital watch."

He handed me a piece of paper that said I could appear in court or mail the fine.

"Any reason you were out here today?" I asked.

"Some guy has been raising hell about speedsters on this stretch of road," he said.

I saw no gain in identifying the complainer. I just folded my ticket and said, "Have a nice day."

October, 2012

AH-CHOO! EXPLAIDING MAH
DUPPY DOSE

For the past week my wife and I have been frolicking at the rhino-virus festival. In other words, we each have a cold. We don't know which kind, because scientists have identified more than 200 different cold viruses. With so many flavors, they say, a person can catch one new cold virus after another and never run out. This daisy chain of cold bugs makes creating a vaccine unlikely.

Jackie Walburn is of Appalachian stock that will try every known old fashioned remedy for cold and cough before taking the last gasp approach of actually visiting a doctor's office. She thinks antibiotics are a hoax created by the same jokesters who made up the fantasy about men landing on the moon. Occasionally, I try to reinforce my image in her eyes by faking similar hill country fortitude and have temporarily agreed to avoid stressing the dwindling reserves of Medicare over some-thing no more sinister than a cold. For example, as I type this epistle at sunrise, I have an ice cube taped to the underside of each big toe. Ac-cording to instructions I must repeat the procedure at noon and night. This is just one of many remedies Jackie excerpts from Dick Frymeir's "Folkology and Home Remedies," first recommended to us by the late radio legend, Ludlow Porch.

Yesterday, in an aggressive assault against my hacking cough and wheezing chest, she dosed me with syrup drained from a concoction of two sliced onions, two cups of honey and a jigger of brandy. I didn't know we had brandy or a jigger, but had not sufficient strength to inquire as to its surprising availability. This morning she became impa-tient to hear a compliment about her medical expertise and ventured, "Your cough seems to be much better."

"It should be," I said. "I practiced it all night." I added, "What else you got in your voodoo bag?" She took it more as encouragement than sarcasm.

258

"Well," she said, "Betty Kuykendahll suggests massaging Vick's VapoRub across the bottom of both feet."

"If my feet have trouble breathing I'll consider it," I promised.

The report I am reading while exploring the frontier of home grown medicine says the average adult will have 2-3 colds per year. My friend, James Archer, pulls the average down without resorting to old-timey cures or modern drugs. He simply aligns seven tooth brushes in a holder and never uses the same one twice in the same week. He says this carefully planned inhospitality to germs accounts for his resistance to the rhinovirus, but Jackie thinks it is because James and Linda Archer are Methodists.

It is well known that Baptists have more colds than Methodists, Presbyterians, Episcopalians and other denominations that don't consider "thou shalt hug and shake hands on the Sabbath" to be the eleventh commandment. Baptists hug and shake hands entering and leaving the sanctuary and a third time during a chaotic hug-and-handshake scramble sandwiched between praise songs and passing the collection plate. Cold viruses adore Baptists.

Personally, I believe the best rhinovirus remedy is to just grin and bear it. I consulted Rome's Doctor of Grinology, Jack Runninger, who prescribed the following dose of humor:

God said, "Adam, I want you to do something for Me."

Adam said, "Gladly, Lord, what do You want me to do?"

God said, "Go down into that valley."

Adam said, "What's a valley?"

God explained it to him. Then God said, "Cross the river."

Adam said, "What's a river?"

God explained that and said, "Go over to the hill..."

Adam said, "What's a hill?"

So, God explained what it was. He told Adam, "On the other side of the hill you will find a cave..."

Adam said, "What's a cave?"

After God explained, He said, "In the cave you will find a woman."

Adam said, "What's a woman?"

So God explained that and said, "I want you to reproduce."

Adam said, "How do I do that?"

God said under his breath, "Geez..." And then just like everything else, God explained that.

So, Adam goes down into the valley, across the river, over the hill, into the cave and finds the woman.

In about five minutes he was back.

God, His patience wearing thin, said "What is it this time?"

And Adam said, "What's a headache?"

I like Dr. Runninger's cure a lot better than ice cubes strapped to the underside of my two big toes.

March, 2013

A COUPLE OF CLOSE BRUSHES

Nudity is not the major focus of this week's composition, but I will lightly touch on that delicate subject as a way of establishing context for remarks about toothpaste.

I gathered from Kim Sloan's September account in our newspaper that the man who jogged into Starbuck's parking lot wearing nothing but a smile didn't mind very much that cell phone cameras were clicking or that tongues were clucking or that Kaitlin Thomas was going to give him exposure on Facebook.

A few weeks later Jeremy Stewart reported that Stephen Lamar Crowe visited a home on Calhoun Ave. The owners might have proved gracious hosts had he not been naked. When they asked him to leave he thought it over and said he didn't think so. His bond was set at $1300.

Now the way I see it, there are two kinds of naked men. There's those that want everybody to take a look. Then there's me; nakedness is by invitation only. In fact, I once was of a mind to severely wound a man over that very issue and likely would have had it not been for toothpaste.

Shortly after moving our family from Macon to Atlanta I was toweling off after a shower one night when my wife began screaming in the den. I thought she was overreacting to a TV show. But when she didn't stop, I walked out of the bathroom to investigate her hysteria. She was pointing and screaming at the window.

The face in the window was chalky white, as was the hair. The eyes were translucent and the intense stare caused hairs on my arms to tingle. I instinctively ran toward the back door, mayhem my intent. But Jackie, a Southern Baptist, caught her breath long enough to gasp, "You can't go out that way! You're naked!"

The face in the window remained. The face grinned. I ran to a closet to get a .22 rifle given to me as a teenager. If I had ever fired it, I don't remember. But because we had young children, I had kept a single bullet for such an emergency as this.

"Where's my bullet?" I shouted at Jackie.

"I think it is in the medicine cabinet," she said.

It was. Unfortunately—or fortunately, depending on the peeping tom's point of view or mine—the bullet was smeared with toothpaste.

Were it not for toothpaste on my only bullet I might have gunned down a man who later proved to be a poor escapee from a nearby mental facility. Had I known his state beforehand I might have been less offended by his continuing to grin at me before finally running away.

Call it coincidence if you will, but years later toothpaste and nudity would collide in another emergency.

It was one of those mornings when nothing was going right and I was running late for work. I stepped out of the shower, grabbed a white tube and hurriedly squeezed the contents onto my toothbrush. My first thought was the toothpaste had gone strangely bland. Neither did it foam. Both reactions apparently are consistent characteristics of hydrocortisone, "excellent for treatment of poison ivy, insect bites, rashes, genital and anal itch." In case of accidental ingestion, the label on the tube warned, induce vomiting and contact your nearest poison control center. I immediately complied with the first instruction, jamming a finger down my throat. I frantically looked up the poison control center number and dialed.

The man who answered the phone said he would have to research the effects. He returned to the phone. "It says here you would probably have to eat the whole tube. You didn't do that, did you?"

"No, I was just brushing my teeth," I said.

"Well, I'll call back later to see if you are having any symptoms," he said.

True to his word, he called back and talked to Jackie. As required, he asked if Mr. Walburn had ever had a similar experience and was told no.

"By the way, is there any indication Mr. Walburn may have not done this by accident?"

Reporting to me about the phone call Jackie chuckled and asked, "Do you suppose they encounter a lot of suicides by brushing?"

So, to sum it up, toothpaste resulted in two things that really irritate me. One is being grinned at by a peeping tom. The other is being chuckled at by my wife.

February, 2013

HIP...HIP...HOORAH!

Edna Biggers called and requested an explanation. She said my several weeks absence from this space had disrupted her Saturday newspaper routine. I explained that for a short while I had been lounging around in narcotic happy land which is a fringe benefit of surgery. I had no inclination toward anything more expressive than an occasional giggle. I further explained that writing while under the influence is almost as dangerous as driving while similarly impaired. Regular pops of pain killers combined with a lingering wooze from anesthesia causes a dangerous disconnect between my brain and Noah Webster's dictionary. To reinforce my alibi to Edna, I cited a case history.

It was in 2005 that Dr. James Riley saved my life by counteracting my wife's diagnosis that I was simply having an unusually painful attack of gas. Notwithstanding my suspicion she might be wrong, a few days prior to meeting Dr. Riley in the emergency room at Redmond Hospital I had, with her encouragement, represented Rome in a state tennis tournament. James Archer and I partnered valiantly in a doubles match until I began to turn funny colors, as did the stuff I was spewing on the court. My wife, as protective of her diagnosis as I was embarrassed by my frailty, continued to spur me on by cheering, "Just hang in there. You're playing great!" Sensing that my on-court death might somehow affect their United States Tennis Association rankings, the opponents offered to quit if James and I were too stupid to forfeit.

I asked Dr. Riley, as aides urgently wheeled me into an operating station, if he thought I might return to the courts in a couple weeks since apparently all I had was appendicitis. Dr. Riley, as realistic as he was concerned, said something I interpreted to mean, "If you are still with us tomorrow morning we will talk about it." As he suspected, the little worm-sized appendage had ruptured. Dr. Riley summarized after he sutured the slice that gave him emergency access to my innards, "It was a mess in there."

I admit that in a literary sense I've managed to go around my butt to get to my elbow, the elbow in this case a metaphor for the previously mentioned disconnect between my brain and Mr. Webster's dictionary while on dope. You see, when my son, Steve, called to inquire about my adventure with Dr. Riley I told him, "The doctor said I had waited so long before surgery that gonorrhea had already set in." After a shocked pause Steve said, "Did you mean gangrene?"

Had I attempted an essay while in that state it's easy to see how fumbling a single word could have caused lots of embarrassment since our family hasn't had cause to explain a case of gonorrhea since Uncle Charlie came back from World War II.

So, as I explained to Edna, once arthroscopic virtuoso Dr. Brandon Busnell posted notice of a command performance in the arena of my left hip I suggested to publisher Otis Raybon that we padlock my computer keyboard for a few weeks as safeguard against a fuzzy-headed blunder besmirching Our Town's printed page.

When I told Pullis Legg that my surgery was scheduled in June if it didn't conflict with Dr. Bushnell's Junior-Senior prom he caught the spirit of my little quip emphasizing that as we age doctors seem ever younger. Pullis said he didn't have a single doctor who still drives a horse and buggy to work. Dr. Bushnell, in fact, rides bikes, skis and probably jogs to work on days when traffic is heavy.

On my recent post operative visit he asked how recovery was going. I said, "Well, pretty good. But my butt really hurts if I sit on it too long."

"So does mine," he said.

I interpreted that to mean I should discard my crutches.

The thing I appreciated most was that Dr. Bushnell never cited my advanced age as a factor in our cooperative venture. Not so with all physicians. I was told about a local lady who reported to her orthopedist that she was experiencing postoperative pain in her left knee. He tried to sooth her by cooing, "Well, you know at your age..."

"Age?" she spluttered. "Well I'm pretty durned sure my left knee is the same age as my right knee and it ain't hurting."

July, 2013

THE UNINVITED GUEST

We have a situation we need to take care of," Dr. Steven Morganstern said. So, having absorbed the verdict of prostate cancer, I slowly lowered the telephone into its cradle, took a deep breath, and prayed.

Some might view prayer as an intense effort to sweet-talk God into a special favor, but even so, prayer seemed a rational means of at least gaining perspective about this reminder of my mortality. It has been said God whispers to us in our pleasures and shouts to us in our misfortunes. That is probably accurate, because Dr. Morganstern's phone call penetrated several layers of spiritual deafness. So, I prayed.

I likely would have embarrassed myself and annoyed God had I asked for privilege among millions of people afflicted with this potentially lethal disease. After all, the desire to live is biologically encoded in us all. I did pray for courage, which seemed reasonable enough. What I meant by courage was simply a determination to not withdraw from the reality of the circumstances, and while earnestly seeking wellness, to not transfer my fear and anxiety to family and friends.

My late mother-in-law, Vivian Miller, had that kind of courage. Less than an hour after doctors revealed a diagnosis of terminal cancer, she walked into our house and said to me, "Lee, can you believe it? I have old lung cancer." Then she asked me to order a load of gravel for her driveway and left for the Glenwood Corners beauty parlor for what she called her weekly hair repair. I never heard her answer an array of sympathetic inquiries about her health with anything other than, "Why, I feel just fine." That was the kind of courage I was hoping for.

A popular theory postulates that every man who lives long enough will either require treatment for prostate cancer or eventually die of some other cause with a degree of cancer present in the walnut-sized gland that surrounds the urethra south of the bladder. My father died in 1984 from the residual effects of prostate cancer three weeks before his seventieth birthday, back when personal courage was more prevalent than medical encouragement. Given the paucity of available treatments and Daddy's failure to acknowledge the consequences of his physician's diagnosis, prostate cancer killed him in a relentless procession of grotesque, painful afflictions. As I watched him suffer month after month, my research into the disease did nothing to assuage his pain and mainly served to alert me that the hereditary nature of this particular disease might represent an actuarial forecast of my own health chart. For a brief moment in the emotional flashback triggered by Dr. Morganstern's message, I pictured myself in the same sequence of devitalization.

I mentally projected a depressing transformation from "just do it" to "don't do it." I barely absorbed the reasons, just the directives. Don't take A, C, E, and selenium supplements or other antioxidants once external radiation treatments start. Don't overexert. After implants, don't ride a bicycle, don't bushhog the pasture on my tractor, don't jostle around on the new little zero-turn lawnmower, don't plan any airplane trips to see the grand-kids in Montana. Don't hold babies in my lap because of exposure to radioactivity. Don't, don't, don't, don't.

I added a don't. Don't become a poster boy for pity. If there is more of a guaranteed way to dampen a good party than by talking about cancer, diabetes, arthritis, and various surgeries, I don't know what it is, although at a certain age such discussions are routinely served up as appetizers before dinner. Besides, I've always wanted to think of myself as brave and self-contained, most likely as compensation for a deep-seated conviction that I am not and would fold once the reality of my new enemy's tenacity sank in. So, I decided to tell no one except my family.

My family gathered for a birthday celebration three days after the telephone call from Dr. Morganstern. "I have good news," I told them, trying to steady the cadence and timbre of my words. "Doctor Morganstern and Doctor Mumber have determined I have prostate cancer. The good news is they think they can whip it."

The room filled up with silence. A granddaughter old enough to understand the implications turned her head away from me. Then her father piped up, "Good news? I thought you were going to tell us you had won that $367 million lottery." Everyone laughed and the moment I had most dreaded passed. We rarely talked about the predicament in the months that followed. If I insisted on feigning indifference, they would honor my charade.

I did amend my list of confidantes to include two friends, plus Reverend Mac McCurry and his associate pastor, Reverend Clyde Hampton. They have worked hard to mold me into a respectable congregant of Pleasant Valley North Baptist Church. I told them I welcomed their individual prayers but asked them to not include my name on the church prayer list. I had proposed an idea for a writing class for church members several weeks before my diagnosis, and I was concerned the coincidental timing of the first session might suggest I was hoping to trade a few weeks of church-sponsored storytelling advice for supernatural favors. Concern with image diminished me, as it often has, although I rationalized I wanted the class to show more concern for active sentences, metaphor, and imagination than sympathy.

I learned, as teachers of writing always do, that there are usually enough demons to fill any room without anyone paying exceptional attention to mine. The protracted suffering of a student named Bettie White, who has endured multiple brain tumor surgeries, touched me in the way it disguised her inner beauty. While I could easily hide my cancer behind a veil of nondisclosure, Bettie's illness, surgeries, and subsequent strokes have altered her face, her equilibrium, her handwriting, and her voice beyond any measure of secrecy. Prior to her enrolling in the class, I knew her primarily from chance encounters after Reverend McCurry's Sunday sermons when she would share copies of her angry letters to then Atlanta Braves general manager John Schuerholz concerning the sad state of his pitching staff.

Bettie's friend, Ann Hardin, brought her to sessions and together we steadied and steered her from car to room. That first night, as best as I could decipher, she was saying to me as we walked, "I love to write."

As an icebreaker the group discussed what each hoped to achieve from the classes. As conversations moved clockwise around the room I grew uneasy. But when the verbal baton passed to Bettie, she did not try to talk. She handed me a sheet of paper that by appearance had been folded and unfolded hundreds of times. She nodded at me and I determined she wanted me to read a poem.

Years ago that poem, beautiful in its innocence, won a prize for Bettie from the *Rome News-Tribune*. I read it to the group through the mist in my eyes. I discovered that Bettie White has composed hundreds of poems and has written for nearly three decades in a journal—so compelling a mixture of her life and world events that I later read the entire diary aloud to my wife. As we escorted Bettie to the car after the first assembly I managed to understand, despite the gravel in her voice, she was saying to me, "I'm so happy."

Dr. Morganstern telephoned at least once per week to encourage me, and if I whined about the symptoms, suddenly I would think of Bettie White and Vivian Miller and feel ashamed. Dr. Morganstern would remind me it was all part of the healing process and one day it finally dawned on me that without the treatments, I might soon be unavailable to feel discomfort or humiliation. That is not to say the epiphany stabilized the ebb and flow of emotions. Thinking became almost as much a disease as the disease itself. Cancer has a way of inserting question marks where exclamation points used to appear, and I found it difficult to dodge the thought that the larger portion of my life is already accounted for.

I was tidying up my office just to fill in some blank spaces in an undistinguished day when I opened a cardboard box stacked to the brim with old newspaper clips and photographs. Several pictures taken before I grew a beard in 1975 lay yellowing with age, and I couldn't even remember exactly why I let hair take over that face. Probably it represented my version of a midlife crisis. For whatever reason, I had trimmed the beard, but not shaved, since 1975. I dug around for other evidence that I was once young. I glanced through high school and college yearbooks and read cryptic notes scribbled by classmates, significance obscured by passing years. I found a caricature that a group of associates inscribed when I left the *Atlanta Journal-Constitution* to edit *Atlanta* magazine in 1987. "I still say you have a great butt," one female reporter had written in defiance of political correctness. Having feasted on that one notation out of scores of less exciting ones, who then would not have eagerly sought a confirming image in a mirror? Alas, if ever my rump had actually sported the slightest provocative curvature, now my khakis drooped like a tarp over a landscape flattened by the tectonic shock waves of time.

A day later, May 2, I decided to shave my beard. I spread a thick white blanket of lather from ear to ear and down toward my collar line. My hand trembled as I raised the Gillette razor. A .45 with a single bullet in one of its chambers would not have caused such hesitation. In less than three minutes it was over. The skin where sun had not penetrated for decades was the color of paste. The fleshy wattle between my chin and Adam's apple drooped in embarrassment over its nudity. Gravity had had its way with the jowls. I gazed in the mirror at a stranger who, innocent of the destruction, nevertheless offended me by his very presence.

I have heard of people, even know some, who have turned intimations of mortality into life-changing decisions. After receiving a diagnosis of lymphoma, Olive Ann Burns, who most of her life endured long episodes of writer's fright, buckled down and wrote the wonderful novel, *Cold Sassy Tree*. Don Maynard, an owner of the Lark & Dove restaurant on Roswell Road, shook off the effects of several heart-related emergencies and converted his passion for making people feel good into a different kind of happy hour. Last year the Methodist Church ordained him as minister, assigning him a little church in North Georgia.

As for me, I conceived of nothing more ambitious than to continue or eventually return to the things I already loved to do… play tennis, read good books, eat good food, drive my tractor, narrate foolish stories and sing off-key songs to my grand-kids, spill some words on paper, pet my dog, kiss my wife.

Many consider the date 7-7-07 the luckiest of the year. Who's to say? I just know that at seven o'clock that evening Jackie shouted for me to come outside to see an amazing double rainbow, our old house centered directly in the middle of their beautiful curvature.

But I suspect omens come and go depending on one's hope or desperation. In the meantime, I just try to make the present tense my friend. Ever the optimist, I even expect that at some point in the future an overwhelming dread of quarterly trips to Atlanta for measurement of my PSA level will no longer hang over my head like the sword of Damocles, and cancer, the stranger that showed up uninvited, will evaporate into the mist of things conveniently forgotten.

May, 2008

EPILOGUE

At times small commercial presses have suggested publication of my writings covering the past 50 years. I have resisted. Chances of commercial success are small and I have arrived at an age when ego is overshadowed by more pressing matters. However, when Cancer Navigators Executive Director Charlotte Atkins zeroed in on the idea of this book as a fundraiser for a wonderful organization, I seized on the prospect of at last doing something worthwhile with my words. Charlotte was a much-admired newspaper editor before answering what she believes was God's call to lead Cancer Navigators. I asked her to prepare the following as an epilogue to this book. It will explain why I joined this project so enthusiastically.

—LEE WALBURN

CANCER NAVIGATORS PROVIDES RESOURCES, RENEWAL AND REASSURANCE FOR CANCER PATIENTS DURING THEIR JOURNEY

By **Charlotte Atkins**

Executive Director of **Cancer Navigators**

"You have cancer." Lives are changed forever with those three simple words. In Northwest Georgia, we are fortunate to be home to an impressive array of healthcare providers and facilities to address the needs of those affected by cancer. But even with state-of-the-art healthcare, the journey can be a challenging one for patients and their loved ones.

Cancer Navigators Inc. was founded as an answer to that challenge. The needs and concerns of those affected by cancer are diverse. They encompass navigating unfamiliar medical processes that follow diagnosis as well as coping with the practical effects a cancer diagnosis has on everyday life. Our goal at Cancer Navigators is to improve cancer patients' experience and quality of life as they go through treatment. It's also vital to find ways to nurture and renew oneself during and after the treatment process.

A dedicated team of nurses, educators and social workers as well as volunteers at our community-based nonprofit have been working cooperatively with area healthcare partners—mainly Harbin Clinic, Floyd Medical Center and Redmond Regional Medical Center—for more than five years and making a tremendous difference in the lives of thousands of cancer patients in Northwest Georgia and beyond.

The goal of our patient-advocacy organization is to provide access to important resources that touch all levels of the healing experience —body, mind and spirit. Attention to the whole person often creates increased endurance and confidence that assists patients' responses to medical therapies.

Our Nurse Navigators work with patients and local healthcare practitioners to provide a single, consistent point of contact for clinical questions and concerns. They advocate on behalf of patients and their loved ones and know where to look and who to call to get questions about diagnosis, treatment, side effects, etc., answered.

Since cancer happens on top of whatever else is going on in people's lives, it can create a daunting array of needs beyond medical services. Patients may need help with transportation to treatments, aesthetic help in the form of wigs or prostheses, help with insurance or other resource paperwork or counseling to help with the emotional punch cancer packs. During one of the most challenging times of patients' lives, our Service Navigators identify and help secure needed resources and services.

Education Navigation provides small-group sessions and retreats focusing on a full range of positive behaviors that may affect clinical outcomes. The aim is to equip patients with the tools and information that empower them to help with their own healing. Quarterly 8-week Sustainable Wellness programs with Harbin radiation oncologist Dr. Matt Mumber allow cancer patients to explore the physical, mental, emotional and spiritual dimensions of dealing with cancer. Renewal Retreats allow time for cancer patients to just focus on and learn more about themselves in a nurturing sanctuary for a whole weekend. Our newest program is From Cancer to Health, a 26-week intervention to reduce the stresses of diagnosis and treatment for stage 2 and stage 3 breast cancer patients and to enhance patients' ability to cope and recover as they move forward. Cancer Navigators is the first in Georgia to offer this program developed by Ohio State University. Our Caring for the Caregiver program aims to support, educate and equip key caregivers with tools for coping and care. A new and exciting piece of our Education Navigation is Cancer Navigators' involvement in creating a federally funded national pilot program MyJourney Compass that offers a health information exchange for cancer patients using mobile technology in partnership with local healthcare providers, the Northwest Georgia Regional Cancer Coalition and Georgia Tech.

Our core mission at *Cancer Navigators is to serve the community as a complement to the medical expertise of cancer care providers by guiding those affected by cancer toward a better understanding of diagnosis and care and connecting them with needed resources in their journey*

Simply put, we are a patient-centered advocacy nonprofit that helps patients navigate their cancer care...sometimes at three or more medical facilities. We are a constant for them no matter where they are being treated. Our patients are what motivate us. They inspire us with their courage and hope and we offer them reassurance, resources and renewal.

All of our services are provided free to patients and their loved ones. Cancer Navigators a 501(c)(3) nonprofit that is 100 percent supported by donations, which are tax-deductible.

The Cancer Navigators team is so grateful to Lee Walburn for publishing this compilation of some of his most endearing and enduring columns from over the decades to raise money for our mission. We are totally supported by donations and we appreciate his dedication to this project.

By making a donation and getting a copy of this book, you are doing more than enjoying and sharing Lee's storytelling mastery. You are also helping cancer patients on their journey. We thank you for being part of our mission.

Donations may be mailed to Cancer Navigators at 3 Central Plaza, Suite 415, Rome, GA 30161 or online at www.cancernavigatorsga.org

The printing of this book was funded through a generous donation by Ethel Evans. She herself is a cancer survivor and a longtime benefactor and volunteer for Cancer Navigators. She's also a huge fan of Lee Walburn and his writing.

ABOUT THE AUTHOR

Rome News Tribune columnist Lee Walburn is former editor-in-chief of *Atlanta* magazine. Under his 15-year leadership the magazine won more than 200 awards for excellence, more than 80 of them national awards. He was presented the Lifetime Achievement Award from the national City and Regional Magazine Association and is a member of the Georgia Magazine Association Hall of Fame. As a writer he has won national, regional and state awards for magazine stories and for his monthly column. In 2003, LaGrange College awarded him an Honorary Doctorate of Humane Letters.

In addition to his career in magazine journalism, Walburn served as editor (1980-1985 of award-winning *Atlanta Weekly*, the erstwhile Sunday magazine of the *Atlanta Journal-Constitution*. In addition to his weekly column in that publication, from 1985-1987 he wrote a thrice-weekly general interest column for the AJC. Originally a sports reporter hired from the *Macon Telegraph* to cover minor league baseball for the AJC, in 1966 he served as Director Public Relations and Promotions for the Atlanta Braves, leaving in 1972 to form his own public relations company, Walburn & Associates, which was purchased by J. Walter Thompson Advertising in 1975.

A graduate of LaGrange High School, Walburn attended West Georgia Junior College and graduated from LaGrange College in 1959 with a B.A. in English. He is married to the former Jackie Miller of Armuchee. They have three children, Shannon Biggers of Armuchee, Steven Walburn of Augusta and David Walburn of Whitefish, Montana. They have seven grandchildren.

16222

DATE DUE

16222

Walburn, Lee
Just My Type

DATE	ISSUED TO

CPSIA information can be obtained at www.ICGtesting.com
Printed in the USA
LVOW06s1315041113

359802LV00002B/2/P